IN

THE

BISHOP'S

SHADOW

A KALEIDOSCOPIC LOOK AT THE SELF-ANNIHILATING WORLD TO WHICH THE BRAVE-HEARTED BISHOP RALPH HENRY HOUSTON WAS SENT TO MINISTER

BY M. LAVERNE BARTON

A CROSSROADS' BOOK - DR. ROBERT C. HILL, EDITOR
BOOK COVER BY BILL TYLER DESIGNS

Library of Congress Catalog Card Number 98-83117
In the Bishop's Shadow
A Kalediscopic Look at the Self-Annihilating World to which
the Brave-Hearted Bishop Ralph Henry Houston
was sent to minister / by M. Laverne Barton

1. Biography. 2. Houston, Ralph Henry 3. Barton, M. Laverne
4. Original United Holy Church 5. Afro-American churches
6. Afro-American Pentecostals 7. City churches
8. City clergy 9. Church and social problems
10. United States -- Church history
I. Title

Published by Crossroads Books, Mt. Juliet, TN USA

PREFACE

*"When Aaron and the others looked at Moses,
they saw his face was shining, and
they were afraid to go near him..." (Exod.
34:29 CEV*)*

The power of God that made Moses' face shine to such an extent that it frightened the Children of Israel, also made Bishop Ralph Henry Houston's shadow one that demonic forces both respected and feared. Few dared to raise their hand against him or those who sought refuge in his shadow.

In the spiritual realm he was widely known as an indefatigable warrior who resided for decades in the graffitied, crime-ridden community of Watts, located just south of downtown Los Angeles, California.

Watts' history was rife with violent gang wars, pandering pimps and their prostitutes, sham businesses dealing deadly drugs and the addictive thrill of playing the numbers. It also included infamous riots that erupted into frenzies of mass destruction and senseless killing sprees,

And Bethel United Holy Church was also part and parcel of Watts' history. Founded by Bishop Houston's mother, the late Daisy L. Houston, it was a lighthouse for those being tossed about in a stormy sea of degrading poverty and paralyzing despair.

"Big Mama," as the Bishop's mother was affectionately known, had lived through worse times and triumphed over them, so she had earned the right to

---

* Copyright (c) American Bible Society, 1995

convincingly encourage her neighbors to keep the faith and press on in their pursuit of a better life. Her unwavering confidence and heartfelt embraces drew them to her, especially the young ones who curled up in her generous lap, laid their head on her ample bosom and felt perfectly safe with her strong arms wrapped around them. While Big Mama loved them, she was also grooming them to follow in her footsteps. And no one got more of that than her son, Ralph Henry Houston.

Her life had been like an awesome comet of light blazing a trail across the dark pages of Watts' history. The Godly fire that consumed her also ignited eternal torches in many, shedding light on their God-given destinies and giving them the courage to live them out. Together they made a concerted effort to right the wrongs of a world gone mad, and the effects were far-reaching indeed.

With his mother's legacy resting on his shoulders, the Bishop had recently watched Montel Williams' shocked audience, gasp and cry during the telling of Robin Byrd's story. And his mind had flashed back to the first time he was approached by the terrified young mother at his church office. That was more than ten years ago when she was running for her life.

The story involved a wild cast of characters who had seemingly leapt right off the screen of Steven Segal's *Marked for Death.* While Bishop Houston had never seen the movie, he had seen their real-life, evil counterparts on the street corners and back alleys of his own community. Still the Bishop had no idea what a sinister situation he was getting involved with when he helped Robin. It would end up being a test of triathlon proportion, which they all faced with courageous endurance.

It is good to tell the Bishop's story of leading his family and church to help Robin and her son. Through an interview with the *Philadelphia Inquirer Magazine*, and during an appearance on the *Montel Williams Show*, Robin made many of the sensational aspects known, but there is more to the story.

Not only does it represent one of the almost insurmountable social problems facing the church today, but many will find the most rare and beautiful aspects of the story to be those of Christians sacrificing their time and money for individuals most of society would have gone to great lengths to avoid. When they gave of themselves to Robin, it was not the only time they had gone out on a limb to help those with unconventional problems.

Perhaps nothing put the Bishop's career more at risk than his decision to minister to Eldridge Broussard, Jr. Although that is not a story the Bishop enjoys talking about, or even remembering, it now seems right to share what he learned from the experience.

While most of the related media coverage dealt with the horror, Oprah Winfrey made a genuine effort to penetrate Broussard's cloak of denial, for the purpose of educating her audience and viewers.

Bishop Houston now shares his own painful recollections of that complex and tragic situation in the hopes of making others aware of the early warning signs so they will be forewarned and forearmed. It has been devastating to see the frequency with which charismatic leaders have enticed followers with messages as seductive as a siren's song and through progressive psychological entrapment, have ended up shipwrecking all those caught up in the nets of their cultic thinking.

There have been far too many autopsies, figuratively and literally, and not enough "preventive medicine" to keep these cults from springing up. Hopefully the proactive education included herewith will prevent others from becoming hopelessly entangled with unhealthy organizations, even if they don't seem that way in the beginning.

Initially, Broussard, a brilliant athlete, envisioned teaching ghetto children the discipline they needed to rise above their circumstances, and he also worked hard to improve deplorable conditions in Watts. For instance, instead of tolerating the low quality of meat being sold at high prices, he brought in high grade cuts and sold them at fair prices to those who didn't have the option of traveling to supermarkets outside of Watts to shop. So, Bishop Houston was heartsick to learn of the virtual meltdown of Broussard's laudable vision. He was also deeply disturbed in his spirit with a feeling that Broussard might be close to the point of no return. So, even though Bishop Houston was criticized for trying to help a man now commonly viewed as an utterly repulsive individual, he did what he could to help him. The pressure was so intense that it was only by the grace of God that he was able to minister to his charge until Broussard died.

It was a harrowing experience that can only be understood by those who have walked right up to the gates of eternity with someone who has made horrid mistakes, as Sister Helen Prejan did in *Dead Man Walking*, and as Bishop Houston did with Broussard.

Supernatural compassion always impelled Bishop Houston to minister to hurting individuals and he did so from the bowels of the inner city to the heart of Africa's bush country. In fact, he was the catalyst for much of the missionary work done by the Original United Holy Church International in Liberia, West Africa, where he personally served as often as possible. During those tours of duty, he defied malaria, deadly flesh-eating ants, and other bodily assaults.

Due to his tireless devotion and arduous work in helping his fellow man enjoy a richer, fuller life, on both a practical and spiritual level, Bishop Houston was elected to the highest office of this Pentecostal denomination in North America, and now serves as its General President. Most members of his denomination are aware of Bishop Houston's servanthood and achievements. Among his circle of friends, it is commonly known that the Bishop owned and operated a successful business enterprise while also making many civic and political contributions on a local, state, and national level. But most of his closest friends do not know of the enormous risks taken by the Bishop's family, members of his church, and most of all, by the Bishop himself.

Their monumental testimony confirms the truth of the following excerpt from former President Jimmy Carter's book, *Sources of Strength.*

"....I want to be known as a good church member. So I'll go to church, teach Sunday School sometimes, maybe serve as a deacon. Activities like this are relatively easy, and they make me feel good. But reaching out to the kinds of people Jesus chose - lepers, the mentally ill, prostitutes, thieves, blind people, the homeless - that's outside the purview of our normal Christian environment. It might put a burden on me, a burden of responsibility for someone else. And that's not nearly so convenient or comfortable.

"....when we open our hearts to other people, particularly those who are different from us, we are opening the door to Him. This is a practical way that Christians can take a major step toward realizing the constant presence of our Savior. He says so specifically: 'As ye have done it unto one of the least of these, my brethren, ye have done it unto me.' (Matt. 25:40)

"When we take such a step, our eyes are opened, as were those of the disciples; we expand our lives, escape from the cages we build around ourselves, and enter a new environment of surprises, adventure, and real gratification."[*]

Bishop Houston has taken that step and by the time you have finished reading this book, you may be challenged to do so as well, or you may retreat even further into the suburbs. Only one thing is certain, you will never forget the time you spend *In the Bishop's Shadow*.

---

[*] Copyright 1997 Random House, Inc.

Dedication

Bishop Houston lovingly dedicates this book to his family, beginning with his mother, the late Daisy L. Houston. Throughout her life, she helped him stay on course while planting precious seeds of promise within his heart and nurturing the God-given visions that sprung from them. She was more than his dear mother -- she was mentor, pastor, and trusted friend.

This book is also dedicated to his beloved wife, Betty, who believes in him and supports him in all his natural and spiritual endeavors.

They both wish to include Minnie, the Bishop's late wife, and Betty's dear friend, as she encouraged him to be faithful and finish his God ordained course.

Like many men of God, the Bishop has agonized over time constraints that have kept him from being with his children as much as he wanted to be. In addition to dedicating this book to them, he also wants to publicly declare their part in the family's ministry.

To each of his precious children, Darrel, Carol, Ronald, Ralph, Jr., Larry, and Kim, he acknowledges that they have shared in the fellowship of Christ's suffering, and will also share in the eternal rewards of the ministry.

But, beyond that, he feels responsible for sometimes making "unwise" choices to address the needs of the church while his children suffered from the need of their daddy's attention, and for those instances, he apologizes to each and every one of them.

Bishop Houston would also like to add Tommy Barton to the dedication list, as Tommy believed in the value of this book enough to give his wife, Laverne, the freedom, support, and encouragement to research and write it. To God be the Glory!

Acknowledgments

Many thanks and plaudits are sent herewith to Pauly and Bill Tucker for their continued encouragement and help during the birthing process of *In the Bishop's Shadow.* It took a saint to patiently proof each rewrite, and to revitalize Laverne with praise, as Pauly did, innumerable times.

We are also grateful for Susan Meredith's valuable input and prayers. Friends like her are among God's most precious gifts.

We wish to credit our editor, Dr. Robert Hill for his sensitive, supportive contributions. He wasted no time moving this project along and was unfailingly kind in the process.

For the final proofreading before going to the printer, we wish to thank Currey Courtney for an expeditious and very thorough job. The author accepts responsibility for all errors as she was still doing re-writes as the car warmed up for the trip to the printer!

Many thanks to the author's husband and sweetheart, Tommy Barton, for his never-ending patience and love. And to Andy and Suzanne Barton, Laverne and Tommy's youngest son and daughter-in-law, for generously providing room, board, and transportation to Laverne during her many research trips to the Federal Courthouse, the library, and even into crime-ridden neighborhoods with razor-wire on second floor balconies.

We also recognize and applaud Robin Byrd and all others who gave us permission to share what the Lord has done in their lives.

CHAPTER ONE

"...the sons of God...
in the midst of a crooked and perverse nation,
among whom ye shine as lights in the world." (Phil. 2:15)

The hot August night grew blacker as clouds drifted across the face of the moon and a ghostly aura of evil wafted down over Robin, paralyzing her with fear. An invisible, but very real and wholly oppressive force settled down over her, suffocating her with terror and freezing her hand in place, making it impossible to turn the key in the ignition. Beads of sweat broke out over her upper lip while her eight-year-old son, Ralph, worriedly watched and waited, as he had so many times before. Sometimes she just couldn't make herself do it and they would finally get out and go back inside, but this time, with trembling hand, she turned the key.

A deafening explosion catapulted her into an ocean of pain as her right hand and arm were ripped from her body. Through the illumination of this lightening strike from hell, Robin saw parts of the dash and windshield flying at her, tearing her to shreds and embedding themselves in her, even filling her mouth with glass and teeth fragments.

In surreal slow motion, Robin saw her right hand fall to the ground along with car parts. As warm, red blood flowed from her wounds, she realized she was dying and thought, Well, it isn't so bad after all.

But then she remembered Ralph. How strange...it seemed someone far away was screaming; then she realized those were her screams. "Ralph...dear God, where is Ralph?"

Robin bolted up from her sleep, wet with sweat and weak as a kitten. Her heart pounded so hard she felt it would come through her chest. Aunt Mary hurried in to find her with arms wrapped around her knees, rocking back and forth, sobbing uncontrollably. Aunt Mary hugged and comforted her niece, "You're okay, you're okay," she whispered reassuringly.

Robin was twenty-eight-years-old, but in her white cotton nightshirt and with tears streaming down a baby face that melted the heart of almost everyone she met, she seemed young, innocent, even virginal. No one would ever have guessed how she had spent the last four years, certainly not dear Aunt Mary.

Robin sheathed her sharp-as-a-cat's-claw mind behind a soft and furry personality, so people generally trusted her. With her engaging personality, along with the ability to think on her feet, she could usually talk her way out of any situation. She was accustomed to swiftly charting a course through even the most treacherous waters, so it was maddening to find herself in such shark-infested waters with no way out. As she thought about Ralph and the risk she posed to him and everyone else around her, a fresh wave of hot tears flooded her eyes. They knew nothing. Robin could get them all killed and they wouldn't even know why.

Aunt Mary was beside herself with worry. While holding Robin close and stroking her back, she pleadingly whispered, "Baby, you've got to get some help."

Her voice breaking, Robin replied, "No one can help, Aunt Mary."

Aunt Mary answered firmly, "Well, we can't go on like this. Now, first thing in the morning I'm calling Bishop Houston. He'll know what to do. Okay?"

Robin nodded in resigned agreement.

Ralph appeared in the doorway sleepily rubbing his eyes. As Aunt Mary rose to go to him, she kissed Robin on the forehead and whispered, "Now try to get some sleep."

Robin nodded while wiping her tears away with the back of her hand. Even though she wanted her aunt to stay with her, she said nothing as she led little Ralph out of the room and back to his bed. She could only hope he wouldn't remember this in the morning.

The next afternoon, Robin stood in the doorway of Bishop Houston's office. She was so nervous she couldn't contain herself. While practically bounding from foot to foot, she wrung her hands together, then anxiously begin rubbing her arms, elbows, and face.

Bishop Houston, had lived for more than fifty years in South Central Los Angeles and thought he had seen it all, but he was stunned at Robin's appearance. As he pulled out a chair and greeted her, he surveyed her arms for needle marks and looked into her eyes for signs of drug use but saw none. At less than five feet tall, she was a pathetic sight.

When he asked how he could help, Robin collapsed into racking sobs. His genuine concern caused an already cracking emotional dam to break and through a torrent of tears, she described beatings and death threats. Bishop Houston had counseled many battered and frightened women before but something told him this might be the most dangerous situation he had ever encountered.

He also had the feeling that she wasn't telling him everything. But, he thought, she might not have the chance if he didn't help her now.

For many years, Robin's Aunt Mary had been a member of the Little Bethel United Holy Church. By example Bishop Houston's mother had taught him to be strong and to stand with members of the church family through every situation, no matter how difficult.   So he assured Robin of his church's help and asked her to wait while he stepped down the hall to see if Ernestine, a psychotherapist and trusted member of his congregation, was still in the building.

Fortunately she was and after meeting with Robin she confirmed what Bishop Houston had suspected regarding the seriousness of the young woman's condition. Now there was no doubt in his mind that Robin was on the verge of a complete breakdown and had to be moved to a place where she felt safe.   Because he already had a full house and a wife who was battling cancer, he made arrangements for Robin and little Ralph to stay with a family living in a house next door to the church.   He wanted them nearby so he could watch out for them and counsel them as needed.

The first night Robin and Ralph were in their new quarters, a Jamaican man came to visit their host family's twenty-year-old daughter. It didn't take Robin long to see things about this man that the young, innocent daughter was totally oblivious to.   Robin had come to know the lingo and mannerisms of Jamaican drug dealers all too well.

So had Ralph and, like most children, he loved to join in every conversation. In their present situation, one childish slip of the tongue could result in fatal consequences, so Robin quickly said good night and took her very bright and sociable son to her room.

She wanted to tell the family she was staying with about the dangers they were exposing themselves to, but she dared not risk it. Too many times she had heard, "If you talk, you're dead...and not only you but your mother, father, brother, sister and kid."

While there was no escaping either the Italian Mafia or Jamaican posses, the latter was totally unpredictable and, due to the influence of crack cocaine, even more violent. No one was safe, not even those who took every conceivable precaution...including flood lights, eight-foot fences, and security guards. Hit men welcomed such challenging hits as a way to enhance their reputations.

They really whooped and hollered over getting the wiseguy who put tape around the hood of his car every time he got out and carefully checked to see if it had been tampered with before he got in. That one was taken out by placing dynamite in the trunk and wiring it to the rear lights.

Even those who entered the government's witness protection program were vulnerable. Louis Bombacino and his new Lincoln were blown up with a blast so powerful that parts of each were found a quarter of a mile away. Much more horrifying than these well-known stories were Robin's personal recollections of the atrocities she had witnessed firsthand. Those were the ones that gave her nightmares and filled her every waking minute with fear legitimately based on indelibly imprinted images that haunted and tormented her. Like a broken record, the memories replayed incessantly, constantly reminding her of tortured, bleeding victims writhing in pain, screaming out, begging for mercy while the horrific smell of burning flesh filled her nostrils. What *was* she going to do?

Frantically her mind raced down every conceivable escape route, slammed into a dead end, wheeled around, and once again began its search for an exit ramp...but there was none.

The next morning as she walked out of the house, she looked down the street and noticed how neat and clean all the yards were. Even though almost every house and even the church, had iron bars over the windows, the properties were well maintained and people greeted each other in a friendly manner as they mowed their yards and trimmed their shrubs.

She didn't think she would ever be able to get rid of the giant emotional weight that kept her from being happy as they were. Tears welled up in her eyes as she realized that every chance she and Ralph had for a normal life was probably gone. While children played in the yard next door and flowers bloomed in a profusion of color, exuding their perfume in response to the kiss of the sun, she felt she was waiting to be executed. The tortuous pressure was eroding all hope, killing her slowly by gouging out little pieces of her life and personality.

She had wanted Ralph to grow up in a place like this where families took pride in their neighborhood's appearance and there was a sense of community esprit de corps, but they had been robbed of that opportunity by her youthful unwillingness to keep working and waiting for the things they needed. Sooner or later she would have to return to Philadelphia to face the consequences of her decisions. She anguished over what would happen to Ralph then.

That was the worry that kept her from turning herself in. Ralph was innocent, bright, and full of promise. She was determined to stay with him as long as she could, but as she considered what Bishop Houston might say when she told him her story, she realized her days with him might be numbered.

She looked haggard, defeated, and ready to give up as she confessed to Bishop Houston that her husband, Robert "Cush" Taylor Smith, had recently been indicted for murder. Swallowing hard, she went on to say that he was a drug kingpin and the head of a violent Jamaican posse. Throwing herself upon Bishop Houston's mercy, Robin explained that because the frequent violence sickened her so, she had on numerous occasions pleaded with him to stop, requests that had usually resulted in him turning on her and beating her mercilessly while accusing her of sleeping with the victim. Worst of all, he now suspected her of turning him in and she now believed there was a contract out on her life! Before Bishop Houston could do more than gasp, she quickly forged ahead, explaining that Cush could find anyone, anywhere. His organization had powerful, far-reaching, octopus-like tentacles and he was the personification of evil! Even his assumed name, "Cush," meant death in seven different languages.

Bishop Houston shook his head in disbelief while trying to assess all the possible ramifications of this absolutely unbelievable situation. Slowly he went over to the window, gazed out, and silently prayed for wisdom. Under his breath, he asked, "*Oh, God, what do I do with this one?!*" Robin sat behind him sobbing, almost certain he had turned his back on her for good...and she couldn't blame him.

Incredulously, Bishop Houston asked, "How did you ever get involved with this kind of guy?"

"Through a friend and at first it was just a romantic involvement but before long he had me under his thumb, and *now he has me under a death sentence!*" she cried.

Wringing her hands, she explained she had met Cush when her son Ralph was only five years old and she was struggling to survive as a single mother who received no help from his father. Like so many, she hadn't thought it really mattered if she was married or not when she got pregnant with Ralph, and in spite of their free and easy relationship, everything seemed fine until his father started doing drugs.

Then their fights began. They escalated as Robin grew increasingly frustrated with the growing list of responsibilities that he shirked and she had to shoulder. Finally she got sick and tired of holding down a job, taking care of the house, and tending the baby while he partied with his friends. She hadn't told him she was pregnant with their second child, but that added to her worries. The next time he came in stoned, they had a major confrontation, which ended with Robin stabbing him.

Robin did not carry her second child to term and developed health problems that prevented her from ever having any more children. In fact, she ended up having four surgeries before little Ralph was four years old. Weak and barely able to keep going, she pressed on, pursuing a degree as a criminal justice major while also working to support Ralph. It was a vicious, relentless cycle in which she got up early to catch the bus, worked all day, went to school at night, and fell into bed dog tired when she got in.

While pacing the floor of Bishop Houston's office, she tried to make him understand how lonely, exhausted, even desperate she had been when she jumped on a plane for Florida to be with a man she had never met. Now it seemed impossible that she did so after only being introduced by mutual friends and talking to him several times on the phone.

The two weeks she spent with him in Florida were a welcome respite from the arduous life she had been living, and even though Cush was arrested for possession of marijuana while they were together, she ignored the warning signs and moved forward to cement the relationship that could set her free from the grueling schedule she had been keeping.

Bishop Houston had heard many different renditions of that sorrowful song. While the women had usually made bad choices, he understood how few choices many of them had and never turned his back on a woman in distress. Yet this was the first time he had been confronted with one who had a contract out on her life. Obviously her husband must be deadly serious and very powerful. This situation was unlike anything he had ever faced before.

An irate husband or boyfriend might come charging in like a bull and yet could possibly be reasoned with, but a professional hit man would probably never be seen. Yes, this was a whole new ball game.

As Robin chewed on her fingernails, he called Aunt Mary and informed her of the situation. Responding with shocked dismay, she advised him not to help Robin any further. Bishop Houston remembered how our Heavenly Father had promised that when our earthly father and mother gave us up, He would take us up. So even though Aunt Mary might have given up, Bishop Houston felt the church should not.

If the U.S. Government could place protected witnesses, ninety-eight percent of whom have criminal records, among its unsuspecting citizens, surely it would be okay for the church to hide this mother and her young son. Aside from that debatable logic, Bishop Houston was sure God wanted his church to protect them. Reaching across the desk to pat Robin's hand, he said, "Someway, somehow, the Lord will help us out of this."

Robin breathed a big sigh of relief that Bishop Houston was still willing to help them and felt a twinge of guilt about not telling him the whole story. What would this 6'5" gentle giant say if he knew *everything*? She wondered just how much she could trust him and thought about unburdening her soul by telling him the rest of it, but decided not to push her luck. Anyway, she was totally wrung out and amazed that he was still planning to help them. As she wondered why, she found herself looking around his office as if there might be some clues there.

His office walls were lined with plaques reflecting his many accomplishments and told her a lot about the man on the other side of the desk. There was a picture of him with Billy Graham as well as a gallery of photos with well-known political figures. She dared to hope that *maybe* this man had the connections to help her out of an otherwise hopeless situation.

As Bishop Houston saw her out, Robin smiled at a simply framed yellowed newspaper photo of him in a football uniform. Beneath the photo, in big bold letters were the words "Iron Man Houston." Bishop Houston chuckled as he told her about being named All League and All City of Los Angeles. His family had been thrilled when he received scholarship offers from several colleges, but those opportunities were circumvented by Pearl Harbor and the draft. After the war, he never again had the luxury of playing the game.

Once Robin was gone, Bishop Houston sat down to meditate and pray. What would his mother do in this situation? As far as he knew, she had never faced anything like this. How things had changed...

The things the church had fought against when he was a boy seemed so innocent now...movies, school dances, and parties with spiked punch...why, they had even objected to his beloved football games!

Bishop Houston's aunts and uncles thought his mother was far too strict on him, but actually he was the one who curtailed his activities, as she did not restrict him from attending any school function. She knew the Lord was at work in his life and could see that he was obedient to the leading of the Holy Spirit.

He was "different" from the other kids, but she had always known he would be, and her father had known it as well. When his fourth grandson was born, he excitedly asked, "What did you name him, Daisy?"

"Ralph," she replied.

Pa said, "Daisy, that boy needs a middle name. He's going to be a bishop. Name him Ralph Henry so when he's ordained, and *he will be*, he can sign his name Bishop R. H. Houston."

It would take fifty-four years, forty-four of them spent in devoted Christian service, before Grandpa's prophecy became a reality.

For a long time, believers in the family waited expectantly to see what the Lord would do in the life of this generous young man who was a good student and an excellent athlete. They couldn't help but notice that he never entered a game without asking God to help him be a good sport who played a hard but fair game. Even when the team lost, they noticed that he did not feel he had. When they asked him about it, he replied, "How can I feel like a loser when I had so much fun playing a game I love?" He felt exhilarated at having given it his best and he loved the team's camaraderie.

He knew his mother prayed for him before every game because, like every mother, she did not want her son to be hurt. Also, as a minister of the gospel, she was sensitive to what the saints might say if he was injured playing a game of which many disapproved.

Games and Youth Night were both on Friday evenings and no matter how tired he was after a game, he had always hid his bruises and went to be with the young people at church. Since that time the church had taken a more reasonable position regarding its youths' activities, and the young athlete's mother had contributed to that by leading the church to change while she also remained faithful to Scriptures. What a legacy she had left him.

At a more appropriate time, and in a discreet way, he would ask Robin about the legacy her family had left her, as he had found that everyone has one and it was not always good. Sometimes, the legacy consisted of vices, strongholds, and "stinking thinking."

Of course, he had also learned that God can and does change all that when a person is willing to let Him, but it isn't always easy. New patterns and lifestyles have to be learned and that takes time. Loving and encouraging people through the process of change was one of Bishop Houston's greatest strengths and another of the skills he had learned from his mother.

Bishop Houston knew his own children had been given a jump-start on life by being born into a family that lived by the good values instilled in him by his parents. He was firmly convinced that the most significant things left behind by older generations were the intangible values on which our lives are built. Yes, those were the most valuable and enduring possessions in life. With faith in God, a strong work ethic, and the ability to get along with others, anyone could reach his or her maximum potential in life.

Bishop Houston was blessed. His parents taught him so many great lessons, including the value of persistence and never giving up. That positive, confident attitude had served him well as a football player, a businessman, and a minister. Like Christ, he stayed right alongside the hurting, never giving up, always encouraging them to have faith and keep on fighting to succeed.

He never burned bridges, realizing it was one thing to have a difference of opinion and quite another to cut the cord of friendship. Because of his extraordinary people skills, he had a wide circle of old friends on whom to call and soon found, with no trouble at all, a new place for Robin and Ralph to stay.

Little Ralph entered school and quickly proved to be an excellent student. But in spite of all the love and support, Robin was still a basket case because of the night terrors that tormented her. Any unusual noise would have her springing from the bed and over to the window.

Even during the day, she stayed in the house most of the time. Behind drawn shades, she peered out at passersby, knowing that if the wrong people saw her, and she was sure they were looking everywhere, she was dead. Sometimes she seemed okay, at other times deeply depressed or very talkative, occasionally getting totally carried away and loud.

Some church members found her stories somewhat inconsistent and came to be suspicious of her motives and trustworthiness. However, Bishop Houston possessing a rare and wonderful kind of faith, steadfastly believed that God could and would help anybody who surrendered his or her life to Him out of any situation, regardless of how hopeless it seemed. He inspired his congregation and family to be patient and follow his lead in helping this young woman and her son. Everyone prayed that Robin realized and appreciated how far out on a limb he was going for them.

When one of the members said as much to Bishop Houston, he gently reminded them that Jesus went out on a limb, and hung there in agony, until He died for all of our sins. Then he simply continued to pray that Robin would finally trust God to help her out of the mess she'd made of her life. He was confident she would.

Street smarts and trust don't go hand in hand, so it took a while for Robin to let her guard down and begin to trust them. Many times the messenger carries almost as much influence as the message, so Robin watched and evaluated Bishop Houston's life. She wanted to see for herself just what kind of man he was. Even though he had rescued them, she still wasn't convinced that he was a man who really "walked his talk."

It wasn't enough that he was widely known as a tower of strength and integrity, a devoted husband, and a loving father of six biological children and innumerable spiritual ones. No, that didn't cut much ice with her, as Cush was also revered and had quite a following. It would take a lot for her to believe that Bishop Houston did what he did for people out of the goodness of his heart while expecting nothing in return. She'd had too much experience with respected public officials, including crooked cops on the take and politicians who are reelected by publicly decrying the dangers of drugs while privately using them.

Many of Robin's peers believed preachers were no better. And recent high profile cases had shaken the confidence of people even more.

Juicy media accounts fanned the flames of cynicism. One particularly distasteful one involved a preacher's son who was eaten up with a desire to even the score for a previous attack on his family by a televangelist. So the son followed the televangelist to a motel and punctured his tires while he was inside with a prostitute. Gang and posse members understood the thirst for vengeance that motivated the preacher's son to then call the press and his father, so that they could all wait together for the televangelist's exit. In fact their modus operandi was very similar.

However, it was harder to understand or trust the loving kindness the Houstons and members of Bethel were bestowing on Robin.

Even before the country was scandalized by the stories of the 1980s, many church congregations were beginning to believe their churches were becoming powerless and no longer had much influence in their neighborhoods or culture at large. Many overworked pastors felt their spiritual vitality being sapped and were increasingly burned out from serving as arbitrators, marriage counselors, social workers, and fund-raisers. Dismay and confusion gave way to serious soul-searching among sincere Christians who were almost as grieved as their Heavenly Father. While they fell to their knees, praying that arrogant, sanctimonious attitudes would give way to humbled hearts that would confess sin and return to God, some people like Robin just watched and waited.

Robin continued accepting every kindness that was bestowed upon her, all the while evaluating people's motives and watching their lives like a hawk. Bishop Houston was not surprised, as he had walked the same mean streets his parishioners walked and had made no effort to separate himself from any segment of his community. He took risks and was vulnerable to every kind of attack as a result of befriending gang members, drug dealers, and prostitutes. In spite of the dangers, he remained approachable and was there for them when they were hungry or in trouble.

Most churches wouldn't give these people the time of day, but when they would come, Bishop Houston took them to church. Even when the visitors smelled of beer, sweat, or worse, the bishop's congregation followed his example, and looking through the eyes of faith, they welcomed everyone with a hug. Many troubled souls found they received better treatment at Bethel than they did from their families.

His neighbors saw the bishop leave for work every day and knew he had the same struggles they had. That made him a more relatable figure to them and more thoroughly integrated him into the community. Many had heard him tell the story of how the Lord elevated him from an employee to owner. It was easy to be happy with him because he had worked so long and hard. He certainly deserved the opportunity that had come to him when the A & A Barrel and Drum Company was offered to him by his Jewish employer, Mr. Holtzman.

Yet it he hadn't obeyed the Lord, he would not have had that chance, because he did not start off on the right track.

When the Houston children were small, their young father worked two jobs without ever being remiss regarding his church responsibilities, but sometimes he would only get two or three hours sleep a night and it wasn't long before he became irritable and short-tempered.   It hurt his wife's heart to see him working fourteen and fifteen hour days, six days a week, and on those rare occasions when he did try to get a little rest, Minnie did her best to keep the children quiet. However, the energetic, irrepressible preschoolers were so excited to have Dad home that they would inevitably slip into the bedroom and wake him.

Suffering from exhaustion and desperately in need of sleep, the overworked husband and father would yell at Minnie to keep the kids out of the bedroom so he could rest. Fatigue would cause him to lash out at her about how hard he was pushing to provide for his family.

Finally, months of patience evaporated from Minnie, and she stood her ground, letting him know that his children needed their father! Then she softened, telling him how much she appreciated the hard work he did for his family and the Lord.

Even when it became clear that something had to change, he stubbornly continued the same grueling pace until the Lord spoke to him one day while he was in prayer, letting him know that it was not right for him to work himself to death. The displeasure of the Lord keenly cut to the heart of the matter. He had been doing what was necessary, according to conventional wisdom, but now he was beginning to understand why the Lord had said, "Be not wise in thine own eyes...." (Prov. 3:7)

Instead of depending on his own understanding, he was going to have to rely on the spiritual wisdom of the ages, from which he would gain the faith he needed to do as instructed and live a balanced life while waiting on God to fulfill His promises.

Surrendering to "In all thy ways acknowledge Him, and He shall direct thy paths" (Prov. 3:6), he decided to quit one of his jobs. Even though he did not see how he could do so and meet his obligations, obedience to the Lord was required of him. So he determined to only work forty hours a week to make a living and trust God to care for them. The next few weeks were very hard as he tried to decide which job to keep and how to readjust his bills. He talked with those to whom he owed money, and to his father, for whom he was working at the time. His father could not afford to pay him any more, and neither of his jobs had any benefits. For his family's sake, it seemed best to continue with the A & A Barrel & Drum Company, where according to his productivity he had the opportunity to make additional income. If he couldn't make enough to take care of his family in that position, he would look for a job with the county or city, where he would have the security and benefits a young family needed.

The Lord was pleased with these prudent decisions and reminded him that He would withhold no good thing from those who walked upright before Him. (Ps. 84:11)

The young husband and father meditated on those words and worked hard. Not only was he enjoying his work, he was once again the kind-hearted, considerate, and caring man Minnie had married. Although he was not earning much money, he begin to be filled with a peace that he couldn't explain and his boss begin to trust him with increasingly greater levels of responsibility. It was inspiring to realize Mr. Holtzman respected his Christian commitment and was treating him like a friend instead of a boss.

It wasn't long before he was given so much freedom that essentially he was his own boss. Because he worked with the company's accounts on a salary-plus-commission basis, he was challenged every day to see just how much he could earn. Soon the commissions doubled his income.

After about two years of working together under this arrangement Mr. Holtzman was diagnosed with cancer. Before he passed away, about a year later, he instructed his wife and son to offer the business to Ralph Houston if they found it too difficult to manage after his death.

According to the Talmud, "If you haven't been persecuted, you are not a Jew." Because of their persecution, most Jews understand and are very sensitive to the pain African-Americans have experienced from discrimination. This may have been a factor in the astute businessman's dying decision to finance Ralph's purchase of the company, which could very well experience a sharp drop in revenues, or perhaps even fail, as a result of being sold to an African-American.

Both buyer and sellers were fully aware of the risks, especially since the '60s had experienced a series of marches, boycotts, and student sit-ins. With the desegregation of schools, restaurants, parks, bus stations, and airline terminals being met with such resistance, would Ralph receive enough God-given favor with the existing customer base to be able to keep the company going?

Some customers would almost surely leave before doing business with an African-American-owned company. Would Ralph be able to retain enough of the business to have sufficient income for day-to-day overhead, provide for his family's needs, and make payments to Mr. Holtzman's family for the purchase of the company?

He never doubted God would provide, and while the devil did attack him through a boycott, by the grace of God, he overcame.

So in 1964, God honored Ralph Houston's request and gave him the desire of his heart by making him the sole owner of the A & A Barrel & Drum Company. At the time he believed it was the only black-owned company in America buying and selling used industrial containers. It was like a dream come true.

For the sum of $6,500, with no money down, and payment of only $50 a week, he had purchased the goodwill of a business that was more than forty years old, a two-ton truck worth about $2,500, and an inventory of stock worth about $800.

Only four or five months after all the papers were signed, he discovered the company had $3,000 in account receivables, reducing his net purchase price to $3,500, which was very close to the value of the truck and inventory.

The company was a gift from God that provided him more free time and discretionary income and enabled him, as his mother's health declined, to assume more of the church's duties and responsibilities. Shortly before her death in 1968, she passed the mantle on to him and he became Bethel's Pastor.

During the next twenty years, he and Minnie enjoyed more extraordinary experiences than they had ever dreamed possible. As Bishop of the Original United Holy Church's Foreign Missions, he and Minnie traveled to more than ten countries including Asia, Kenya, Nigeria, Taiwan, Hong Kong, and Switzerland and made more than twenty trips to Liberia.

The Houstons had a passion for missions and all of their travels were part of their ministry for the Lord. The A & A Barrel & Drum Company had grown from a business with $35,000 in gross annual receipts to one with over $250,000, so the Houstons certainly could travel wherever they desired. But they never went to the popular vacation resorts. Instead, most often they followed their hearts and spent time with the very loving and appreciative people at the rather primitive Salala Mission in Liberia, West Africa.

While the work in their own back yard was also a mission field, and the people at home were also loving and appreciative, the needs of the people on foreign shores seemed much greater. Perhaps that was the reason they longed to help them and be with them.

However, regardless of where they were, it seemed the demands on the church were increasing. In fact, to some it seemed that both home and foreign missions were being flooded with torrents of destruction, challenging them as never before.

CHAPTER TWO

"...when the enemy shall come in like a flood,
the Spirit of the Lord shall lift up a standard against him..."
(Isa. 59:19)

Bethel's work with street gangs grew significantly after Leon Watkins joined the church in 1978. Before Leon found God, while watching the *700 Club* television program, he had been an alcoholic and drug addict who guzzled a fifth of whisky every day while smoking pot and snorting cocaine. In spite of those destructive habits, he was elected president of his class at Pepperdine University. But his misery could not be dispelled by recognition or anesthetized by mind-altering substances.

When God delivered him from the misery, he no longer needed the crutches. He quit everything--cold turkey. Then God filled that hole with unspeakable joy and called him to share his victory with others. Leon answered back with a resounding, "Yes, Lord!" The spiritual echo sent shock waves throughout South Central Los Angeles. Demons shuddered at the thought of this newly empowered 300-pound recruit to the Heavenly Army.

Even the meanest of the mean paused when they encountered him. He spoke with a soft intensity filled with conviction about how God could and would free anyone from their problems. He didn't wear a collar or hit gang members over the head with the Bible, but they knew they were talking to a man of God who understood them and cared for them.

Leon knew that as dysfunctional and destructive as the gangs were, they still possessed certain family characteristics. By banding together, members were not alone in a world filled with hate, anger, and violence. Together they were a force to be reckoned with, not just so much flotsam to be tossed about, washed up, and kicked around by others. So, Leon didn't just walk in and tell them their gangs were no good.

Instead, he showed them the love of the Father by trying to help them. His friendship made them feel better about themselves. With Leon's acceptance and approval clearly evident, they didn't have to prove anything, and the anger subsided. The value he bestowed by being genuinely interested, resulted in their trust. So they opened up when he asked them about their hopes and dreams. Then he cultivated their destinies by imparting faith and confidence into them. His respect for the latent talents and abilities he saw in each individual caused them to see themselves in a new light.

Like so many in the inner-city, Leon had also grown up without a father, so he was aware of the need to be believed in, encouraged, "prized," and loved. He knew the results of being deprived of those essential ingredients for a lifetime. Instead of looking at the personality deficiencies that resulted, he was able, through the eyes of faith, to see them as healthy and whole individuals. When they began to see themselves in the same light, they came out of the gangs and grew into productive members of society.

Without the Father and a vision, they were perishing and taking others down with them. But with their Heavenly Father and a vision, they were succeeding.

Many churches didn't want these gang kids coming to be with them but Bishop Houston welcomed them and supported Leon Watkins' work both prayerfully and financially. He became Leon's mentor, taking him with him to meetings, introducing him to key individuals and sharing with him like a father many of the things he had learned about God since being saved at the age of ten.

Bishop Houston was the perfect mentor, offering suggestions and assistance but never attempting to control Leon's decisions regarding his work. He listened, loved and encouraged.

The greatest thing Leon received from Bishop Houston, was the same thing he gave the gang members, faith that they could realize their dreams. Then he rejoiced with them, as Bishop Houston did with him, when they achieved them.

Families in crisis could reach Leon, or one of the volunteers he recruited, anytime day or night via the Family Helpline, which Leon established. Initially he operated it from a pay phone until he could get properly set up. Currently, they assist more than 11,000 of their neighbors each year with counseling, referrals and other resources.

Friends and strangers caught his vision of redeeming the neighborhood's children and, among other things, helped him tutor thirty troubled youths every school year to keep them from dropping out. They arranged tours, field trips, camp-outs and film-industry excursions. Anything to broaden the horizons of their young people and set them ablaze with hopes and dreams for the future.

After every field trip, Leon now tells the young people, "I'm counting on you to get out there and succeed," and they believe they can. What's more they look forward to the day, when they are a part of the work places that Leon brings the next wave of youngsters to on future field trips.

Leon had brought together gang members and businessmen to form the San Pedro Street Businessmen's Association for the purpose of keeping kids off the street and out of trouble by putting them to work. He suggested and helped implement a program to get kids designing and marketing graffiti T-shirts instead of wasting their energy defacing the neighborhood.

Even prior to doing so, Leon noticed the "boyz in the hood" always passed over the A & A Barrel & Drum Company, sparing it from vandalization, as a sign of the enormous respect they had for Bishop Houston.

Respect and love were all Leon received for his efforts, but he couldn't stop. The work was too important to be measured in dollars and cents. It was being measured in lives and he was compelled to continue his work for fifteen years before he was finally able to draw a salary. During times like that, it meant a great deal to have the friendship of Bishop Houston, who did everything he could to help. In their own ways, both literally waged war on the forces that sought to destroy their community's future generation.

Bishop Houston was as proud as any father could be when Leon's programs came to the attention of many state and national leaders, including President Ronald Reagan, who invited him to the White House to discuss them. Later President George Bush toured the riot-ravaged neighborhood of Watts and listened respectfully as Leon emphasized the importance of rebuilding not just the physical structures but the people and their spirits as well.

Leon's legacy for his children and grandchildren, is attested to by a plaque bearing his image at the Will Rogers' Park Promenade of Prominence, right next to Johnnie Cochran's. He couldn't have done it without his wife, Evelyn, who shared in the sacrifice, as did their four children. Some thought he was a fool for letting her work and support the family while he poured eighty hours a week into street kids but it didn't matter, he couldn't quit.

Even when the payments on their tiny house had not been paid for almost a year and the bank gave them fourteen days to bring everything current or get out. Leon just kept on working and trusting God to provide. It was hard on the family's nerves, but in the end, everyone agreed, it had been the right thing to do. Once a friend wrote them a check for all the back house payments, enabling them to persevere a little longer, and finally they got the mortgage paid off.

Bishop Houston enjoyed all of Leon's accomplishments. He loved to see people overcome as Christ overcame and sacrifice as Christ sacrificed simply because they loved as He loved and not for any other reason.

Observing these things, Robin and Ralph knew that was Bishop Houston's reason as well. They were learning to trust, and an interest in God was beginning to sprout as a result of the spiritual sunshine emanating from Bethel church. Robin's emotions slowly settled down and she began growing physically stronger every day. She was also beginning to believe Bishop Houston's Jesus just might be able to help her too, but she still wasn't ready to make a commitment to Him.

As Bishop Houston was nearing the end of his long and illustrious tenure at Bethel Church, he was reflecting back over what the Lord had given him the privilege to do. His service to the community had resulted in numerous honors being bestowed upon him. Among these honors was a personal invitation to participate in an event presided over by Pope John Paul II, one of the most recognized and admired people in the world. Imagine that! It still seemed like the stuff dreams were made of. Even though there were times when it seemed almost unbelievable to him, he knew it wouldn't have surprised his mother.

On her deathbed, she said, "Ralph, remember...your gifts will make room for you and bring you before great men...and you don't have to push it."

How could he ever thank God enough? His life had been full, rich and closely intertwined with the lives of his church members and neighbors. He had married the children of couples his mother had married, conducted funerals that celebrated the lives of their loved ones, visited the sick, led the church in prayer and praise to the King, but his greatest joy was in preaching the gospel that set the captives free.

As he contemplated retirement, he realized how much he would miss preparing his weekly sermons and wondered what the Lord had in store for him. Was he being turned out to pasture, or did the Lord have more work for him to do? He was content with whatever it was.

His work in Watts had been most rewarding and his church family made him beam with pride. They had survived great trials and tribulations, including the Watts riots of 1965 when 34 people were killed and more than 850 injured. Over and over again he had witnessed his people triumphing over adversity and emerging stronger, especially the members of Bethel, who possessed a richer and deeper sense of responsibility toward one another than most Christians. They were certainly more willing than most to help people like Robin, Ralph, and the gang members Leon Watkins brought in.

Yes, they did plenty of missionary work at home and much of it was done by the strong women Christ had raised up for the tasks. Maternal vigilance was maintained in their neighborhoods, not just by blood mothers, but also by mothers from the church who watched over the children living around them, teaching them to be respectful and to do what was right. There was such a sense of community.

Maybe it was because there was a time when none of them could have survived by themselves, a time when a neighbor needed to borrow a cup of flour to make bread for dinner.

Whatever the reason, they had pulled together and they were their brother's keepers in spite of drugs, crime, or whatever else the devil had to throw at them. And he always had something up his sleeve.

Noted author and theologian Marcus Dods, as an old man, said: "I do not envy those who have to fight the battle of Christianity in the twentieth century." Then, after a moment, he added, "Yes, perhaps I do, but it will be a stiff fight."[*]

Yes, it was, and in October of 1988, the fight heated up for Bishop Houston when he received devastating news of little eight-year-old Dayna Broussard's senseless and tragic death. She was the daughter of Eldridge Broussard, Jr., a charismatic young man who had been a basketball star at Pacific University before returning to Watts in the mid '70s, with plans to help ghetto kids escape the poverty and despair of the inner cities. He had intelligence, personality and education along with great ideas that thrilled the hearts of public officials and clergymen throughout Los Angeles. Like so many, Bishop Houston had helped Broussard get established.

As long as one of Bethel's elders were there to observe, Broussard was allowed to hold Sunday afternoon services at Bethel. He was a dynamic speaker and developed a strong following among eight- to fifteen-year-olds who wanted to follow in his footsteps and become outstanding athletes. As a strong advocate of

---

[*] Marcus Dods, quoted by Henry E. Fosdick, *Christianity and Progress*

self-help, he taught them to study and work hard. Parents were delighted at the improvement in their children and rallied around in support

As he had done with Leon Watkins and innumerable other young people, Bishop Houston introduced Broussard to very influential people like Peter Ueberroth, President and CEO of the Los Angeles Olympic Organizing Committee (LAOOC) and later the sixth Commissioner of Major League Baseball.

Broussard left that meeting with fire in his eyes and began assembling a team of athletes to train for the Olympics. Unfortunately, his priorities got out of balance and he gradually strayed further and further from the straight and narrow way.

Initially, though, it seemed to be a good thing. He brought together a group who used their own money to refurbish the gymnasium at Will Rogers Park, putting in glass backboards and hardwood floors that looked as good as those on which the pros play.

Carolyn Van Brant became so involved in Broussard's activities that she lost her job with the LAOOC, then joined him full time and became a key person in his organization. They had big ideas for the Olympics, planning to get corporate sponsorship and official endorsements. The work on the gym brought a lot of good publicity as well as visits from basketball star James Worthy and football's O. J. Simpson.

A 34-team basketball league was formed. All the players and many kids in the neighborhood were given shoes from a 1,600-pair donation, worth approximately $50,000, made by the New Balance sportswear company as an indication that they found Broussard's plans to be worthwhile.

Broussard was a hard taskmaster, requiring his followers to rise at 3:00 a.m. every morning to run and perform strenuous drills including hundreds of push-ups, sit-ups and 1,000-5,000 jumping jacks.   Of course, drinking, smoking and profanity were strictly forbidden.

The first indication Bishop Houston had of Broussard getting off track was when he began instructing his flock to do controversial things like getting out of second marriages if their first spouse was still living. Bishop Houston counseled with him, to no avail, and in spite of continuing in error, Broussard's flock grew.

Finally, in the late 1970s, they pooled their resources to buy an old bakery at 7700 S. Avalon, which they did a beautiful job of renovating.   Then everyone moved in and began to live communally. Bishop Houston had known some of these people all their lives and was astounded to learn they were selling their property, cashing in pension funds, and turning over their salaries to Broussard.

In 1987, Broussard moved to Oregon for the purported purpose of taking his organization's young people to a more wholesome rural environment. He had his own daughter and fifty-three other children in The Ecclesia Athletic Association camp. Even after Danya's death, the parents of most of the children remained loyal to Broussard. They did not make any effort to take their children away. They had come to rely on Broussard for everything. He was absolutely in control of their lives, their sole authority figure.

What had happened to them, or him? Had he lost his mind? Oprah Winfrey interviewed him but got only smirking responses to her questions.   He blamed the media for blowing everything out of proportion and did indeed seem crazy when he blamed *them* for the death of his daughter who had been beaten with more than 500 blows.

A broken-hearted Bishop Houston would have to deal with many consequences of this tragedy in the near future.

Who could understand what had happened to Broussard? Had he moved to Oregon to escape the checks and balances of his peers? Had he become a god unto himself? It wouldn't be easy to get to the bottom of this or to help the survivors get over the betrayal of their trust or the crisis of faith that was sure to follow.

Would Broussard's followers even be able to re-enter society and function independently again? Bishop Houston knew the failure rate was high for those attempting it. It was surely one of the most tragic situations the sad bishop had ever come in contact with. He had always desired to be an agent of healing, but this was almost unapproachable.

When Bishop Houston was a teenager, he had lived a clean, wholesome life. While many of his peers were partying, he was on his front porch conducting Bible study classes for sometimes as many as fifteen to twenty young people from the neighborhood. Many were still his friends to this very day. He had helped countless friends and relatives stay out of life's ditches but when someone did swerve off the road and crash, he would be the first one there to pull them out, give them spiritual first aid and encourage them on their way.

This thing with Broussard was like a train derailment, with so many injured and such a mess to clean up, that it was hard to know where to start. The bishop just prayed and made himself available to those who called on him.

In the midst of the breaking Broussard debacle, Robin, after hearing a sermon entitled, "There Is Yet Hope," gave her heart to the Lord. Carol Houston, who would later follow in her father and grandmother's footsteps to become Bethel's pastor, had been telling her parents she felt there was still more to Robin's story. She was certainly right!

Robin floored the Houstons by confessing she had actually been hiding for two reasons. Not only was there a contract out on her life but she was also wanted by the FBI, as she was actually the underboss of the Jamaican drug organization! Well, the family couldn't harbor a fugitive and they couldn't abandon her either; so Bishop Houston called attorney Johnnie Cochran, a friend of many years, for advice.

Mr. Cochran contacted an attorney in Philadelphia, Robin's hometown, and wheels were set in motion for her to return and face a mountain of federal charges.

Because of the deteriorating health of the Bishop Houston's wife, Sister Minnie, plans were made for Carol to become legal guardian to Robin's son, Ralph. Little Ralph would live with Bishop Houston's nephew and niece since they had a son close to his age...one who would be like a brother to him while his mother was away.

Bishop Houston also made arrangements for a Philadelphia Bishop to accompany Robin and her attorney to the federal building. She needed the reinforcements.

When Robin's lover, Cush, was previously indicted on state murder charges, he had retained the services of Chuck Peruto, Jr., a flamboyant attorney well known by those frequently needing a criminal lawyer.

While it was not known at this juncture if Peruto would be representing Cush again, Robin was fairly certain it would someone equally as qualified, or better. As she remembered the qualifications of Chuck Peruto, Jr., she wondered what kind of representation she might have; certainly it would not be equal to Cush's.

Chuck Peruto, Jr. was a member of one of Philadelphia's most prominent legal families. His father was a dignified and conservative pillar of the legal establishment. In his own way, Chuck, Jr. was considered by some to be equally powerful.

He had built a high profile for himself by representing defendants such as Gary Heidnik, who had kept six women chained to his basement walls as sex slaves. He murdered two of them, one by electrocution in a water filled pit; the second one he boiled and fed to the others.

Chuck's legal fees for the Heidnik case were reported to be in the $150,000 range. It was a much publicized trial that resulted in Chuck becoming well known. Chuck had arranged publicity shots of a wild, unkempt and crazy looking Heidnick, who had taken his advice not to shower, shave or cut his hair for three months, hoping it would help convince the jury of his insanity.

Heidnik was found guilty, given two death penalties, and sentenced to 320 years in prison. Chuck was a guest on *The Morton Downey, Jr. Show*, as well as numerous others. In January of 1989, he appeared on four different television programs in a single day.

Heidnik's trial received considerably more attention, but the results of Cush's trial also made the newspaper with an article that appeared under the heading of "N. Phila. 'Drug Kingpin' Guilty in Slaying."[*]

Interestingly enough, Cush who, through a reign of terror deterred most of his workers from using drugs, said his own actions were the results of drug and alcohol use. Robin did not believe that was the case and claimed it was a defense tactic.

She had arrived in town on the eighth of January, 1989, to find the city in an uproar over police corruption tied to the drug trade. Just five days earlier, a dramatic federal trial had begun to unfold. Six former members of "Five Squad," a once-elite city police narcotics unit, were charged with extortion, robbery, bribery, racketeering and

---

[*] Dave Racher, *Daily News* Staff Writer

filing false income tax returns. Between 1980 and 1984, these officers had allegedly stolen drugs and approximately $400,000 in cash from drug dealers.

In her own case, Robin was one of twenty-three individuals named in a seventy-two count, one hundred and nineteen page federal indictment. Four of them, Robin and Cush included, faced life sentences on more than one count.

Cush was identified as the posse's drug kingpin and Robin as his longtime lover and underboss.

Robin faced nine counts of distributing cocaine base, with each carrying a twenty-year penalty, and two counts of possession with intent to distribute cocaine base, carrying penalties of forty years each. Numerous other charges included three counts of distributing cocaine base near a school with penalties of forty years each, one count of traveling interstate and foreign commerce to facilitate narcotics transaction, carrying a five-year penalty, and three counts of employment of persons under eighteen years of age, each carrying forty-year penalties, and more! All together, she faced charges totaling 505 years!

As U.S. Marshals were summoned to take Robin into custody, the Bishop and Robin's attorney said their farewells and departed. Soon Robin was being escorted out of the building. The cold January wind cut through her like a knife. She was all alone, totally vulnerable and separated from anyone who cared about her. Her life would not be her own for a long, long time. A strange and frightening feeling came over her as she realized her son's fate and her own were out of her hands. Fear of the unknown gripped her. It seemed a thick emotional fog was descending upon her and the tears began to flow, blinding her and causing her to stumble. "Oh God, what is going to happen to me and my son?" she prayed.

The marshals looked at each other and sadly shook their heads. To them it was like watching a reckless driver go over the side of a cliff and tumble down the mountainside. There was nothing they could do but hope, against all odds, that the driver lived past the tragic results.

Robin also felt her life was tumbling out of control, and her heart cried out for Ralph. She needed him, his precious, warm hugs and funny little ways of making her laugh. She knew he needed her too. The bond between them was strong and tight. What would happen to that love connection if she was sent to prison for the rest of her life?

Where would she be sent? How long would she be there? Would she be shuffled around the country from institution to institution? Would little Ralph *ever* be able to come see her? It didn't seem likely with him now living on the other side of the country with people who were totally unrelated to her.

Even though she felt physically sick at the thought of him seeing her in prison, the thought of not seeing him at all was worse. Through bitter, salty tears, she prayed, "Please, God let me be with my son again."

CHAPTER THREE

"...Rescue my soul from their destructions...(and)
I will praise thee among much people." (Ps. 35:17-18)

Bethel's church members had mined through tons of dirt to get to the diamonds in Robin's life. It was funny but Bishop Houston never really saw the dirt, just the diamonds. He saw diamonds in everyone's life and knew they were there in Robin as well. As a result of receiving the confidence of such an honorable and well-respected man, Robin's opinion of herself began to slowly change as she stretched to meet his and the church's expectations. Bishop Houston was pleased. Little by little she had become more like them...following them as they were following Christ...until she had finally grown enough to be honest with them.

Had she grown enough to face the lions alone? No, but in spite of how she felt, she wasn't alone. The church's heart was there with her and they were sending up fervent prayers for her yet nobody's prayers touched the heart of God like little Ralph's. Before Ralph was three years old, he could recite Bible verses extensively. He had been taught them at the Christian day-care center to which Robin took him while she worked. The seeds planted there were being nurtured at Bethel, and Ralph was growing into a strong young Christian.

However, Ralph missed his mom terribly and at times, the normally talkative little guy, would lapse into long silences broken only by heavy sighs. Every night he faithfully said his prayers, beseeching God to take care of his mommy and send her back to him soon. It made him feel good when the Houston family prayed together with him, as they often did.

Feeling it was time to devote himself to caring for his beautiful bride, Bishop Houston made arrangements for church and business to be taken care of by others. Then he and Sister Minnie moved to Nashville, Tennessee, one of the friendliest and most spiritually rich places on earth.

After working hard to raise six children and faithfully serving her church and community for almost 50 years, Sister Minnie deserved all the beauty Middle Tennessee had to offer. Joyous yellow daffodils sang to her of His Glory and dogwood tree blossoms proclaimed His resurrection power and promises of eternal life.

She had cancer, but cancer didn't have her. She regularly attended church, always standing tall and looking strikingly attractive in her Sunday best, which usually included a fashionable hat. Her long graceful hands were beautifully manicured and every hair was in place. However, she wasn't so elegant as to be unapproachable. Quite the contrary, she exuded a warmth that drew people to her.

With the greatest of ease, the Houstons moved from a predominately black neighborhood into a predominately white neighborhood; from a small church to a "mega-church" where The Judds, Charlie Daniels and other celebrities were in attendance. The Houstons didn't have to work at winning the hearts of everyone they met; people were just simply attracted to them.

Bishop Houston and Sister Minnie immediately felt right at home at Christ Church, which had the greatest choir this side of heaven and a strong missions department, two features both of them loved. The Senior Pastor, L. H. Hardwick, Jr., and Associate Pastor, Dan

Scott, both recognized what a truly humble, yet absolutely remarkable and spiritually influential couple the Houstons were and welcomed them with open arms.

Friendships developed quickly. Pastor Hardwick, like Bishop Houston, had began his work for the Lord at an early age. In 1949, at the tender age of 18, he was pastoring a little church at the corner of Rose and Saddler. It eventually grew to a flock of more than five thousand. His congregation basks in the unfailing love of the Lord that emanates from him continually. Some have been with him since the beginning of his ministry and in all those years they never had a difference of opinion they didn't work out.

Bishop Houston and Pastor Hardwick were both too busy unifying people, within their own churches and within the body of Christ at large, to be caught up in divisive issues. Both grieved over the racial division among Pentecostal believers that had started back in the 1920s. They felt it was time for God's children, black, white, and every other color, to leave their differences behind and work together. Having decided to do all they could, they started working together to improve interracial cooperation in Nashville.

Their first project was to assist Exum Chapel CME, a fledgling inner-city church, pastored by Bill Smith and his radiant wife, Charisse. A more deserving young couple couldn't be found anywhere. Both held down full time jobs and spent all their free time working with families living around their tiny, un-airconditioned church located in a high crime area of Nashville. On more than one occasion, gunfire interrupted church service, reminding them of the risks they took in coming there.

Across the street, crack houses sucked in beautiful brothers and sisters from the neighborhood and spit them out as twisted, mangled, wrecks. Some became addicted in as little as three weeks while others might be able to be casual users for as long as six months. But most discovered rather quickly that the drug owned them and was the cruelest of masters, demanding they come back with the money for another fix, regardless of what they had to do to get it. Crack drives its addicts to sell their bodies to strangers...steal from their mothers...kill their neighbors...whatever it takes to get another fix.

Crack mothers abandon their children and crack fathers are among the most violent predators in the country. While their babies shriek from the pain of being born with the claws of that demon tearing at their insides, many experts wonder what those children will be like when they are grown.

In Watts, Bishop Houston and Sister Minnie had seen the power crack can have over a neighborhood and wanted to help Exum Chapel persuade as many youngsters as possible to decline that deadly dance with the devil. The Houstons' support and encouragement helped keep Bill and Charisse going. Bill had been serving there since 1984, when he was still a senior in college. Upon graduating from seminary in 1992, he realized there were many "better" opportunities for him, but he and Charisse stayed with Exum and the people they loved. Their unswerving devotion touched the hearts of many.

When there were needs, Bishop Houston prayed and also did everything he could to see they were met. The first thing Exum needed was air conditioning, so Bishop Houston talked with Pastor Hardwick and a man was sent out to install it.

Before the work was completed, the air conditioning contractor was stabbed, but thanks be to God, he was only slightly injured and did not even require medical treatment.

Bishop Houston and Pastor Hardwick invited Bill and Charisse to ministers' meetings and church conferences, introducing them to people who could help them.   Many volunteers from Christ Church were soon assisting Bill and Charisse in organizing neighborhood sports programs, field trips, summer camps, and many other activities.   Allowances were given to the neighborhood children who worked at the church so they could be taught at an early age to save and budget their money.   If they could just develop the mindset of working and waiting while saving, they would not be so vulnerable to the recruiting efforts of drug dealers on every corner.

Christ Church drama and music teams began providing free entertainment, and the 50+ class began furnishing cupcakes for monthly birthday celebrations throughout the year.   Thanksgiving and Christmas baskets were made up and prayed over before being sent to Exum Chapel for distribution to needy families.

Realizing how wonderful it would be for every large church in America to take a small inner-city church under its wing, Bishop Houston and Pastor Hardwick hoped their efforts would be duplicated many times over.

In some communities, large established businesses help develop small businesses by giving them assistance during an "incubation" period.   Many inner-city churches would benefit from that concept being put into practice by the religious community.

And that is precisely what happened when Bishop Houston spoke to Pastor Hardwick about another young, dynamic African-American minister named Rodney Beard. Rodney's young and vibrant congregation needed a place to hold services temporarily, until they could buy property and build a church of their own.   Pastor Hardwick graciously offered Christ Church's Wallace Chapel, and Rodney gratefully accepted but said his congregation was a prosperous one and they wanted to pay for the use of the Chapel.

Pastor Hardwick wouldn't hear of it. Furthering the cause of Christ was his mission in life. Because of Pastor Hardwick's magnanimous heart, Christ Church and many other churches are growing larger and making the world a better place in which to live.

Bishop Houston and Pastor Hardwick shared a vision of churches working together in a spirit of unity and brotherly love. Both were wondering how many years they had left to lead while growing increasingly aware of how much work there was to do. Younger ministers would soon be filling their shoes and become caretakers of the nation's souls. The most important thing statesmen of the faith could do was to counsel, develop, encourage, and love them. They would be satisfied with their work if they could teach the younger pastors how important it was to cooperate, not compete; to have a spirit of generosity and openheartedness toward all, regardless of denominational background, race, creed or color.

Freed from the daily demands of running a business and pastoring a church, Bishop Houston was not only enjoying being a counselor and mentor, he was also enjoying more free time with Sister Minnie than they had ever had in their entire lives. They did puzzles together, traveled and enjoyed their children and grandchildren. He faithfully took her to the doctor and did everything he could to lighten her load so she could get the extra rest she needed.

Sister Minnie curtailed her activities but was still very influential. Actually she didn't need to work at teaching, as her quiet life of devotion to God and family spoke volumes. She and Bishop Houston's most important work was done just by fellowshipping, being available and obedient to the Lord.

Sister Minnie kept their home spotless and open to anyone who wanted to drop by for a cup of coffee and a piece of freshly baked cake. She cooked without using recipes, the way some people play instruments without sheet music, and it was always great.

No one dropped by more often than Tommy Barton, husband to the author of this book. From the first time he met them, Tommy loved Bishop Houston and Sister Minnie. It wasn't long before he sampled Sister Minnie's cooking and came to love it as well. He shamelessly took second helpings of Sister Minnie's cake and Bishop Houston's encouragement from the scriptures. After every visit, Tommy came home a better man.

Tommy and Laverne were the Realtors who delighted in helping the Houstons find a new home in the Nashville area and became good friends with the Houstons in the process. They delighted in seeing them at Christ Church, where they had become members after moving to Tennessee from Texas.

Sister Minnie was also from Texas originally, so they had a lot in common and enjoyed talking about what it was like growing up there...the places they knew and things like that. At one time, the Bartons had lived just a few miles from Waxahachie, where Sister Minnie was born in 1923. Both families were very familiar with the picturesque area, dotted with Victorian mansions built by cotton and cattle barons around the turn of the century. They talked about the marvelous red sandstone Ellis County Courthouse, which was showcased in *Places of the Heart,* a Hollywood movie starring Sally Field.

Sister Minnie didn't remember the local folklore about the Courthouse being haunted, but Tommy insisted some Courthouse visitors had seen a woman's face floating down the hallways. The ones who stayed around long enough to ask were told it was the face of Mabel Frame, who had captured the heart of the Italian stonecarver brought in to do the exterior carvings on the building in the late 1800s. Sister Minnie didn't believe a word of Tommy's story, but it was good for a laugh!

She had moved from the area long ago and enjoyed Tommy's funny stories and also news of how the place had developed. Before going to beautiful Southern California in 1936 with her mother, four sisters and three brothers, Sister Minnie had moved from Waxahachie to Amarillo, where it was dry, flat and *hot*.

They all had a lot in common. Tommy had been born in San Angelo, Texas, and later lived in Monahans where he played on sand hills and helped his father herd sheep through mesquite trees and cactus. When Tommy grimaced at the recollection of the distinctive and never-to-be-forgotten odors associated with shearing sheep, Bishop Houston laughed knowingly, as he had spent the first ten years of his life herding sheep and working on a farm in Watonga, Oklahoma.

Tommy wasn't familiar with where Watonga was but was interested in learning it was the place where the famous author Edna Ferber had gathered most of her material for the novel *Cimarron*. Another of her best seller's, *Giant*, had been made into a movie that was filmed in Marfa, Texas, about 150 miles from Tommy's hometown of Monahans.

It seemed that every time they got together, they discovered they had more in common. Tommy reveled in Bishop Houston boyhood stories but shuddered when told of pulling burrs from sheep's wool.....without gloves! At the end of a long hot day, with backs aching and fingers bleeding, Bishop Houston said his mother was paid 50 cents, while he and his brother George would be paid only 25 cents each.

Bishop Houston was born just three years after one of Oklahoma's most famous territorial governors, T. B. Ferguson, died in 1921. Gov. Ferguson's contributions included pressing for the statehood of the

Oklahoma Territory and implementing the "herd law" which required land to be fenced to prevent livestock from destroying settlers' crops. During Bishop Houston's lifetime, the world would undergo phenomenal change, while the things that remained constant were love of family, friends, and God.

Times were hard, in the '20s and '30s, especially for a Black sharecropper with a wife and three children, but Bishop Houston's Dad was resourceful and his family never missed a meal. Sometimes it was only molasses and bread, or beans and cornbread, but they never went hungry.

The family lived in a little three-room home that was sparsely furnished, but overflowed with love from Mom, Dad, and extended family who lived nearby and visited often.

Some would say it was a coincidence that Sister Minnie's family in Texas and Bishop Houston's family in Oklahoma both moved to Los Angeles in 1936, but they knew the Lord had brought them there to be together and establish them for their life's work.

Sister Minnie's preparation started at the age of 14, when she accepted Christ under Mother E. J. Dabney. She was attending the Emmanuel Church of God in Christ, pastored by the late Bishop Samuel M. Crouch, Andre Crouch's great uncle. She taught Sunday School to the "Cradle Roll" and served as junior President of the Young Peoples Willing Workers.

Through the fellowship of Emmanuel Church of God in Christ and House of Prayer United Holy Church, she met Ralph Houston and in June 1948, they were married by Bishop Crouch.

Over the years, Sister Minnie's work in the church and community grew, but her priorities never changed. First there was her personal time with the Lord and then she was Ralph's wife and mother to their children before tending to the many duties and responsibilities of being *the Bishop's* wife.

Young pastors and their wives always found a visit to the Houstons helped them immensely with their own priorities, but they weren't the only ones. A group of young Doctors met regularly at the Houston's home for Bible study and found the teaching to be pure gold.

Neighbor Hilly Hicks, who produced the television show *Catch the Spirit*, stopped by regularly to get his word for the day. Dr. Charles Oakes, a health care consultant, and his wife Carolyn often came by to visit and almost always brought freshly baked bread. All who came by found the fellowship sweet at the Houstons and left having observed people whose lives were dedicated to, and shaped by, serving Christ. More lessons came from simply observing their well-ordered, hospitable lives than anything they ever said.

The Bartons, and other members of Christ Church, often checked in to see how Sister Minnie was doing with her cancer therapy. And it wasn't long before the Bartons were among those asking Bishop Houston to accompany them on visits to other friends who needed prayer.

The Houstons also asked them to pray for some of those they still ministered to in California. Of course, they did not mention Robin's situation to anyone, but later they would learn of it and discover it had been a matter of constant prayer during that time. Bishop Houston had assured Robin she would have her son back with her someday and encouraged her to just tell the truth and trust God. As a result, she had come completely clean without having any idea about what to expect in return.

For the next several months, she cooperated fully with the Drug Enforcement Agency (DEA), U.S. Marshals and U.S. Attorneys. Having never been addicted to drugs herself, she had an excellent memory and after more than four years of living with Cush, was able to furnish them with a wealth of information.

In fact, they soon realized she would be their star witness. In preparation for the trial, Robin accompanied U.S. Marshals and Drug Enforcement agents into neighborhoods where Cush's posses had operated and supplied them with the information they needed to solidify their cases. All the while, Robin was looking over her shoulder, as even with all the government's protection and firepower, she did not feel safe.

The group were actually chased out of one neighborhood after being spotted by members of the posse. Of course, the U.S. Marshals and DEA agents could have fought it out, but under the circumstances, it made more sense to make a high-speed exit and protect their witness.

DEA agent Patsy Matthews was a constant source of encouragement during Robin's many bouts with loneliness and illness. Throughout the years Robin spent with Cush, he had beaten her, thrown her down stairs and in many other ways subjected her to outrageous physical and verbal abuse, compounding her health problems.

Robin's health problems began in 1983 when, following an episode of excruciating pain, she was rushed to the hospital and underwent surgery for a ruptured ovarian cyst. After the operation she was never really physically sound again. Frequent periods of severe constipation and nausea overtook her, causing her to vomit until she was completely debilitated. With her weight dropping dramatically, she had to remain hospitalized and continue with intravenous feedings until her condition was stabilized.

Even after being released, reoccurring periods of intense suffering resulted in her being sent to a specialist for a battery of tests. Some of the tests were more painful than the condition that originally brought her in, but Robin was relieved to finally have a diagnosis. It was a relief to know she might finally be free from the complications of intestinal nerve damage by having a section of her intestines removed.

However, she had barely recovered from that surgery when another ovarian cyst sent her back to the hospital. Following those episodes, she had never fully recovered her health. So it wasn't unusual for another surgical procedure to be required. However, this time there was the added pressure of the upcoming trial.

Everyone was very kind to Robin during this period, especially Patsy, who went above and beyond the call of duty by doing her hair and other little things to make life more pleasant. Patsy's caring companionship bolstered Robin's spirits during her stay in the hospital and through the tough days that followed.

There wasn't been much time for convalescing, as Robin was on the witness stand just one week after surgery. It wasn't easy to sit there day after day facing eight defense attorneys who tried to discredit her by questioning every word of testimony she uttered.

Question: "You are in prison...?" Answer, "Yes."
Question: "You never actually saw the home in Florida, did you?" Answer, "No, I did not."
Question: "You never saw a home in California, did you?" Answer, "No."

Day after grueling day she testified and withstood attacks on her credibility and for almost every mistake she had ever made in her adult life. It all came out for the whole world to see. She felt naked, stripped of all rights. probed and prodded until she would have been psychologically decimated, except for Christ. In her weakest hour, she felt Him there with her and in spite of confessing to some of the most egregious mistakes a human being can make, she was not despised by the judge and jury.

From the expressions on the faces of the jurists, she could see they couldn't comprehend how she could have been a party to such unseemly deeds, especially when she was examined about who her husband really was. Jury members just shook their heads in disbelief as she explained that she had gone to Jamaica and married Cush's brother in order to help him gain entry to America. In spite of the humiliation, she pressed on. How she wanted to tell the judge and jury she was forced into complying with Cush's demands, but how could she explain that to their satisfaction? She had willingly entered into a personal relationship with him, willingly allowed his friends and workers to move into her apartment. But once she was under his control, she could not leave when she wanted out.

How she wanted to be understood on this point, but what were the chances of her lawyer, a public defender, adequately communicating it? Even the great attorney F. Lee Bailey had not been able to do so for heiress Patty Hearst after she had been snatched and literally brainwashed into converting to her captors' ideology.

Robin couldn't explain it, but she had been under the control of something bigger than herself until she accepted Christ. It was very frustrating, but all she could do was press on. So she continued and provided rare insights into the inner workings of a drug operation that employed more than fifty individuals who manufactured and distributed cocaine, crack, and marijuana.

From 1985 until December 1988, their organization sold well in excess of two million vials of crack, for $5.00 to $10.00 each, from over twenty locations, some of which were heavily fortified.

The federal government began tracking Jamaican posses in 1984 and estimated they had killed more than 1,400 people in the US by 1989. The devastating effects of their various enterprises on America's communities were well documented but not well known to the public at large.

Cush's organization was one of the first groups to distribute crack cocaine in an organized fashion in that part of the country. While the communities suffered, Cush profited handsomely from his illicit trade. Robin testified about the lavish lifestyle Cush enjoyed, driving expensive cars, and purchasing a $250,000 home with a swimming pool in Florida. Robin had helped him make the money to buy it and enjoyed some of the benefits but still couldn't prove much of his holdings existed. Cush had promised to take her to see his hundred-acre estate in California but said he would have to blindfold her first so she wouldn't be able to tell anyone else how to get there. Paranoia is rampant in the drug business, and Cush didn't trust anyone.

Sullen and tight-lipped, he did not allow anyone to take his picture, and if anyone slipped up and disclosed anything about his business, they paid dearly for doing so. Wanton violence was part and parcel of the drug business.

In the courtroom, Robin could feel his hate and would not even look in his direction as she testified about driving him to a street corner where he opened fire on several men, murdering one in cold blood and wounding another because he believed they were rival drug dealers.

She was reliving the horror of the past each day she was on the witness stand, recounting for the jury the many times she had seen him brutally beat workers senseless.

On one occasion Robin, nauseated and scared stiff, had driven the car through a black, moonless night while Cush and one of his cohorts wrestled "Mikey," a sixteen-year-old they had beaten bloody, down onto the backseat floorboard. As he struggled to get up, they grabbed his right hand and attempted to cut off the thumb and index fingers. Cush liked to leave visible evidence of his retribution on those who smoked up his dope and profits. But Mikey was desperately and frantically struggling to escape. The intensity of the fight finally caused Robin to "lose it" and she hit the brakes, throwing the men in the back of the car forward.

Momentarily loosened from the grip of his captors, Mikey bailed out of the car and ran at breakneck speed toward a passing police car. As Cush yelled at Robin to get the h--- out of there, she hit the accelerator of the pearl-colored Mercedes throwing the cursing men in the back seat off balance. Knowing every street like the back of her hand, Robin sped through the blackness like a professional race-car driver. Jamaican expletives assaulted her as she screeched around corners while catching glances of Cush's fierce face in the rearview mirror.

When they realized they did not have a police car on their tail, the men started laughing at Mikey's terror-filled cries. Satisfied the kid would never again steal from him, Cush's rage subsided.

Relieved that she was escaping retribution, Robin's heart gradually settled down, but she was very cautious and did not dare enter into the laughter or conversation, as Cush was totally unpredictable. She did not want to re-ignite the anger of this proud, dangerous and easily offended man who could be extraordinarily generous with her one minute and cruel as the grave the next.

Cush's dreadlocks reached down to the small of his back and he strictly adhered to Dreadlock traditions, even restricting his diet and drug use accordingly. The Dreadlock organization descended out of the Rastafarian religion and aside from marijuana (ganja), which they consider to be medicinal, they *did not* believe in using the drugs they sold. If Mikey hadn't escaped, it's likely that he would have lost more than his fingers, the state of which remains a mystery. As did many other things in which Cush was involved.

In typical Caribbean fashion, he had ongoing relationships with at least four different women at the same time, by whom it was said that he fathered as many as ten children. According to Rastafarian custom, the women were assigned an inferior status in his organization. Typically they were "mules and go-fers" -- except for Robin, who more valuable to him because of her high intelligence, American citizenship, disarming baby face and engaging personality. He and Robin had no children together, but they were very close in spite of the other women in his life.

Robin knew of five children he had with one of his "baby mothers," two with another, one with another, and there were rumors of others.

The women and younger workers were the most vulnerable and expendable ones, so they were placed in the most dangerous positions. Most had not been in the country very long, had no money and were desperate for work of any kind. It was not uncommon for workers to be picked up in New York, given some drugs to sell and dropped off at a trashed out, abandoned house that stunk to high heaven of garbage and human excrement.

Of course there was no electricity or plumbing, but they were given candles for light and a kerosene heater to keep them from freezing to death. They had no money to go anywhere and didn't know where to go if they did, so they stayed and sold drugs for Cush until they were arrested or figured a way out. Cush allowed them to use some of the drug money for food and they would walk to a convenience store to wash up and get something to eat.

It took an awesome level of fear to keep people in such dire straits from dipping into the till, but Cush's legendary skill with guns, swords, and the martial arts kept them in line. Very few risked falling into his bad graces by taking any more than they needed to survive. Even then they were always nervous about what they took, as he was very dangerous and would not tolerate them taking any liberties with his money. In one instance, believing a man had robbed him, he poured gasoline around his house and set it on fire.

Some of the young people who found themselves under his dominion came from extremely poor but caring homes with hard-working parents. They were in this predicament because a violent Jamaican civil war in the mid-'70s resulted in them growing up in a politically unstable and war-torn environment, where people were often killed in the streets.

In addition to the violence, they had to cope with a severe food shortage that forced rural residents to migrate into Kingston to survive. Away from their family and friends with whom they might otherwise have left their children, some resorted to tying their young children to trees while they worked.

By law, children of school age were required to attend until the age of 14 and if not for the fees imposed by the "free" public schools for books, supplies and other items, many children might have continued beyond that. However the economic pressures placed further education beyond the reach of the average family, leaving them unprepared to be useful members of society.

Getting to the United States or Canada, where the streets seemed to be lined with gold, was the dream of most young Jamaicans, and about 13,000 a year made it.

Even though he came from these conditions himself, Cush seemed to have no compassion for his fellow countrymen. When they were arrested, he only bailed out the ones who were most useful to him. Even the woman who had borne him five children found he had made no provisions for her legal defense. She had to rely on a court-appointed attorney to plead her case and ended up with a prison sentence to be followed by deportation. Cush did not seem to care if his own children were left without benefit of father or mother.

Jurors were aghast and pained by the testimony they heard. Most of them knew nothing of the Jamaican culture that was now seriously impacting their own city. Sunny beaches, tropical tans and exotic drinks were how most of them had formerly thought of Jamaica. A few had seen movies like Steven Seagal's, *Marked for Death* but hadn't realized this social poison was moving into a community near them. Now their eyes were being opened as to how the drug business provided outrageous extravagance for some, desperate poverty for others, and peace of mind for no one, least of all innocent bystanders and taxpayers like themselves.

They were keenly interested in how Robin, a young woman with enormous potential, became involved. She told them Cush had initially been wonderful to her and Ralph. He bought her clothes, took her to nice restaurants and on one occasion he gave Ralph a one hundred dollar bill to get an ice cream with and told him to keep the change!

So Robin was shocked to discover how quickly Cush turned on her when she found a suitcase full of drugs and money, and ran to her mother's house. Cush countered by taking Ralph from day care and from that point forward she was so terrified of him that he had no trouble controlling her every move. It wasn't long before she was deeply involved in his organization's burgeoning drug business; collecting money, transporting drugs, negotiating property leases, purchasing cars and weapons.

It was only after Cush was arrested that Robin found the courage to take Ralph and run as far from Cush's henchmen as she could get. She knew their modus operandi all too well. She shuddered at the memory of one man being stripped naked, tied to a straight-back chair and tortured by having hot burning plastic dripped all over him. Somehow he managed to break free and jumped from a second story window.

Another worker was just lying on the floor watching television when without warning, Cush begin to kick him in the head and back. As his rage built, Cush stomped him repeatedly, then grabbed a stun gun and shocked him into a coma-like state. The price for tampering with Cush's merchandise was high, and this kid had been filling the caps with candle wax while smoking the crack that he was supposed to be putting in them.

All manner of weapons were used to intimidate and terrorize underlings. Prosecution attorneys requested permission to bring the defendants' swords into the courtroom, and the judge flatly refused them. He knew the defendants were all martial arts experts and had no intention of having his courtroom look like the last scene of Camelot!

In spite of everything, Bishop Houston, Sister Minnie and Bethel members continued to pray and stand in the gap for Robin. Interceding for such a desperate situation is not easy, but they had little Ralph before them every day as a constant reminder to keep praying and asking God not for justice, but for mercy.

There was no denying the load was heavy for the Houstons at this time.   Thank goodness Sister Minnie was holding her own and even felt like accompanying Bishop Houston on an upcoming mission trip to Liberia. They were looking forward to this welcome break and were in high spirits, until the subpoena arrived.

"Oh, dear God, please help me and my family to deal with this," Bishop Houston prayed.   Being called to testify in the Broussard trial was one of the hardest things he had ever faced in his life.   As he stared at the subpoena, he noticed the date did not interfere with their mission trip and for that he was grateful, as they really needed the time away before facing that ordeal.

CHAPTER FOUR

*"...Go ye into all the world, and
preach the gospel to every creature..." (Mark 16:15)*

On the long flight to Liberia, Bishop Houston read Marie Rice's book about Sister Bertha and Sister Ruth, two women missionaries who went to Liberia in the 1920s...

"One day as I (Sister Bertha) was sitting on the verandah, a heavy, hairy something hopped on my shoulder. Startled, I screamed and jumped to my feet.

"Mr. Zeussli laughed. 'Don't be afraid, Miss. That's only Jimmy, my pet chimpanzee. He won't hurt you - will you Jimmy?'

"The chimp hopped over to Mr. Zeussli, looked appealingly at me, and shook his head "no." In a friendly gesture, he extended his hairy hand.

"I hesitated and drew back for a second. With one quick movement, the animal stole my handkerchief from my dress pocket and immediately blew his nose into it. Then he grinned at me as if expecting my approval. I was flabbergasted.

"'He's one smart chimp.' Mr. Zeussli said. 'I've been training him. He's a good student, and has a great sense of humor.'

"He began to brag about his pet and Jimmy listened attentively as if he were agreeing with every word. It was uncanny.

"The chimp had been taught to wear clothes. He had a complete outfit, exactly like his master's, and when the two of them were together, the chimp looked like a miniature Mr. Zeussli.

"It was a comical sight - the two of them walking together and puffing on cigars, or sitting at a table sharing a meal.

"Jimmy had his own bed and wouldn't go to sleep unless he was wearing clean pajamas. If he didn't like the way the girl made his bed, he would tear it all apart. If he didn't like the way she ironed his shirts, he'd tear them apart. Truly, Jimmy was an amazing animal.

"One day, Mr. Zeussli planted several cabbage plants in his garden. Like a sidewalk superintendent, Jimmy watched every move. After he finished planting them, Mr. Zeussli went back into the house. The chimp studied the garden for awhile. Then he meticulously pulled up every cabbage plant and replanted each one upside down.

"Mr. Zeussli became very angry and spanked Jimmy. The chimp was mortified and shamed to such an extent that his heart was broken.

"After that, Mr. Zeussli tried every way to pet the animal and make up with him, but the chimp never responded to him. Jimmy finally died of a broken heart."[*]

As Bishop Houston read on about the experiences those two remarkable ladies had when they went to Liberia more than 50 years ago, he couldn't help asking himself how in the world these two white ladies coped with life in Africa.

In an age when most American women didn't even work outside the home, how did two single, white, Christian women ever get the courage to go live in Liberia?

---

[*] *Sister Bertha, Sister Ruth*, author Marie Rice, Jonathan Publisher

Before going, they would surely have read about the experiences of those who had gone before them. Best known was Dr. David Livingstone who went to Africa in 1838. At times, Dr. Livingstone, was half-starved and suffered from jungle fevers, malaria, and dysentery, but he continued to share the message of Christ as long as he drew a breath.

While he was not inclined to write of the difficulties, others had. "On the job training" for new recruits included instructions on how to deal with charges from water buffalo. He told them it was best to throw themselves to the ground and grab hold of the grass so the water buffalo could not get their horns under them to throw them in the air! He also felt the best way to deal with lions was to look them right in the eye and not back down. It worked for him most of the time but on one occasion, he was attacked and severely mauled, causing permanent damage to one arm. However, he reported, a dreamlike state and numbing effect kept the actual attack from being too bad.

At the conclusion of more than thirty-five years of thrilling and well-documented, adventures, Dr. Livingstone's reputation was legendary. There probably wasn't a missionary who came to the African continent after him who hadn't read every word he had written. He had traveled over 29,000 miles of Africa's terrain and was as respected for his remarkable exploration feats as for his highly successful work for Christ.

After surviving every manner of ferocious beast, poisonous snakes and deadly insects, he died peacefully on May 1, 1873, in his Chitambo hut. He was found about at 4:00 a.m., down on his knees. What a fitting conclusion to life totally consecrated to Christ. His African converts wanted him buried there with them, but the English wanted his body buried in his homeland. The debate was resolved by the natives burying his heart near them, under the shade of a majestic tree. Then they further demonstrated their enormous love and respect for him by carefully preserving his body and transporting it over thousands of miles to a seaport. The journey took months and from there, his body was shipped back to England where he was buried in Westminster Abbey with royalty and others of renown. These early pioneers didn't have the luxury of flying in, but came via long, rough sea voyages. In our modern culture, very few people can understand the commitment it took to leave behind families, and everything else that was familiar, to brave such challenges. Missionaries who have done so are sure to have the seats closest to the throne on that great and glorious morning when the dead in Christ shall rise. Bishop Houston thought it was wonderful that Sister Bertha and Sister Ruth had been able to persevere and get along with each other well enough to work together for fifty years.

During his years of leadership, he concluded that very few talents need to be developed more conscientiously than the ability to get along with each other. This more than anything else determined one's ability to succeed in life. In cross-cultural situations as complicated as Liberia's, it was doubly important.

To Bishop Houston, it seemed, Liberia hadn't changed all that much. Even today, about ninety percent of the population retained their tribal way of life, and even though English is the official language, most people still speak one of the African languages.

Bishop Houston enjoyed studying Liberian history beginning when the country was founded by the American Colonization Society (ACS) in 1816 to repatriate freed Negro American slaves to Africa.

In Bishop Houston's conversations with Liberians, they told a far different story than those recorded by the

Library of Congress. Some Liberians said philandering, guilt-ridden white men who had fathered far too many mulatto children were eager to see the physical evidence of their sins shipped to foreign shores.

Others said it was because some Americans were afraid their own slaves would be influenced by a growing number of free African-Americans. So they set about helping freed slaves leave the country in order to protect their own interest.

While there was some truth in these stories, Bishop Houston felt God was the real reason for the development of the ACS. President James Monroe and Supreme Court Justice Bushrod Washington were among the distinguished founders of the ACS as were Andrew Jackson, Francis Scott Key, Henry Clay and Daniel Webster.

According to the African Repository and Colonial Journal, Robert E. Lee freed most of his slaves before the Civil War and offered to pay expenses for those who wanted to go to Liberia.

In November 1853, Lee's former slaves, William and Rosabella Burke and their four children, sailed on the *Banshee*, which left Baltimore with 261 emigrants. A person of superior intelligence and drive, Burke studied Latin and Greek at a newly established seminary in Monrovia and became a Presbyterian minister in 1857.

He helped educate his own children and other members of his community and took several native children into his home. The Burkes's letter describing their lives in Liberia shows that they relied on the Lees to convey messages to and from relatives still in Virginia, and the letters also reflect affection for their former masters.[*]

---

[*] Library of Congress, Internet Edition

After five years in Liberia, William Burke wrote, "Persons coming to Africa should expect to go through many hardships, such as are common to the first settlement in any new country. I expected it, and was not disappointed or discouraged at anything I met with; and so far from being dissatisfied with the country, I bless the Lord that ever my lot was cast in this part of the earth. The Lord has blessed me abundantly since my residence in Africa, for which I feel that I can never be sufficiently thankful."[*]

A letter from Mrs. Burke to Mrs. Lee demonstrates personal warmth between the two women. Mrs. Burke shows concern for Mrs. Lee's health, tells Mrs. Lee about her children, and asks about the Lee children. "Little Martha" was Martha Curtis Lee Burke, born in Liberia and named for one of the Lee family. Repeating her husband's enthusiasm for their new life, Rosabella Burke says, "I love Africa and would not exchange it for America."[*]

Many others also considered it a great privilege to go to Liberia in spite of having no idea of what to expect when they got there. It became easier still when the civil war was over and African Americans did not have to face some of the terrible decisions that confronted them prior to it. For instance, when Timothy Roger of Bedford County, Virginia, freed his twelve slaves in his will, under the condition that they go to Liberia, one indicated he preferred to remain a slave if he were unable to take his wife, the property of another owner, with him.

By 1866, the ACS had sent approximately 13,000 of these "settlers" to Africa's West Coast. Then in 1892, a new direction was announced as the ACS turned its attention to the question of how best to strengthen Liberia

---

[*] Ibid, Excerpts from 7/16/1858 letter to ACS President Ralph Gurley
[*] Ibid, Letter from Mrs. Burke to Mrs. Robert E. Lee

and make it self-sufficient. It was decided that future colonists should be selected according to the needs of Liberia and the next wave of emigrants were hand-picked from the candidates most qualified to help the country.

An example of this preferred type of colonist was Miss Georgia Patton, described in an early issue of "Liberia," "Well-educated, Miss Patton planned to practice medicine and teach school in Liberia. She also shared the ACS goals of doing good for others and spreading Christianity and civilization in Africa."[*]

Because the character of emigrants was an issue the ACS was very concerned with, applicants had to submit letters of recommendation. Excerpts from a highly favorable letter came from officials of the Citizens Bank of Vian and J. H. Dodd, M.D.: "Henry Bonds has a host of friends in all the races," and his family is "regarded as one of the very best in the country."[*]

As these fine people came to Liberia to establish new lives, missionaries (primarily from Baptist, Presbyterian and Methodist denominations) came to help them. Together they faced fierce resistance from the natives and lethal diseases like malaria, tuberculosis, yaws and leprosy. They learned to contend with the humid, equatorial climate whose rainy seasons (June to July and October to November) sometimes produced as much as 200 inches of rainfall in a year.

There was a heavy mortality rate and only about half of the newcomers survived the adjustment period. But with the support of the United States, the settlers rose to power and established a democracy. They designed a Declaration of Independence, Constitution and flag that closely resembled America's and chose the dollar as their currency.

---

[*] Ibid, Nov. 1893 edition of *Liberia*
[*] Ibid

Monrovia, named after President James Monroe, became the country's capitol, and many other places were given American names as well. These settlers became known as Americo-Liberians whose elite educated their children in American colleges before guiding them into positions of national leadership, including sixteen of the next nineteen Liberian presidential posts.

Now, in 1990, as Bishop Houston and Sister Minnie flew toward Liberia, he contemplated the gap that still had not been bridged between the emigrants and the indigenous African population. There were many contributing factors including the thirty-four different languages spoken in a country that is about the size of Tennessee and the less than sixty-five percent literacy rate. In addition to the communication problems, most Liberians lived in abject poverty, so it wasn't hard to understand why tensions ran high between the ruling class and the majority of the country's 3,000,000 citizens.

Bishop Houston was among those who believed that education could bring about understanding and raise the standard of living for those toiling under such a heavy burden. For that reason, he and Sister Minnie had brought business consultant Ms. Berleter Hall to the Salala Mission in 1987 to research the feasibility of adding a high school and junior college to the mission's educational program that presently stopped at the ninth grade level.

It had been wonderful to have Ms. Hall come help, even though her offer was contingent on them not pestering her to regularly attend church! The Houstons decided to leave that to the Lord and accepted her offer.

When they left the Roberts Field Airport and the flat coastal areas of the country that were developed, the Houstons watched closely for Ms. Hall's reactions. She was every bit the modern, professional woman and they wondered how she would feel about entering a culture that would make her feel she was stepping back in time.

The Salala Mission, about sixty miles out of Monrovia and two miles off the main road, was in the bush country where only seven acres had been cleared from the dense growth of cotton trees, fig, mahogany, ironwood and various kinds of palms, as well as trees providing rubber. Some of the surrounding villages could only be reached by walking through thick tropical forests that reduced transportation routes to mere trails.

At the mission, food, clothing and other physical needs were met and, as often as possible, basic treatment was given for illnesses or injuries. However, evangelism and education were also of the utmost importance. Students came from various parts of Liberia for the Kindergarten through ninth grade classes, the twice-a-day prayer services, Bible study and Sunday worship services.

Others were ministered to through outreaches to the villages that included taking as many of the mission's services as possible out to the people in the jungle.

Over the years, the Houstons had brought many people to the Salala Mission and they almost always left a big part of their hearts behind in Africa when they went home. Ms. Hall was no different and quickly came to love the country and its people.

As they met with government officials and church leaders, Ms. Hall became increasingly impressed with Bishop Houston's respect for her abilities and his support of her work. When she commented on it, he explained that because his mother had been a great woman, he never questioned a woman's ability to do an outstanding job.

Ms. Hall thought, how refreshing it was to be treated as a *consultant* instead of a *woman*. So many businessmen had a tendency to patronize women, treat them as an ornament, or take pains to make sure everyone understood *they were in charge.* That type of posturing made it difficult for everyone else to operate freely or have their competency recognized.

But Bishop Houston was different. He was totally relaxed in who he was and felt no need to assert himself. Ms. Hall wished some of the chest-beating businessmen she worked with could simply observe Bishop Houston and see how a truly great leader didn't need to control, dictate, and call attention to themselves. So much more was accomplished when the *project* was the focus of attention. Ms. Hall's respect and appreciation of Bishop Houston's fine qualities grew with each passing day.

She found that Bishop Houston had a deep and abiding commitment to do his part in fulfilling Jesus' final earthly request about "going into all the world and preaching the gospel." As she looked at the financial picture, she realized Little Bethel provided the lion's share of the funds to support the Salala Mission. At this point, she did not know how many churches there were in the entire United Holy Church denomination, but clearly Bishop Houston was the person in whom the mission's vision burned the brightest.

Many times, she noticed him reach in his pocket and discreetly pay for many of the things that needed to be taken care of, including the repair of the mission's pick-up truck. It was good to see his sacrifices were appreciated by the people benefiting from his gifts. In fact it moved her deeply to see how much love and respect the people accorded Bishop Houston.

His desire to help these people was genuine and contagious. She soon found herself wanting to be a part of what was happening here.

Upon returning to the states, Ms. Hall started attending church and was welcomed into Bethel's family. Bishop Houston's sermons were like seminars and she loved seminars! But most of all, she felt she was a part of something good and wholesome, something larger than herself, a world-changing force.

So many people sit around criticizing the work others are doing while doing nothing themselves. Of course it is easier to do that, or to sidestep a call to courage by philosophizing about why people have needs, but that accomplishes nothing. Bishop Houston and his congregation at Bethel were looking for ways to help and worked to change things for the better. Ms. Hall found it very refreshing to be with people who cared, and not about what the members wore, but about their brothers and sisters in Christ.

Ms. Hall had first heard about Bishop Houston after seeing a newspaper article about a new ministerial alliance called "The Gathering." She liked a statement he made about how the church's role included ensuring economic well-being for its members here on earth. This was startling! A preacher? A *black* preacher?

She had never been able to understand how all cultural groups, except African-Americans, used their religions to address this area of the "church body's" needs, so she was excited to find one who felt as she did and made arrangements to meet him.

She was delighted to find Bishop Houston was an understanding man regarding where people were in their life and accepted them as they came.

Her confidence in men of the cloth was restored as she observed the love and respect he had for his family. He was a devoted family man who always praised his wife and children for their accomplishments.

She noticed it was Bishop Houston's habit to go home at 4:00 p.m. every afternoon for the delicious supper Sister Minnie always prepared for him. She also quickly learned that there was no point in attempting to schedule an appointment around that time.

However, on several occasions, she was invited to come by and join them for dinner. Before long she realized it was okay to just drop in, as others did. As a consultant, she would be the official "taster" which would help keep the cooking skills sharp and make sure the fixins' were delicious. Everyone teased her about her way of helping out!

Like so many, she admired Sister Minnie's social graces, etiquette and openness. What a fine family the Houstons had produced. The men were strong, hard working, and wore their Houston name proudly -- but without any pretenses.

It was also easy for Ms. Hall to see why Carol was the entire family's bright and shining star. Her parents and her brothers unanimously acknowledged her rare and rich gifts without any hint of sibling rivalry.

They were all certain--and Ms. Hall (who they were now affectionately calling "B") concurred--that Carol, a dynamic woman of God, would be used in a mighty way. She was a powerful preacher, teacher, coordinator and counselor as well as an astute businesswoman and all around nice person.

If Bishop Houston left this world with unfinished business, he was sure Carol would be able to finish them properly. However, there were some things he would like to get done before his work on earth was through and he hoped to finish some of it on this trip.

As the coast of Africa came into view, he wondered why he had not been able to get his denomination to go ahead and construct the much needed high school and junior college. The feasibility study Ms. Hall had done was excellent and all the groundwork had been laid for it on his last visit. But for some inexplicable reason, his denomination had refused to move forward.

Well, this time, he had personally raised and brought enough money with him for a smaller project and hoped to see it well underway before leaving. Wages were quite low in Liberia and for $25.00 per month, he could get excellent workers who would work from the time the sun came up in the morning until it went down at night. In Liberia, they simply agreed to work from "sun to sun." These Liberian men worked hard and steadily so Bishop Houston expected to make significant progress on this trip.

It grieved Bishop Houston's heart to think of the limited opportunities the Liberian men had. Some had to work for as little as fifteen cents an hour while others raised their families in rubber plantation huts and spent their whole lives eking out a living by "milking" latex from the trees.

Many times, the Houstons had stopped and watched these industrious men and their families at work. Starting at about eye level, they made a slanted cut, about a third to halfway around the tree, so the exuding latex would trail down and into a cup.

The tree would be continually retapped (usually on a daily basis) by shaving a thin strip of bark away, just below the original cut. When the bark had been stripped away all the way to ground level, the tree was allowed to renew itself before being tapped again.

Men, women and children would quickly empty the cups, holding only about an ounce of latex each, into buckets secured to the ends of a pole and carried on the shoulders of workers who ran all day collecting the precious substance.

The lives of families toiling together in Africa's rubber plantations were much like those of their counterparts who worked America's farms. If a man was working his own farm, it was a satisfying way of life, but if he was working for someone else who wanted to get the most out of a person for the least amount of money, it was miserable.

Since 1926, Firestone had operated the world's largest rubber plantation in Liberia. As might be expected, there had been labor disputes and scandals. Liberia's elite had accused Firestone of taking advantage of the country's work force and natural resources while not doing much to help the working class.

Under such conditions, the peasants had grown increasingly unhappy over the class disparities and felt the ruling elite, who had formerly been oppressed in America, were now their oppressors. Decades of poverty-driven despair were hardening into anger, which Liberian leadership would temporarily appease with various development programs and, when those didn't work, by retaliation.

America had a vital interest in Liberia's stabilization as the country was useful as a base from which regional terrorism could be fought and as a CIA "listening post." Under President Reagan's leadership, America gave more than $400 million in aid from 1981 to 1985, which was more than Liberia had received during the entire previous century. Unfortunately, this did not trickle down to the working man, and civil strife continued.

In late 1989, a small group of rebels had crossed the border and there were reports that the fighting was escalating, but from the information he had received, Bishop Houston understood the Salala Mission was unaffected. Hopefully a peaceful resolution would be forthcoming shortly.

After arriving at the mission and recovering from jet lag, Bishop Houston and the mission's director, Dr. Raymond Johnson began working with a group of Liberian men to clear the land and prepare the site for the clinic they planned to build.

It was needed more than ever since the beautiful, three-story John F. Kennedy Hospital in Monrovia had been stripped of all of its equipment. Thieves just carted some of it away in the night, and many suspected the doctors themselves had taken some of the larger equipment to their own clinics in outlying areas. Corruption was rampant and massive mismanagement of public resources was raising the levels of tension.

Bishop Houston was heartsick to find there was not enough gasoline or cement available to complete the clinic. Nothing could be done about it, and this project too would have to wait until some future date.

About halfway through their six-week visit to Salala, Bishop Houston was awakened very early one morning and went out to sit on the screened porch. He asked himself, "After thirty-six years of marriage to such a wonderful wife, why aren't you at one of the popular vacation resorts instead of deep in the bush country of Liberia?"

A divinely inspired answer came as quickly as the question, "You're in the right place and you're right on schedule." Then came the scripture, "Many are called but few are chosen." Joy filled Bishop Houston's heart as the spirit of the Lord continued to minister to him, "I've chosen you to lead and you're on schedule."

It was about 4:30 a.m. and a bright moon illuminated the dew-covered trees and bushes with tinges of liquid silver. Fragrant wild flowers perfumed the air of a serene, peaceful and profoundly silent world. Bishop Houston sat very still and contemplated what had just been revealed to him, as the precious presence of the Holy Spirit gently surrounded him with a feeling of loving approval and comfort. Moments like these were why he continued to come back to this place.

With the spirit of the Lord lingering upon him and the stars fading from the sky, he was inspired to get up and get a notebook. In the coolness of the morning, it seemed the Holy Spirit moved his hand as he outlined the course of his life's experiences from his early conversion up to that moment.

Bishop Houston then reviewed the outline to the sounds of the waking forest and the rising of the sun over the tree top. As he looked up at the heavens lightening up with luminous streams of peach, blue and gold, something stirred within him confirming the dawning of a new day in the life of his ministry.

He was moved to write about his life's journey with the Lord, and as he did so, he praised the Lord for all His blessings and marveled at what God had already done in his life.

Then came the sweetest part of all as the Lord showed him that the course of his ministry was about to change and that larger responsibility lay ahead.

Bishop Houston was humbled and honored to be chosen of the Lord and to have the promise of a greater leadership role in His Kingdom. He smiled and wondered where the Lord was taking him. Wherever it was, it would be fine, just as long as the Lord kept assuring him he was in the place He wanted him to be.

During the remainder of their stay at the mission, the Houstons received an outpouring of love from everyone. Sister Minnie had fresh flowers and fruit brought to her daily along with precious handmade gifts from the students who noticed she was thinner and weaker than the last time they saw her.

Their own future was as uncertain as hers because no one knew what would happen in Liberia, but regardless of what lay ahead, they all felt this was a time to be cherished. The singing was sweeter, the sermons more meaningful and the communion with each other and God richer than they could ever remember.

Each moment was treasured and as their departure time grew near, the Houstons prayed for the Salala Mission as never before. Liberia was like a powder keg with a short fuse, and they didn't want anything to happen to their dear friends.

They were also praying for their friends back in the states. Robin and Ralph were in their prayers daily as were those involved in the Broussard case. In all his life, Bishop Houston had never seen the kind of spiritual warfare the church was facing while dealing with things like the Broussard situation. The church just could not afford to be ignorant of the increasingly deceptive tactics being used by the enemy of our souls.

CHAPTER FIVE

"...Why eateth your master with publicans and sinners? But when Jesus heard that, he said...'They that be whole need not a physician, but they that are sick.' " (Matt. 9:11)

Numerous messages awaited the Houstons when they returned to their home in Nashville. Robin's trial was over. After eighty witnesses had testified, Cush was found guilty on all counts and sentenced to life without the possibility of parole.

But Robin had lost her good friend and confidant, DEA agent Patsy Matthews. It was a great shock to everyone involved in the case, but especially to Robin, who lived in constant fear for her own life and was certain Cush could get to anyone, anytime he wanted to.

Patsy's body was found in her bedroom on the upper level of her two-story home. She was slumped over in her bed with a bullet wound in the left side of her head. A .22 caliber automatic pistol was found on the floor near her body.

Patsy's son said he was sleeping in his own bedroom when he was awakened by the sound of a gunshot. He went to his mother's bedroom and found her. No suicide note was found and he did not feel she had been depressed or had any reason to kill herself. There were no signs of forced entry or assault inside the home.

Patsy had been a policewoman since April 1977 and had most recently been doing undercover investigations for the narcotic unit's Jamaican task force. Robin mourned the loss of her friend and knew she could very well share the same fate.

The prayers of Robin's family and friends were all that kept her sane during this time. As she watched members of the drug organization receive their long sentences, her hope of ever having Ralph with her again wavered and almost died. Especially when the mother of five of Cush's children received a stiff sentence that would be followed by deportation orders. Who knew what would happen to those children? Or all the others who would be punished along with their parents?

However, prayers were answered and Robin found mercy in the eyes of the Lord. When Robin told Bishop Houston that the Judge, Robert S. Gawthorp III, had referred to her as one of the most convincing witnesses in the trial, Bishop Houston was proud of her for redeeming herself with the truthful and courageous testimony that contributed to so many violent felons being taken off the streets.

Most of all, they were overjoyed at Robin's light sentence (only 16 months). After that, she and Ralph would enter the government's witness protection program. She was elated and felt she could do her time standing on her head as long as she would have Ralph back with her soon.

She was sent to the Rochester Federal Medical Center in Minnesota, which had to be the coldest prison in America, but Robin's thoughts were with her dear son in sunny California and that warmed her soul, even when her hands and feet were freezing. They were able to talk often and speculated about where they would be re-located when she got out.

Of course she was still afraid of the Jamaican Mafia and knew they could get to her here, too. In addition to always looking over her shoulder, she also had to contend with strip searches, rigid rules that changed at a moment's notice, and the chilling view of an electric fence topped with razor wire that could cut a body to shreds.

Robin managed to stay out of harm's way and passed the time visiting with other inmates. The facility she was in had originally been a mental institution and still housed some prisoners who fell into that category.

Particularly sad was a man who kept talking about going home to see his family. His words expressed the poignant longings of a deluded man whose mind had obliterated the horrifying memory of having murdered them himself many years ago!

Prison was a strange place. The ultimate melting pot that held within its confines individuals who would seldom, if ever, meet outside this bizarre institution. People like Jim Bakker, who had been invited to the White House and flown with Presidents on Air Force One, were housed with people who had never received respect or love from anyone.

Those who had enjoyed the luxury of screening every call were now rubbing shoulders with violent, habitual offenders. However, most of the prisoners were much like the country's average citizens. The well-known and the unknown all shared the same loss of freedom, dignity, and self-respect. The greatest misery came from feelings of abandonment when visits tapered off and mail quit coming.

Some prisoners hadn't heard from anyone on the outside for years. Like the country's elderly who were institutionalized in nursing homes, many were largely forgotten and dropped from their circles of family and friends.

After about two years, married prisoners usually found their spouses couldn't cope and were on the verge of filing divorce papers. Holidays were the hardest to face, as they reminded everyone that life was going on without them. Usually they had nothing to give their loved ones and were consumed with guilt and a sense of total worthlessness.

Just when Robin thought she could not stand this cold, gray, depressing place another day, she received news of a transfer to California! It would be so good to be near her son Ralph and in a warm climate.

It wasn't long before Robin was telling the Houstons about meeting hitman Jimmy "The Weasel" Fratianno, former leader of the Los Angeles Cosa Nostra. She couldn't believe he had defied all the rules of the witness protection program by writing a book, giving interviews or doing whatever else struck his fancy.

Fratianno had been the Justice Department's star witness against the mob and felt he should be treated better because of it. He complained about everything, including all the name changes he and his wife had to go through, having to move every five or six months and the money he lost by having to trade cars so often to keep from being found. Basically he felt the government owed him a living for his "immeasurable contributions to society."

When talking with women, it was his habit to smile confidently and charmingly, calling them "Honey" or "Hon." He gave Robin a signed copy of his book, and a lot to think about.

Meeting him may have contributed to Robin's future decisions regarding the possibility of breaking the rules of the witness protection program without consequences. While Fratianno got away with it, Robin did not.

Many individuals, especially those with an established work ethic, were able to make the transition to a new way of life. Counselors who wore many hats acted as bodyguards, social workers, employment agents and financial advisors who did everything possible to help protected witnesses get established.

But to Jimmy the Weasel, and others who had made easy money from a life of crime, a steady job was inconceivable. He had bragged about grossing $1.4 million in the trucking business and making $15,000 a week out of a dress shop and two bars.

For some incorrigibles, nothing would help, but for those who were willing to work hard at building a new life, it was possible to have one. In fact, the government reports a recidivism rate of only 17 to 23 percent among protected witnesses, at a time when it was almost twice as high for other convicted criminals.

Robin and Ralph would soon join the ranks of more than 15,000 other Americans who disappeared into the government's witness protection program. Like the rest of them they would have to learn to stop themselves from automatically signing their old names or sharing a personal experience from their past. Every single detail of their lives up to this point must remain a secret from new acquaintances.

Would Robin ever be able to get over the fear of being recognized and murdered by the Jamaicans? Would she be able to get her physical strength back and discipline herself to holding down a job? Extensive testing indicated she was a good candidate for the program.

Soon Robin was told she would be flown to Washington's International Dulles Airport and taken to a secluded location for orientation, but she was given no more information about exactly where she was being taken.

The flight was smooth enough and all the routine activity of flight attendants seemed normal, but this trip was anything but normal for Robin. She was about to divorce herself from her past and undergo an identity crisis to which few people could relate.

Through the dark, foggy night she could barely see the lights of the airport down below and wondered if they would be able to land with visibility being so limited. After circling a few times, the seat belt sign came on and they were told to prepare for landing, but she still couldn't see much.

It seemed the Federal Government was able to control everything, including the weather, to make this trip a top secret affair. Finally she heard the sounds of the landing gear being lowered and hoped this ghostly ride would soon be over. As they descended and then touched down, she leaned into the window for a better view of what it looked like out there but couldn't see much past the runway lights and a little open field. As the huge 747 braked, turned and headed toward the terminal, she wondered if it had been an instrument landing.

At the gate, Robin, as instructed, sat still as the other passengers gathered up their belongings and deplaned. She had been told she would be the last passenger to leave the plane and she was.

Trenchcoated men escorted her quickly through the foggy night and into a van with windows covered so tightly that nothing could be seen from them. They drove for quite a while. Robin listened closely for clues as to where she was being taken but finally gave the game up. This was much like being driven somewhere blindfolded. After a while the sounds of the city faded away and it got quieter and quieter outside.

Then she felt them drive slowly down an incline, and it seemed they proceeded for a while in a tunnel, but she couldn't be sure about that. However, when her escorts stopped the car and helped her out, they were in an underground garage.

She was taken to a room that was secured so that she could not enter or exit without assistance. When left alone, she went over to the drapes and pulled them back. Beyond the balcony's sliding glass door, there was nothing but a high brick wall obstructing the view to all landmarks. She was glad she wouldn't be here long.

She had previously been given physical and dental exams as well as psychological tests to determine what, if any, potential risk she would pose to the community where she would be relocated. She had also taken a battery of vocational tests.

A Memorandum of Understanding was read to her, and she initialed each page of the enormous and terribly restrictive document. By far the hardest rule to abide by was never returning to the city where she had grown up and given birth to her son and where all her immediate family, except for Ralph, still lived. That was now referred to as the *danger zone*, and she was told she could never go back there.

Her family and friends could never know which state she was living in, much less have her number or know how to reach her directly. She could call them but was prohibited from even discussing how the weather was in the city she was calling from, as that would provide a clue to her whereabouts. As a matter of fact, she was advised, for her own safety, to sever *all* contacts with the past.

If a family member passed away, they could notify her through the Marshals Service but she would not be allowed to attend the funeral with the rest of the family. She might be ushered in secretly to pay her last respects either before or after the funeral, but she would not be allowed to be there to comfort, or be comforted.

All mail was to be channeled through "Marshal Mail" and no packages were allowed, as they were a security risk for all concerned. She was advised to expect delays in the forwarding of her mail so birthday and Christmas cards might arrive months after the event.

The good news was that the witness protection program claimed to never have lost anyone who didn't break the rules. She hoped she could remember all of them and not break the walls of security they were building around her. She also hoped she didn't emotionally smother within them.

Finally Robin exited the tunnel with a new name that she had repeatedly practiced signing. Soon, she would be receiving a birth certificate, driver's license and Social Security card reflecting her new identity.

In California, Ralph's things were being packed, and he would soon be joining her. He also had a new name and background story to learn.

Ralph had been with the Houstons now for almost two years and was a part of the family. They were relinquishing a child whom they had grown to love. His photos were a part of their family album. Tears flowed at the thought of never seeing him again. Letting him go was as much a test of their faith as any part of this ordeal.

Feelings of uncertainty filled their minds with questions. How in the world would this friendly, outgoing child ever learn to think twice before he spoke of anything? And if he did develop that trait, what would the experience do to him?

Still, it was a joyful reunion for mother and child. Afterwards, though, they suffered through an extremely difficult transition period. It was almost impossible to suppress every spontaneous impulse to talk freely and easily to new acquaintances. Every lie they had to tell made them feel bad, and they both became depressed. Ralph started to cry every time it rained and when it rained at night he was inconsolable. If the wind blew branches against the windows, they were both up for hours.

Initially, U. S. Marshals were with them all the time, but Robin had never felt they were much of a match for the Jamaican posse, and she doubted it even more after Patsy's death..

Some of the Marshals were wonderful and tried to help Ralph adjust by taking him fishing or playing ball with him, but others were condescending. Robin hated it when some of them tried to be cool by using street slang or jive talk. Ralph didn't talk that way, and Robin didn't want him talked to like that, but a protected witness doesn't have much recourse.

Taxpayers shell out over $53,000,000 a year to support a witness protection program that is shrouded in an impenetrable cloak of secrecy. Thorough and fair evaluation of such a clandestine operation is almost impossible, but leaks of abuses do occasionally come to the surface.

For a long time, Robin would be on her own to deal with these issues, even though the Houstons continued to pray for her and Ralph. For the Houstons and members of Bethel, it was a time to marvel at what the Lord had done. Jesus gave them strength to deal with the situation as it was needed and usually not in advance of it. Jesus told His disciples that they wouldn't even be able to bear it all if they knew of their spiritual battles in advance, so Bishop Houston and Bethel probably would not have been able to help Robin and Ralph if they had known the whole story all at one time.

They also realized that the Lord gives the harder battles to seasoned warriors whom He has prepared. They concluded that while no one should seek involvement in some of the risky situations they had encountered, that such situations should not be feared if the Lord brings them into one's life. If He divinely and supernaturally places people in the middle of them, He will see them through, but others had better beware or they will find themselves in the same shape as those who were trying to emulate Paul.

"And God wrought *special* miracles by the hands of Paul. So that from his body were brought unto the sick handkerchiefs or aprons, and the diseases departed from them, and the evil spirits went out of them.

"Then certain of the vagabond Jews, exorcists, took upon them to call over them which had evil spirits the name of the Lord Jesus, saying, 'We adjure you by Jesus whom Paul preacheth.'

"And there were seven sons of one Sceva, a Jew, and chief of the priests, which did so.

"And the evil spirit answered and said, 'Jesus I know and Paul I know, but who are you?'

"And the man in whom the evil spirit was, leaped on them and overcame them, and prevailed against them, so that they fled out of that house naked and wounded.

"And this was known to all the Jews and Greeks, also dwelling at Ephesus, and fear fell on them all, and the name of the Lord Jesus was magnified." (Acts 19:11-17)

God will not put more on us than we can bear, so those trusting in God can rest in the knowledge of His ability to bring us through any situation in which we find ourselves.

Christ sometimes leads His own dear children to follow in his footsteps in dealing with critical situations. To understand the depths to which He will go and to which He may lead His children to go, it is worthwhile to remember that after His crucifixion, He even descended into Hades. As Bishop Houston frequently says, "Praise Him!"

If our eyes were open to the spiritual world, we would see the devil duck and jump back each time the Bishop punctuates one of his praises with a jab of his powerful right hand.

While Bethel was rejoicing and praising God for what He had done, Robin and Ralph were facing a new set of problems since being separated from the body of Christ and the support system it had provided them.

Most U.S. Marshals are not spiritually minded individuals and while some are understanding, most view their charges with a jaundiced eye. In this new climate of distrust, cynicism and secrecy, Ralph's whole demeanor changed. The previously happy, outgoing youngster began to withdraw. In order to stop his downward spiral, Robin requested and received counseling for both of them several times a week.

Robin was also able to call the Houstons for prayer and encouragement but she had to watch every word she said.

The Houstons hoped and prayed Robin and Ralph would make it through the difficult transition period and be able to build new lives for themselves. The Broussard trial had given Bishop Houston a small taste of what Robin had been through and for all parties, right or wrong, he had discovered a lengthy trial is a harrowing ordeal.

For Bishop Houston there been the stress of being called to testify plus the strain of dealing with the wide spectrum of anguished emotions with which Broussard's followers were struggling, and also the criticism from some of his peers. The critics could not understand why he did not distance himself from these people.

Bishop Houston had been Broussard's friend in the early days of his ministry, before his vision became corrupted. It had been easy to be his friend then and many were. It wasn't easy now, and except for those who were defending themselves in the process of defending him, very few people would allow their names to be linked with him. Among some of the church community, Broussard was a pariah, and understandably so.

Of course, Bishop Houston did not like any of Broussard's mistakes, but it went against his Christ-like nature to abandon anyone in their hour of need, so the kind and courageous Bishop absorbed the criticism and stood by Broussard and his followers in their hour of darkest need.

Since he did not turn his back on them, some of Broussard's followers finally turned to Bishop Houston for help, giving him the opportunity to help them find their way back into mainstream society.

Those in Broussard's "family" had kept their dark secrets just as effectively as many incest victims do and the more Bishop Houston learned, the more he realized just how sick the situation had become.

As it was revealed, Bishop Houston grieved and privately wept over the way God's message of hope for mankind had been twisted and used to emotionally imprison this group of people.

Very few things move people like helping children born into unfortunate circumstances, and it was for that purpose that Bishop Houston and many others had initially helped Broussard.

Broussard knew the Bible backward and forward, as his father was a minister who had him teaching Sunday School by the time he was fourteen. How had Broussard gotten so far from the truth? What kind of madness had he and his followers given themselves over to?

The pattern of excessive discipline originated from Broussard's background. His father openly admitted striking his son with an extension cord until he cut right through the teenager's pants. People wondered why in the world he would do such an inhumane thing. They also wondered why he would confess to it and why a strong, athletic young man would tolerate it. People wanted to understand it so they could prevent it from ever happening again.

With the charges Broussard was facing, he was much more guarded than his father in discussing what had happened to his daughter. However, when he was a guest on the Oprah Winfrey show, she worked hard at shedding some light on the tragic cycle of violence that still exists in America today and must be stopped. That will happen when other people are as courageous as Oprah, who was willing to reveal her own painful family history while trying to draw out Broussard.

In response to Oprah asking if the children were beaten, Broussard replied that they weren't. She then asked if they were whipped or spanked, and he acknowledged they were. Then a discussion of the difference between a whipping and beating ensued.

Broussard was adept at confusing the issue with semantics, but deeming it important to get to the heart of the matter, Oprah persisted. She reminded Broussard that authorities reported some fifty-three to fifty-five children had been examined upon being removed from the home. Some of those children said they had been beaten with up to 800 lashes.

Broussard countered by saying the authorities were only human, alluding to the possibility of a mistake. He expressed a desire for someone to come to Los Angeles and examine the children there, especially someone who knew what kids in the projects look like. He believed that would be a more balanced approach and would result in conflicting reports.

Seemingly, Oprah really wanted Broussard to come to terms with the reality of the situation and told him that when she was growing up, some children were given whippings that were brutal by today's standards. Broussard agreed and seemed relieved to hear that Oprah had insights that many did not have.

Oprah appeared to understand the cycle of violence that subjected children to such brutality. Some viewers were hoping Oprah could get Broussard to acknowledge how horrific and wrong these excessive whippings were, but whether he did or not, they felt Oprah's candid and persistent examination of the problem might shock those who shared the same background into getting help before such a tragedy occurred again.

Oprah once again re-emphasized that it was brutal, then went on to say that she had been one of those children whipped until she had welts that bled.

Thanking her for sharing that, Broussard said he was beaten as well. Again Oprah said she considered that brutal. Twice Broussard started to speak but Oprah pressed for the truth, asking him to concede that it was brutal to be spanked to the point of bleeding. Again Broussard started to say something else, but Oprah seemed to want him to admit it was child abuse.

To make it easier for him to acknowledge it, she once again referred to her own personal experiences and said that by today's standards what their relatives had done to them was abuse. Oprah believed the grandmother who beat her also loved her and believed she was doing the right thing for her, but it was still abuse.

Finally, Broussard agreed that it was. Then Oprah referred to the children who had been in Broussard's care in Oregon and asked him if they were abused. He denied that they were but said his dad had kept him out of a lot of trouble while he was growing up by half-killing him with whippings.

It was a sick way of thinking. Before this sickness had run its course, many would believe the legacy of those beatings were the basis for Dayna's death and, in the not too distant future, for the early demise of her father as well.

It was all a tragic waste of enormous talent and potential. Broussard had the intellectual prowess to awe audiences. He could recite long passages of scriptures and eloquently persuade people to his way of thinking but he had trouble maintaining a steady course.

For a while, his message was along the lines of the prosperity gospel, and that appealed to large groups of people who wholeheartedly believed it.

Then reports begin to surface about those who had gone to the grocery store and filled their carts while expecting to miraculously receive the money by the time they got to the checkout counter. Of course, they left the store embarrassed and chagrined.

However, the prosperity gospel's message was so seductive that people didn't want to give up on it. Just one testimony of success could have folks buying back in to it and doing foolish things like mixing up buckets of hot, soapy water to go wash the new car they were sure would materialize in the driveway.

Faith is a very important part of the Christian's walk with the Lord, and only those who walk where angels fear to tread will dare discourage anyone from stepping out in faith. However, Bishop Houston discovered that *error is often truth out of balance*. He believes one of our greatest challenges as Christians is keeping the faith while also keeping our balance.

In Bishop Houston's experience, *he has seen miracles*. Most often they have occurred in relation to God's work -- usually for eternal purposes. He had not found God to be a Santa Claus type figure or a "Genie" waiting to give us our three wishes.

He is the Almighty Creator of the universe and while He is concerned about, and does meet, our physical needs, He cannot and will not be manipulated for our pleasure or our glory. We were created for His pleasure and not the other way around.

The Bishop believes God created a marvelous world for us to live in and is available to us when we seek Him in spirit and in truth. If mankind had not opened the door for sin, we would still be walking through the garden of Eden enjoying continual communion with God. We would not have to worry about working or struggling to survive. But mankind did open the door to evil, and so we must work and as Bishop Houston says, "do all we know to do."

To walk with God, we must fall into step with Him, He will not fall into step with us, and our God is marching on toward the fulfillment of all He revealed in times of old to the prophets.

We serve a God who created a universe so vast our most brilliant scientific minds admit they cannot take the measure of it. As they struggle to understand His marvelous creation God constantly reveals to them how far off they are with their scientific estimates of its age, size and origin.

Technology that was unimaginable only a decade ago is revealing His creation to be larger and more complex than previously believed and of course, the Creator Himself is greater still. How loving He is to reveal Himself, as He always has, through His word and by His spirit to those who seek Him with humble, honest hearts, in order to seek and do His will. God does not reveal Himself to those seeking to build *their* kingdoms but to those seeking to build His.

To Bishop Houston, it seemed Broussard had mistakenly intended to have things *his own way*, instead of praying humble Christ-like prayers of *"not my will but thine be done"* for him.

On one occasion, Broussard prayed until he was hoarse for God to raise a person from the dead, and when it didn't work he stopped preaching his brand of the faith message.

When he went from one extreme to another and tried to persuade those following him to take vows of poverty, his following melted in size. Those who remained were very loyal and his organization became very "leader centered." Unfortunately, it was clear to Bishop Houston that Broussard had become their leader, not Christ.

To the casual observer, and even to their neighbors in Watts, everything appeared well-organized, immaculate and picture perfect, but inside it had gotten stranger than fiction. Broussard possessed a high level of personal magnetism and with all of them living under the same roof, it wasn't long before some of the women begin to fall in love with him. So he begin to take various women with him when he left to take care of certain things. And of course he left his wife at home.

His power over these women grew until one day he publicly asked them to choose between him and their husbands. To the utter amazement of their husbands, some of the wives left them and lined up behind Broussard. He later asked seven of the couples to sign divorce papers he had obtained from the Dominican Republic. Some of them did sign, but no one would say who or how many.

These were not the kinds of things Broussard wanted known, and so he forbade his followers to associate with their families and friends who lived outside the commune. No visitors were allowed to see the interior of the building where they slept and lived. Visitors were kept to a minimum and at arm's length.

Broussard increased his control by requiring members to stop reading the newspaper and watching television. They were to answer no questions from outsiders, but in spite of this some concerned family members on the outside became alarmed at the direction things were taking.

Some noticed the children were not growing properly and looked sickly. Requests for permission to take them to the doctor was flatly denied.

Then, Broussard's little nephew, Alvin, who was not quite two years old, died in California of an acute upper respiratory infection, followed by the death of Faith Hendrick, age 30, in Oregon.

Hope and her sister, Faith, had previously sold property they owned together and given the proceeds of $20,000 to Broussard. Faith suffered from epilepsy but felt she could do without her anti-seizure medication and did not want to ask Broussard for the money to purchase it. The corner ruled the death was due to natural causes due to a blood clot to her lungs.

These two incidents increased the unfavorable attention Broussard's group was receiving in both California and Oregon. The welcome he had received upon returning to Oregon, where he had once enjoyed happiness as a basketball star at Pacific University, begin to evaporate quickly.

Oregon residents had already been badly burned by the effects of Indian mystic Bhagwan Shree Rajneesh's commune. His fleet of more than eighty Rolls-Royces had driven down their highways, trailing rumors of sex orgies and murder plots while the enigmatic, bearded leader waved benignly as he went past.

They wanted no part of another wave of deception. Oregonians cherished the work ethic that built this great country and the traditional family values that sustained it.

Initially the 3,000 or so residents of Sandy, Oregon, did not recognize what they had in their midst when the Ecclesia Athletic Association took up residence in a two-story farmhouse in their community. So, being friendly, country folks who were accustomed to giving their neighbors a helping hand, they loaned Broussard and his followers farm equipment, gave them trees and helped in a number of ways. But the loaned items were not returned.

And when the group's code of silence was occasionally broken, conflicting stories begin emerging that raised neighbors' suspicions, so they gradually withdrew from the newcomers and watched from afar.

As growing numbers of people moved to the farm, Sandy's residents felt their stomachs tightening. Then when they saw the grueling exercise regiments the children went through, they thought it was excessive and cruel. Word got out that some of the kids worked all day in the fields before having to run ten miles, after which they were often required to drop down and do as many as 500 push-ups and then leap up to do 1,000 jumping jacks.

As the weeks passed by, tents were pitched and twelve portable toilets were moved in to accommodate the nearly 100 people now living on the farm. At this point about thirty-five families signed a complaint against Broussard's Ecclesia Athletic Association and presented it to the Clackamas County Planning Director, who had already received dozens of letters from concerned individuals.

The brutal death of Broussard's eight-year-old daughter, Dayna, proved that their concerns were well founded.

Dayna's funeral was attended by about 200 mourners, but her parents weren't among them, having decided they couldn't face the intense media attention. The pastor obliquely referred to circumstances surrounding her death by acknowledging that no one there had ever experienced anything like it before and that at least little Dayna was free from the suffering of this world.

Fifty-three children were placed in protective custody as a result of the light Dayna's death shed on the situation. Their parents were forced to provide better lives for them in order to get them back. In life, Dayna had fought against the situation she lived in and would have been pleased that the other children were now free from it.

It is not pleasant to review such painful events, and Bishop Houston is not attempting to simplistically put a silver lining on this tragedy. But without reviewing the effects one person's mind control can have over others, history is more likely to repeat itself. Reminders of the tragic results, combined with proactive teaching may motivate others to be on the alert. It is worthwhile to encourage vigilance, as it isn't likely that cult members will intercede for others to stop the suffering. Once inculcated in the group's doctrines, the majority of cult members seem incapable of extracting themselves from the evil web in which they have become spiritually and psychologically entrapped.

It is hard to believe that members of Broussard's organization had, upon joining, received an information packet that included an application form whereby the applicant agrees to: "...declare all of my ambitions, desires, past and future commitments, relationships, expectations, assets, gifts, talents and connections under the total control of Eldridge John Broussard, Jr. All of my decisions - financial, social, recreational, educational, dietary, romantic and any not mentioned in the above, must pass his scrutiny and obtain his approval. I relinquish even the rights of decision-making."[*]

Those who signed did not inform their family members outside the group of their radical decisions. These were not ignorant or deranged individuals making them. They were people life had made vulnerable. They were capable of functioning normally, and many did. One

---

[*] *The Los Angeles Times,* June 1994

of them had an income of $60,000 a year and several others had good-paying jobs.

Before Broussard died at age 38 in September 1991, he had done immeasurable damage to his followers. All the control he sought in life couldn't save him in death. He died in the same farmhouse in which his 8-year-old daughter, Dayna, had been killed by his followers three years earlier.

When he returned to Oregon with the large following from Watts, he was as fit as he was when he played college basketball at Pacific University. After Dayna's death he became reclusive and overweight. He died alone, with every dream having degenerated into a nightmare. There were no signs of a struggle or foul play. The bearded giant died facing federal charges of enslaving 29 children in his Ecclesia Athletic Association.

A deep sense of hopelessness is often the reason people become involved in cults. Individuals desperately in need of hope are vulnerable to a seemingly caring and certainly confident leader. Excessive devotion to an extremist cult leader allows him to control them. Often convinced their leader's authority comes directly from God, they dare not question him, especially since physical or psychological punishment is frequently the price. Limited freedom and isolation increases the leaders ability to instill and reinforce a radical, rigid belief system that further imprisons his followers. It is not uncommon for the belief system to hold its captives hostage after the one who taught them is gone.

Those who realize they were manipulated, must deal with the pain of having allowed it to happen. When tragedy results from staking excessive hope in an extreme solution, the one who has made such a serious mistake may never be able to trust themselves or others again.

A proactive approach by churches could limit the number of people left with this lamentable legacy. According to *Modern Maturity Magazine*, "87 percent said they had some religious affiliation before joining a cult..."[*]

It is easier to deceive people with lies that contain some truths than with blatant lies. By getting out of balance with Scripture, or contaminating Scripture with lies and untruths, cults can effectively deceive people who have been taught a little of the Word, but who do not know enough of the Word to recognize the lies and subtle but deadly deceptions. Perversion or contamination of truth is common. That is what Satan did in the garden of Eden and what many cult leaders are doing now to pull members from churches. A familiar message with a new twist is always intriguing but not necessarily true, so we must be vigilant.

The most important message to remember, is that with God, anything is possible. Even though many of these cults are brought down by a tragedy, some members do exit and get the help they need. We must keep the faith, continue praying, and educate our families and friends.

The cult phenomenon is growing and in order to keep people we know and love from falling victim to masters of deception and manipulation like Jim Jones, David Koresh and Marshall "Do" Applewhite, we must be informed and vigilant. Margaret Thaler Singer, Ph.D., is a clinical psychologist and emeritus adjunct professor at the University of California, Berkeley, as well as an expert on post-traumatic stress and cults. She writes, "Most people believe that cult members are mentally unbalanced or are misfits...Often people take comfort in the fact that the influences of cults are far removed from their everyday lives. *Yet nothing could be further from the truth.*

---

[*] *Modern Maturity Magazine*, June 1994

"Over the past decades, in the United States alone, an estimated twenty million people have joined cults. Often a cult is disguised as a legitimate organization or business: a restaurant, self-help group, psychotherapy clinic, leadership training program, hobby club, or nonprofit community group could be a front for a cult. Anyone - no matter what age or income level - could be susceptible to the covert and seductive nature of a cult. During periods of life changes or transitions, people are especially vulnerable to these masterful manipulators: a college student away from home, a grief-stricken widow in need of support, a recently divorced man or woman, or a businessperson relocating to a new and unfamiliar community."

Bishop Houston believes churches should pay particular attention to its members who fall into these categories. Unfortunately, churches are often more responsive to those suffering from physical problems than to those dealing with grief or other equally devastating changes in life.

Bishop Houston encourages parents, Sunday School teachers, and pastors to educate those in their care to the dangers of cults, while they are emotionally healthy and strong. Then, they aren't as likely to fall prey to a cult during the periods of their lives when they are more susceptible. There are many sources of material.

In Dr. Singer's book, *Cults in Our Midst*, written with former cult member Janja Lalich, she "explains what cults are, how they recruit and operate, and what techniques are used to retain members. This compelling book debunks commonly held myths and answers perplexing questions about these exploitative groups."*

---

* *Cults in Our Midst: The Hidden Menance in Our Everyday Lives* by Margaret Thaler Singer with Janja Lalich. Copyright 1995. Published by Jossey-Bass, Inc., San Francisco, CA

Janja Lalich writes, "We were new and different - an elite force. We were going to make the world a better place for all people." Among other things, she soon discovered their leader was an unbending, ultra-authoritarian, and almost always angry individual.

"All cults, no matter their stripe, are a variation on a theme, for their common denominator is the use of coercive persuasion and behavior control without the knowledge of the person who is being manipulated. They manage this by targeting (and eventually attacking, dissembling, and reformulating according to the cult's desired image) a person's innermost self. They take away you and give you back a cult personality, a pseudo personality.

"They punish you when the old you turns up, and they reward the new you. Before you know it, you don't know who you are or how you got there; you only know (or are trained to believe) that you have to stay there. In a cult there is only one way - cults are totalitarian, a yellow brick road to serve the leader's whims..."[*]

Bishop Houston believes we are our brother's keeper and that we should be accountable to one another. Cult leaders do not subscribe to this philosophy, giving them much latitude for leading people further and further astray until they all end up entrapped in a powerful, evil web.

According to the American Family Foundation, Inc., people really need to be wary of individuals who are "not accountable to any authorities (as are, for example, military commanders and ministers, priests, monks, and rabbis of mainstream denominations)." They also caution

---

[*] *Repairing the Soul After a Cult Experience* by Janja Lalich. Copyright 1995. Originally published in Creation Spirituality Network Magazine 1996, vol. 12, no. 1

against groups that have "a polarized us-versus-them mentality, which causes conflict with the wider society."[*]

Just as in the matter of the prosperity gospel, the accountability doctrine can be taken to the extreme. For that matter, anything can be taken to the extreme, even the desire to fight against cults.

Some believe the previous owners of the Cult Awareness Network (CAN) lost their organization as a result of getting out of balance themselves. (By a bizarre twist of fate, CAN is now owned by members of L. Ron Hubbard's Scientology Movement!)

Prior to that development, *The Christian Century* reported on January 31, 1996, "The Cult Awareness Network (CAN) has been found guilty of violating the civil rights of Jason Scott, a member of the United Pentecostal Church, in its attempts to 'deprogram' him. CAN has appealed the decision, but the $4.8 million damage award may mean the financial end of the group."[*]

Surely this is one of the most perverse and complex deceptions with which the church must contend. Almost every Christian will be frustrated (or blindsided) with their first encounter with a cult.

According to Jan Groenveld of Freedom in Christ, "Anytime you say anything negative about the group, whether justified or no, it is regarded as "persecution." Any criticism of the individual is also seen as persecution because they are the "true Christians" or "enlightened" ones - not because they, as individuals, have done the wrong thing. However, at the same time they will feel free to criticize whatever you believe, say and do because they are the only ones who are right.

Groenveld continues: "They lose their ability to socialize outside the group. This can go so far as to not

[*] American Family Foundation's Website
[*] *The Christian Century*, January 31, 1996 v113 n4 p102 (1).

being able to structure their time or make simple decisions for themselves when they leave. Their world-view alters and they perceive the world through their leader's eyes. They become very naive about life in general."[*]

It may take someone coming out of a cult one to five years to recover, during which time they may experience suicidal tendencies and/or severe psychological problems.

Seeing results requires endless patience while trust is slowly established, the mind renewed and the soul healed. Bishop Houston has that kind of patience. He made himself available to Broussard, his followers, and others who have been caught up in similar situations.

While he prays for them, he encourages himself by remembering what the Lord has done in other tragic situations that required infinite patience.

Janice Riley McCree was a precious soul he kept interceding for over many years. Approximately half a century ago, she was the flower girl in Bishop Houston and Sister Minnie's wedding. In fact, Bishop Houston and Sister Minnie had known Janice all of her life. So, it was sad to see her leave the church when she was grown. However, they were glad she stayed in touch with them even when she wasn't attending church.

They were happy for Janice when she married and had a family, and they grieved with her when she was widowed. The Houstons could see how hard it was for her to be a widow and single mother at the tender age of twenty-one. The difficulties in Janice's life were soon exacerbated when she started drinking and eventually became an alcoholic. All during this time, Bishop Houston reached out to her and encouraged her to return to the Lord.

---

[*] Jan Groenveld's Freedom in Christ Website

Janice loved the Houstons and often turned to them for emotional support, appreciating the fact that they always received her with open arms. Since they never condemned her, she was comfortable returning to church even though she was still struggling with serious problems. They were aware of how hard she was trying to get her life back together and after she remarried, it seemed that she might. Then at age 31, she was widowed again and her problems worsened.

Bishop Houston continued to stand by her side, pray with her, and give her Godly counsel. With absolute conviction, he told her God's grace was sufficient and that Satan was a liar. Janice knew it was true, but her pain was overwhelming. Finally, she sought escape in the world of crack cocaine.

The Houstons refused to give up on her. They continued to love her and pray. And they were always available for Janice whenever she called, just as Jesus is always there for each of us when we call on Him.

Finally at the age of 49, she was delivered from twenty-five years of alcoholism and ten years of drug addiction which she attributes to the love and Grace of God, as shown to her through the Houstons.

Spiritual warfare is very real. We must "be sober, be vigilant; because your adversary the devil, as a roaring lion, walketh about, seeking whom he may devour: whom resist steadfast in the faith, knowing that the same afflictions are accomplished in your brethren that are in the world." (I Peter 5:8-9)

Bishop Houston was interceding for Janice while Satan was seeking to utterly devour her. That intercession kept faith flickering within her even while Satan tried to quench the work of the Holy Spirit. When the battle was over and victory won, Janice believed it was due to, "...the effectual, fervent prayers of a righteous man..." (James 5:16)

While interceding for the most critical cases, Bishop Houston finds it helpful to recall the victories God has given him. From them, he draws strength to continue to pray for, and minister to, all those brought into his life, regardless of how hopeless they may seem, or how long it takes to win the battle.

CHAPTER SIX

"Yea though I walk through the valley of the shadow of death, I will fear no evil: for thou art with me; thy rod and thy staff they comfort me." (Ps. 23:4)

Are we tested according to our strength? Do some of our latent, God-given, strengths and abilities only rise to the surface under fire? After we have overcome one battle, do we have a higher spiritual ranking and more important campaigns scheduled for us?

During the years of his ministry, Bishop Houston went through many trials of testing. He leaned heavily upon the Lord for his strength and gleaned help from other brothers who had experienced similar trials.

In the angelic realm, he learned, there is a hierarchy for good and also for evil, as internationally recognized Bible teacher Derek Prince explains in *Spiritual Warfare*. "For instance, there might be one king over each major city of the Persian Empire, one over each major ethnic group, perhaps one also over each of the various religious and pagan cults of the Persian Empire. We get a picture of a highly organized, structured kingdom with various areas and descending levels of authority with headquarters in the heavenlies and which is a kingdom of rebellious, fallen spirit-beings."[*]

---

[*] Used by permission of publisher, Whitaker House, 30 Hunt Valley Circle, New Kensington, PA 15068. Copyright 1987 Derek Prince, author

How do we overcome spiritual battles? How do we fight an enemy we can't see or even begin to understand? Do we actually defeat the enemy by accepting, being transformed and testifying to the suffering our Lord and Savior has brought us through? Bishop Houston believes we can triumph over the enemy by accepting the crosses we have been given to bear in our lives and going on with God, as Christ did. "And having disarmed the powers and authorities, He made a public spectacle of them, triumphing over them by the cross." (Col. 1:15 NIV)

Many ask, "Why is the struggle necessary? Why must we suffer? Why do we feel like spiritual kindergartners when we ask why? Is that also a tactic of the devil? One that keeps us from exploring and learning about the spiritual metamorphosis that occurs during suffering?"

Bishop Houston suggests that there is no better place to start searching for answers to those questions than in the book of Job. "Now there was a day when the sons of God came to present themselves before the Lord, and Satan came also among them. And the Lord said unto Satan, Whence comest thou? Then Satan answered the Lord, and said, From going to and from in the earth, and from walking up and down in it. And the Lord said unto Satan, Hast thou considered my servant Job, that there is none like him in the earth, a perfect man one that feareth God, and escheweth evil?

"Then Satan answered the Lord, and said, Doth Job fear God for nought? Hast not thou made an hedge about him, and about his house, and about all that he hath on every side? Thou has blessed the work of his hands, and his substance is increased in the land. But put forth thine hand now, and touch all that he hath, and he will curse thee to thy face.

"And the Lord said unto Satan, Behold all that he hath is in thy power; only upon himself put not forth thine hand. So Satan went forth from the presence of the Lord." (Job 1:6-12 KJV)

The preceding passage of scripture and the rest of Job gives us intriguing insights into the realm of the supernatural. In addition to the promises and joys of knowing God, we will also have trials and tribulations. It goes with the territory and we should not be afraid of it, as the battle is the Lord's and we are simply called on to be good soldiers.

Who would volunteer to be Job for the sake of all who follow? Consider his anguished cry, "Have pity upon me, have pity upon me, O ye my friends; for the hand of God hath touched me." (Job 19:21) Neither Job nor his friends had any idea what God was doing. Job only knew that he was in great overwhelming, physical, emotional and spiritual pain. And it wasn't for a day. Except for Jesus, who bore the sin of all mankind, has anyone suffered as much as Job?

God often takes what Satan meant for evil and transforms it into something good. Nothing brings that into focus more clearly than the martyrdom of the saints, which the Bishop read about in the book of Hebrews.

"Who through faith subdued kingdoms, wrought righteousness, obtained promises, stopped the mouths of lions, quenched the violence of fire, escaped the edge of the sword, out of weakness were made strong, waxed valiant in fight, turned to flight the armies of the aliens.

"Women received their dead raised to life again: and others were tortured, not accepting deliverance; that they might obtain a better resurrection:

"And others had trial of cruel mockings and scourgings, yea, moreover of bonds and imprisonment: They were stoned, they were sawn asunder, were tempted, were slain with the sword: they wandered about in sheepskins and goatskins; being destitute, afflicted, tormented; (Of whom the world was not worthy:) they wandered in deserts, and in mountains, and in dens and caves of the earth. And these all, having obtained a good report through faith, received not the promise. God having provided some better thing for us, that they without us should not be made perfect." (Heb. 11:32-40 KJV)

Bishop Houston preaches about the foundation of the Church being laid with the lives of those saints and even more so with the manner of their deaths. A deathbed testimony carries more weight than the testimony of a healthy person, even our legal system recognizes it as almost above question.

Those who would not deny Christ, even when the air reverberated with the roar of hungry lions or flames melted the skin from their bones, sent forth an eternal testimony that indelibly imprinted itself on the hearts of kings and peasants alike. The stories were so awesome that they lived on from generation to generation causing tremors, spiritual-quakes and aftershocks.

Those saints left us a great spiritual legacy and they are the great cloud of witnesses who watch us to see what kind of stewards we are in our generation. The very idea that we are somehow exempt from pain and suffering is both preposterous and unscriptural. Consider this excerpt from Foxe's Book of Martyrs:

"Christ our Saviour, in the Gospel of St. Matthew, hearing the confession of Simon Peter, who, first of all other, openly acknowledged Him to be the Son of God, and perceiving the secret hand of His Father therein, called him (alluding to his name) a rock, upon which rock He would build His Church so strong, that the gates of hell should not prevail against it. In which words three things are to be noted: First, that Christ will have a Church in this world. Secondly, that the same Church should mightily be impugned, not only by the world, but also by the uttermost strength and powers of all hell. And, thirdly, that the same Church, notwithstanding the uttermost of the devil and all his malice, should continue."[*]

When we suffer and surrender to the will of God, the veils of our humanity are drawn aside and we become windows through which people catch "Glimpses of Glory." The veils of our humanity usually obscure our spiritual eyesight. When we are strong in the flesh, we don't seek and find God, but when we are weak and transparent, holding to Him for dear life, people can see Him through us. Suffering saints are radiant, resplendent, awe-inspiring reflections of Jesus Christ Himself but for some, that state of transfiguration may last only for a short while. Being chosen for suffering is something very few people can accept.

Acceptance of suffering defies logic. It flies in the face of our most basic survival instinct and even conventional wisdom about the blessings God's people have come to expect.

However, some of us will share in the fellowship of Christ's suffering. "Beloved, think it not strange concerning the fiery trial which is to try you, as though some strange thing happened unto you: But rejoice, inasmuch as ye are partakers of Christ's sufferings; that, when his glory shall be revealed, ye may be glad also with exceeding joy. If ye be reproached for the name of Christ, happy are ye; for the spirit of glory and of God resteth upon you: on their part is evil spoken of, but on your part He is glorified. But let none of you suffer as a murderer, or as a thief, or as an evildoer, or as a

---

[*] Used by permission of publisher, Whitaker House, 30 Hunt Valley Circle, New Kensington, PA 15068. Copyright 1981 by Whitaker House, author John Foxe

busybody in other's men's matters. Yet if any man suffer as a Christian, let him not be ashamed; but let him glorify God on this behalf. For the time is come that judgment must begin at the house of God: and if it first begin at us, what shall the end be of them that obey not the gospel of God? And if the righteous scarcely be saved, where shall the ungodly and the sinner appear? Wherefore let them that suffer according to the will of God commit the keeping of their souls to him in well doing, as unto a faithful Creator." (I Peter 4:12-19)

Suffering for the cause of Christ is one of those divine, esoteric mysteries, and it may be one of life's greatest honors. Keeping the faith through suffering and after it is certainly one of the greatest challenges mortal man will face.

However, without faith, we will not heal properly because we cannot, with our natural mind understand these deep supernatural mysteries. We can only "see through a glass, darkly" (1 Cor. 13:12) until we have passed from this world and into the one to come.

Then all the veils of our own humanity will fall away and we shall truly be like Him. With our new name and body, we will have eternal, celestial vision so that we can understand Him and why it was necessary for us to suffer. Once we can see what He sees, we will no doubt apologize for the times we sobbed and through hot, anguished tears, just barely managed to whisper, "Amen to the will of God."

Bishop Houston has noticed that some of God's children have a will of iron that God must temper while others are naturally more predisposed to follow God without complaint. According to Isak Dinesen, author of *Out of Africa*, our African brothers and sisters are spiritually more attuned than the white man. "The Kikuyu are adjusted for the unforeseen and accustomed to the unexpected. Here they differ from the white men, of whom the majority strive to insure themselves against the unknown and the assaults of fate. The Negro is on friendly terms with destiny, having been in her hands all his time; she is to him, in a way, his home, the familiar darkness of the hut, deep mould for his roots. He faces any change in life with great calm."[*]

Bishop Houston's friends have observed that great calm in him. It is a part of his rich heritage, his roots. We have seen him face life's most fierce storms with equanimity, and it has inspired us to be more accepting.

They watched him stand like a giant oak while the dark flood waters of death raged and rose around him in 1994 and 1995. He never doubted that they would finally subside and he never changed. During those days, he made many think of Paul, who wrote, "...for I have learned, in whatsoever state I am, therewith to be content. I know both how to be abased, and I know how to abound: every where and in all things I am instructed both to be full and to be hungry, both to abound and to suffer need. I can do all things through Christ which strengtheneth me." (Phil. 4:11-13)

This represents the very essence of Bishop Houston, who exemplifies the love of Christ when he is in full regalia presiding over a convention or when he is doing some mundane task like painting his son's house. Many saw Christ through him when he was joyous over his daughter's (Pastor Carol Houston) ordination service and when saddened by the death of loved ones. His Christian testimony has remained the same in every situation.

It is easy to rejoice and stand tall in the Lord in the good times, but during the trials of our faith, when we sit

---

[*] From *OUT OF AFRICA* by Isak Dinesen. Copyright (c) 1937 by Random House, Inc. and renewed 1965 by Rungstedlundfonden. Reprinted by permission of Random House, Inc.

down and Christ stands up, that is when we are the most beautiful.

Those who watched Bishop Houston manage one tragedy after another in 1994, had even greater levels of respect and love as a result of seeing his unswerving faith in God. Paul said, "Those things, which ye have both learned, and received, and heard, and seen in me, do: and the God of peace shall be with you." (Phil. 4:9)

Bishop Houston was not aware that, in the midst of his trials, he was teaching. As he simply trusted God and continued on with his Father's business, many watched and learned how Christ would have us handle similar situations in our own lives. Even while he was caring for Sister Minnie and dealing with the ebb and tide of his own emotions as he watched the toll cancer was taking on her, he continued on, strong in the faith.

Then, his brother, George, after losing his wife of forty-six years, came to see Bishop Houston and Sister Minnie. It was a comforting and satisfying visit, a time of coming to terms with the mortality of man and the immortality of the soul. Sister Minnie was becoming more translucent and peaceful by the day. She had asked the Lord for the opportunity to live out seventy years and the Lord had granted her that request. Now she was in a lovely grace period, encouraging Bishop Houston, her five boys and daughter to go on with God.

For a long time, the family had relied on her to intercede for them, and her work was almost through. She would soon be passing custodianship of her spiritual baton on to them, and she wanted them to be ready to receive it.

In addition to her family, others were privileged to have Sister Minnie encourage, care and pray for them during those golden days of her life. Tommy and Laverne were grateful to be among them. As veil after veil fell away, her great beauty and dignity were enhanced with greater measures of purity and holiness.

George and Bishop Houston were cherishing Sister Minnie's sweet spirit and each other during that time. It was good just to be together and occasionally feel a loving hand on the shoulder. An unspoken understanding flowed between them all as the angels whispered to their souls, "Your race is almost run."

The two brothers leaned on each other and felt closer than they had since childhood. George had great respect for Bishop Houston's Christian walk and was very pleased with his achievements. He was delighted to have the opportunity to accompany him on a trip to Stantonburg, North Carolina, where Bishop Houston presided over the General Mission Convention. George's heart swelled with pride and tears of joy came to his eyes as his august brother, attired in all the accouterments of his office, rose to imposingly deliver the opening invocation. No one doubted that he had been born for this role.

Privately, Bishop Houston shared with George the joy and honor of being chosen to lead. He confessed to feeling unworthy and yet so grateful that he made himself available to serve even when he was tired or already heavily committed. George had never realized the demands and pressures of living in the limelight and it meant a lot to him to have Bishop Houston share from his heart. George just shook his head in amazement as Bishop Houston confessed to struggling with the inability to say, "No," whenever he was called on for help. Maybe it was a season of reflecting upon one's life as Bishop Houston was very open and transparent with George. He acknowledged that he had occasionally been overzealous toward good works without getting true direction from Christ who had called and ordained him.

He told George he had constantly prayed for wisdom and discernment concerning the balancing act required of him as a husband, father, man of the cloth, businessman and civic leader. His greatest challenge was striving to make contributions in all those areas.

It warmed the cockles of George's heart to hear his brother tell young mentorees, "I am sure no parent could love their children more than I. Being a parent is a first for every father and mother, and learning how to set priorities in relationships is an experience learned after some damage has already been applied through ignorance. Separating or blending one's commitment to Christ and family can sometimes be confusing. Being zealous for the work of Christ can easily become another tool Satan uses to throw you off course. I have learned and am learning that while Christ is first, we must also heed the instructions He has given us on how to care for His gifts, the most important of which are our children, and the family structure."

As the mentorees nodded understandingly, Bishop Houston continued, "I have been able to see in the lives of my five sons and one daughter the effects of my sometimes being over zealousness for the work of Christ at their expense." But I give thanks to God that He is healing these mistakes. As I confess, I am being healed and pray my loved ones will be healed of the effects my transgressions, mistakes, and the over zealousness that has caused pain in the lives of those I love.

"Darrel, Carol, Ronald, Ralph Jr., Larry and Kim are the most precious gifts the Good Lord has bestowed on their mother and me. I have this confidence that my Lord will honor my confession and prayer and grant my heart's desire that "My house will be saved."

The Holy Spirit was bringing forth this type of confession in 1994 and it was only the beginning of what He was doing. That was the year Bill McCartney gave up his coaching career to tend Promise Keepers.   He realized and confessed, "The sharp edges of my personality had inflicted heavy damage," He discovered it was time for him to "shut up and listen to his wife." He also took responsibility for some of his daughter's actions, believing his own behavior may have been a contributing factor.

These public confessions strengthened Bill McCartney's credibility and gave other religious leaders permission to face their own demons and contradictions. One is the paradox of doing the "Lord's work" at the expense of the family. Another is the collusion of mass audiences who crave a faith leader without regard for the emotional, ethical cost to that leader."

His wife, Lyndi McCartney, encourages other spouses to be patient and keep the faith, "If your husband is a Promise Keeper, you may grow cynical if his walk at home doesn't match his talk. Don't be hasty. God works relentlessly toward having him possess in reality what he professes by faith. I pray it doesn't take thirty years for you."*

This was a message the church needed to hear and as George observed his brother ministering his own very similar message to others, he remembered when his brother was born again at the tender age of 10 and how he became active in the work of the Lord just a couple of years after that. George smiled at the memories of his brother helping Mother Hammock fill her old 1935 Dodge with children to carry them to the House of Prayer United Holy Church on East 25th Street. At the young age of 15, his brother had been Sunshine Band Leader and shortly thereafter, the assistant secretary of Sunday School.

The brothers took a stroll down memory lane, recalling that while there were very few young people in

---

* *The Tennessean*, Ray Waddle's Religion article 11/23/97

that small church, that the adults fellowshipped with them so much that the generation gap was bridged by the closeness.   Brother Samuel Catley was a very caring deacon and a lathing subcontractor who took Bishop Houston under his care and taught him how to "lath." He soon became quite good and was placed on jobs with the best in the trade. He was called a good "lath-er" and in spite of being so young, he was able to hold his own with the most experienced men.

When Brother Catley received a bid to do an entire subdivision, he assigned Bishop Houston to work in a house all alone. It was a big responsibility, and it pleased Brother Cately when he rose to the occasion and even completed the job much earlier than expected. Brother Catley appraised the job "well done," and from that time on, Bishop Houston was respected as one of the finest lath-ers in the area. Now, more than a half a century later, Bishop Houston still likes to build as a hobby and George had heard him attribute it to the confidence Brother Catley's placed in him as a young lad.

George wondered why their lives had been so different and finally decided it went back to decisions made in childhood. When they were growing up, prayer was taught and encouraged by Pastor H. D. Green. During the summer and on Saturdays, he would come by every morning, except Sunday and take their Mom to prayer at 11:00 a.m. Most of the time Bishop Houston went with them, but George usually declined, even though he saw the effect prayer had on their lives and was happy about it.

Then when Bishop Houston was sixteen years old, the pressure of teen life begin to grow as he was the only teenager in their group who was open and up front with his Christian testimony. At one point the peer pressure became so great that he decided to give up the struggle. When he told his Mom, she did not scold or rebuke him, she only advised him to hold back on the decision until he could pray about it. She advised him to give thanks to God for having saved him and to thank Him for all the blessings he had been given. She also suggested that he be open and honest with the Lord, telling Him of the pressures and his subsequent decision to leave Him to follow the ways of the world. On the way back home, George asked him if he remembered that.

Bishop Houston chuckled and said, "Yes and I'm sure you know what happened. As I began to thank Him for His goodness, the joy of salvation began to flood my soul and I repented. That was about a half century ago and since that time I have never again had a desire to let go of His hands. God was already becoming my all and all, my very present help in times of need."

Bishop Houston's decision was like that of young Moses, of whom it is recorded that he chose "...to suffer affliction with the people of God, than to enjoy the pleasures of sin for a season; esteeming the reproach of Christ greater riches than the treasures of Egypt: For he had respect unto the recompense of the reward. By faith he forsook Egypt, not fearing the wrath of the King: for he endured as seeing him who is invisible." (Heb. 11:25-27 KJV)

Bishop Houston was concerned about George's spiritual standing with the Lord but did not want to hurt his brother's feelings, so he gently explored the sensitive issue by asking George if he was ready for the Rapture. George said he believed he was but honestly confessed to feeling convicted about smoking cigarettes. He reminded Bishop Houston that he had started smoking at age 14 and admitted that he was hopelessly addicted. He felt the Lord was not pleased with him being a slave to such a harmful habit.

Bishop Houston reminded him of I Cor. 10:13 (CEV): "You are tempted in the same way that everyone else is tempted. But God can be trusted not to let you be tempted too much, and he will show you how to escape from your temptations. "

As Bishop Houston watched closely for his brother's response, he noticed that George was actually quite thin and asked him to go to the doctor for a checkup. George responded with a little joke about it being a result of eating his own cooking. They both laughed but Bishop Houston couldn't shake the feeling that George needed to see the doctor and made him promise he would do so when he got back to L.A.

When they arrived in Nashville, Bishop Houston had many calls to return; one of which concerned an invitation from Bob Dorsey, a friend from Christ Church. George had always been amazed at how easily and comfortably Bishop Houston intermingled with people of all races and stations in life. He was the same man with the street walker or drug dealer peddling their wares on a corner in Watts as he was with the most respected leader of Congress, having long since learned that we all have our problems and we all need God to help us deal with them. Doors closed to many were always open to Bishop Houston because he genuinely cared about hurting people of all races and ethnicities and from all socioeconomic backgrounds.

George, having not fully come to terms with the pain and humiliation he had experienced from white people during his childhood, declined the invitation Bob Dorsey extended to him through his brother. That bothered Bob, as he had grown to love the Houston family and really wanted George to join them. Bishop Houston assured Bob it was nothing personal and told him what the problem was. After prayer and thoughtful consideration, Bob made a personal call to George and jokingly offered to blacken his face if it would make him feel more comfortable. George laughed at the thought of it and said he would come. That was the beginning of an enduring friendship between the two men.

When George returned to L. A., he went to see the doctor and was diagnosed with cancer. During the months that followed, Bob made long distance calls on a regular basis to see how he was doing and to encourage him in the Lord.

Early one morning, Bishop Houston was awakened at around 4:00 a.m. with a feeling of urgency regarding his brother's condition. He felt it was important for him to go see George, who had been in the hospital for a week, right away. Sister Minnie encouraged him to go, and by 9:00 a.m. of the same day he was boarding a flight to L. A. During the flight, he sought the Lord on his brother's behalf, and the Lord spoke to him about what he was to say to George. It wasn't easy, but when he arrived, he told George that God was preparing him for heaven and that he did not need to pick up a cigarette now.

George broke down and cried when he heard the message. Just before Bishop Houston had arrived, he had tried to get his grandson and eldest daughter to get him a pack of cigarettes in spite of being under doctor's orders not to smoke. Bishop Houston could see George had received the message God had given him and thanked God for it.

Sister Minnie was fighting her own battles back in Nashville, and it was hard for Bishop Houston to be away from her to spend a week with George as he planned. He kept reminding himself of the excellent care three young doctors, who were like daughters to the Houstons, were giving Sister Minnie. One of them, Dr. Pam Williams, lived within a block of the Houstons and was especially attentive to Sister Minnie's every need. Of course, family members who lived in the area kept a close eye on her as well. Especially the Houston's son, Ron, and his wife,

Vicky.   They often dropped by with the best tonic of all...the Houston's youngest granddaughter, Brianna.

Just when it seemed that everything was going as well as could be expected, and only two days into his visit with George, Bishop Houston received the most shocking call of his life. His only sister, Lil, had driven home from a prayer meeting, pulled into her downward sloping drive and, as she had done a thousand times before, left the engine running while she got out to unlock the gate. Somehow the car suddenly slipped out of gear and started to roll toward her. A friend in the front passenger seat, frantically tried to reach the brake but accidentally hit the accelerator instead, causing the car to hit Lil with a fatal force, killing her instantly.

George told Bishop Houston he would not leave him to face this sorrow alone. Both were heartbroken and very concerned about the impact this tragic news would have on their 90-year-old father, who had also been diagnosed with cancer.

However, even at his lowest moments of grief, the dignified patriarch proved to be a tower of strength for his very large family. Bob Dorsey was among those who were called and, like so many, began to make his plans to attend Lil's funeral.   He and his wife, Jo, would be attending as friends of the family and also as representatives of all those friends from Christ Church, whose hearts and prayers traveled with them.

During Bob and Jo's flight, they prayed for the Houstons and also talked about their own deepest feelings regarding death. Jo told Bob that she hoped her manner of death would be quick as Lil's had been, as she did not want to linger and suffer. Little did they know that before the year was out, Jo would have a sudden heart attack and also be with the Lord.

Bob told Jo that he wanted to see George as soon as it was convenient to do so and she agreed. The two of them were among the Lord's most faithful, kind and considerate followers. What Bob did when he agreed to blacken his face was so like Paul who said, "....I am made all things to all men, that I might by all means save some. And this I do for the gospel's sake, that I might be partakers thereof with you." (1 Cor. 9:22-23)

Together, Bob and Jo often entered into an empathetic identification with others. They had never read *The Rewards of the Personal Worker*, but they performed those duties to perfection, "With Christ's compassionate LOVE and a hearing ear, we can flow in the Spirit as we identify with those who have hurting hearts by letting Jesus come forth from within them to deliver, to heal, to reconcile, and to restore them to a unity with Him (and with all others) that brings a peace that passeth all understanding. Jesus is there doing the work through His word...Our reward is to see HIM at work. Hallelujah!"[*]

As the plane touched down, Bob recalled what Pastor Carol had said about how to identify the person who would be meeting them and taking them to their room. After picking up their luggage, Bob and Jo walked out the doors and immediately saw Bishop Houston getting out of a car. When he saw Bob, the big man just shook his head sadly. Bob's heart broke for him.

As Bob gripped his giant hand and hugged the Bishop at the same time, he thought, When we spoke on the phone, he sounded stronger than he looks now. Then, Bishop Houston told him that George had just passed away. Bob and Jo were absolutely stunned. Bishop Houston went on to say that they were planning a double funeral for his only brother and only sister. Bob thought,

---

[*] *The Rewards of the Personal Worker* by Gerald Easterly, Printed by Crockett Commercial Printers, Crockett, Texas

No wonder Bishop Houston seemed so much sadder than when they talked last.

People were calling from all over the country to express their sympathy, and many were planning to come. Bishop Houston thought of his mother and was glad she had gone on to be with the Lord before this happened.

On the day of the funeral, the little church Daisy Houston had built was packed to overflowing. More than 600 people were there to hear Bishop Houston eulogize George and Lil. Bob was also asked to share his story of offering to blacken his face, and that lightened things up. Then in the tradition of black churches across the country, a celebration of George and Lil's life unfolded. People of faith recognized that even while the family was shot through the heart with a double barrel of sorrow, that they offered up a sacrifice of praise for the blessings of the lives that had enriched their own. Along with the family, the congregation rejoiced to have known George and Lil here on this earth and for the reward to which they had gone on to receive.

The celebratory service might have seemed strange to anyone who had never attended a funeral conducted by African-Americans with beliefs similar to the Houstons. But those who understood their traditions and beliefs about the hereafter joined in with the singing and heartfelt affirmations generously offered by the congregation as remembrances were shared by family and friends. It was a lively, revival type service that confirmed their faith as few other things could.

As beautifully expressed in Isaiah 51:11, "So the ransomed of the Lord shall return and come to Zion with singing, with everlasting joy on their heads; they shall obtain joy and gladness, and sorrow and sighing shall flee away."

As the Bishop reminded them that Christians do not sorrow as those who have no hope, people of other races noticed that their African-American brothers and sisters in Christ were *fully confident* of the eternal bliss their loved ones had passed on to. It was for that reason that they could *celebrate* the life of their loved ones who had just passed away.

Even while grieving their own loss, they celebrated for the ones who had gone on to a place where, as the Bishop described by reading, "...They shall hunger no more, neither thirst any more; neither shall the sun light on them, nor any heat. For the Lamb which is in the midst of the throne shall feed them, and shall lead them unto living fountains of water: and God shall wipe away all tears from their eyes." (Rev. 7:16-17 KJV)

"And they shall see His face..." (Rev. 22:4) Nothing expresses the joy of that phrase better than the old hymn that declares..."What a day that shall be when my Saviour I shall see, when I look upon His face, the One who saved me by His grace, then He'll take me by the hand and lead me to the Promised Land...What a day, wonderful day that will be..."

For those left behind, to finish their earthly race, God promises, "weeping may endure for a night, but joy comes in the morning." (Ps. 30:5) And, "...for I will turn their mourning to joy, will comfort them, and make them rejoice rather than sorrow." (Jer. 31:13)

Bishop Houston's spiritual pantry was well-stocked with these and many other promises of God. Even at such a time as this, it was as natural for him and Sister Minnie to encourage their family of believers with these promises as it was for them to prepare a meal for them. "Your words were found, and I ate them, and Your word was to me the joy and rejoicing of my heart; for I am called by Your name, O Lord God of hosts. (Jer. 15:16)

George and Lil had moved into the land of milk and honey, and that is what they emphasized. Jesus had promised that He had gone to prepare a place for His own and if it were not true, He wouldn't have said it. Eye has not seen and ear has not heard what our Lord has in store for His own.

Bishop Houston's very life had been built on the Word, and it never meant more to him than it did on the day he buried his only brother and sister while holding the hands of his fragile wife and elderly father. If the Word was true, as he knew it was, these separations were only temporary. All through eternity they would be living in mansions in the most prestigious Master-planned community ever conceived because when THE MASTER plans one, all others pale by way of comparison.

If one could believe John the Revelator's description, and Bishop Houston certainly did, there was no need to weep for George and Lil, who had already gone to the place John saw and wrote about in detail.

"And he carried me away in the spirit to a great and high mountain, and shewed me that great city, the holy Jerusalem, descending out of heaven from God, Having the glory of God: and her light was like unto a stone most precious, even like a jasper stone, clear as crystal; And had a wall great and high, and had twelve gates, and at the gates twelve angels, and names written thereon, which are the names of the twelve tribes of the children of Israel: On the east three gates; on the south three gates; and on the west three gates. And the wall of the city had twelve foundations, and in them the names of the twelve apostles of the Lamb.

"And he that talked with me had a golden reed to measure the city, and the gates there of, and the wall thereof. And the city lieth foursquare, and the length is as large as the breadth: and he measured the city with the reed, twelve thousand furlongs. The length and the breadth and the height of it are equal. And he measured the wall thereof, an hundred and forty and four cubits, according to the measure of a man, that is, of the angel. And the building of the wall of it was of jasper: and the city was pure gold; like unto clear glass.

"And the foundations of the wall of the city were garnished with all manner of precious stones. The first foundation was jasper; the second, sapphire; the third, a chalcedony; the fourth, an emerald; The fifth, sardonyx; the sixth, sardiuis; the seventh, chrysolyte; the eighth, beryl; the ninth, a topaz; the tenth, a chrysoprasus; the eleventh, a jacinth; the twelfth, an amethyst.

"And the twelve gates were twelve pearls; every several gate was of one pearl: and the street of the city was pure gold, as it were transparent glass.

"And I saw no temple therein: for the Lord God Almighty and the Lamb are the temple of it. And the city had no need of the sun, neither of the moon, to shine in it: for the glory of God did lighten it, and the Lamb is the light thereof. and the nations of them which are saved shall walk in the light of it: and the kings of the earth do bring their glory and honour into it. And the gates of it shall not be shut at all by day: for there shall be no night there. And they shall bring the glory and honour of the nations into it. And there shall in no wise enter into it any thing that defileth, neither whatsoever worketh abomination or maketh a lie: but they which are written in the Lamb's book of life." (Rev. 21:10-27)

The good Bishop believes that none of us know the day or the hour when we will meet our Maker, and so it is best to have our names written in the Lamb's Book of Life as soon as possible.

Sister Minnie was almost overwhelmed to be at George and Lil's funeral, as it had seemed that her own passing into glory would certainly supersede theirs. Evidently God knew Bishop Houston would need her by his side and did not leave him to face this without her. Some considered it a miracle that she had the strength to fly out and be with him, and perhaps it was.

In the days that followed the funeral, Bishop Houston often reminisced about the childhood days he had shared with Lil and George. And Sister Minnie enjoyed hearing the stories she had heard so many times that they were part of the joint memory bank they had established and shared for almost half a century now.

With the passing of all his siblings, the Bishop's stories became more valuable, like old and well-worn pieces of furniture that have survived long enough to become invaluable antiques, keepsakes of a by-gone era.

Bishop Houston told her, "I shall never forget when news came to George and me that Grandma was going to bring us a little sister. Grandma had come to visit us from Boley, Oklahoma, and we had to spend a few days with Aunt Rosa. At that time, we did not know where babies came from...can you believe at seven and nine years old that George and I didn't know where babies came from? Anyway, it was exciting spending the time with our aunt and cousins. Then, one evening Uncle George came home and told us Grandma had brought us a little sister. We ran all the way home, more than half a mile down the road, screaming, 'we got a little sister...we got a little sister!'

"Our cousins were very jealous because there were three of them without a sister. Well, Grandma stayed with us a week. Then she stayed at our cousin's house while they stayed with us, and Grandma delivered a girl for Aunt Rosa. During the weeks that followed, we were five very proud country boys, walking around with our chests puffed out and bragging about Lillie and Vila, the two little girls that had invaded our ranks." His voice trailed off and tears ran down his cheeks as Sister Minnie patted his hand.

Listening to another can be a way of giving of yourself to them, and no one knew this better than the very wise and insightful Sister Minnie. She knew Bishop Houston needed to replay the childhood tapes that were stored in the recesses of his mind, and she quietly waited to see which one he would select.

Bishop Houston's mind had retreated to the agricultural community he grew up in. The small Northwestern Oklahoma town of Watonga was the perfect place for boys to explore Indian trails and have imaginary encounters with vengeful Cherokees who, a century earlier, had been the prey of the white man and the scourge of the black man. A strange triangle had existed between the three, and slavery was right in the middle of it. As the book *Trail of Tears* reveals, "It was the deepest scar on the body of the Cherokee nation, and while that nation pleaded with God for deliverance from its own enslavement, it allowed the enslavement of another people" (approximately 2,000 blacks).[*]

Local folklore fired the boyhood imaginations of Bishop Houston, George and their three cousins. When the Cherokees set up camp near them, they were both fascinated and somewhat afraid. At first they watched from afar as the agile Indian boys rode their bareback, paint ponies at breakneck speed. Then, upon learning that the Indian lads liked to eat the land turtles, the African-American youngsters took them some. The Indians boiled them whole, like crabs, then cracked their backs to get the meat. The African-Americans watched the Indians extract the eggs from the turtles and eat them, and decided to try it themselves, only to find they couldn't bring themselves to eat the eggs after they had extracted them.

---

[*] Copyright (c) 1988 by John Ehle, author, published by Doubleday

All the boys had dogs and, at very early ages, went hunting for rabbits and squirrels. It was especially exciting during the winter snow when they would beat the bushes and almost always flush out a rabbit or two. They were easy to catch because of the snow, and they would almost always catch more than they could eat right away. So the boys would skin and clean them, then their Moms would "can" them.

Bishop Houston's mom usually used lard rendered from hog fat. Sometimes, she used the meat grinder to make ground rabbit, then she would shape it into a patty like sausage and preserve it in sealed fruit jars.

Between hunting and raising meat and vegetables, the Houston family was almost totally self-sufficient. Dad would start turning the garden soil as early as February, when the ground was still rock hard. Later, following behind their old mule, he plowed it into rows. Onions, Irish and sweet potatoes, corn, tomatoes, okra, peas and beans were planted and prayed over. For a good harvest, they needed the right amounts of rain and sunshine, but no hail and not too many bugs.

Turnip greens taken right from the patch, cooked with salt pork and eaten with hot cornbread, provided a tasty and economical meal for their growing family. George and his dad would usually leave for the fields very early, while mom finished up the household chores and put on some beans for supper. Then she would leave Bishop Houston to watch Lil and tend the simmering pot while she went to the field to toil alongside the rest of her family.

In the hot summer time, they would "shock" the wheat; cutting it and tying it in bundles that stand upright in the field until the spring of the following year when they would haul it in out of the fields. Young George was terrified of the snakes and would always run from them, even if he had a stick in his hand. Their mom had no fear of them. She would whack off their heads and keep working, reminding her family that God has given us the "...power to tread on serpents and scorpions, and over all the power of the enemy: and nothing shall by any means hurt you." (Luke 2:14)

Of course, she did not believe in tempting God by playing around with snakes, but when she reached out for a shock of wheat and one was coiled up under it, she knew no fear, confident that God's protection was with her.

After a long, grueling day in the sun, she would come home, clean up, feed her family and if the circuit preacher was holding a revival, take her family to church. Some property owners were so prejudiced that they would not allow them to take a shortcut across their fields so they had to walk the long way. Wonder what God thought about that? One thing was sure, He met them at the church and blessed them while they worshipped. His presence was so sweet that they would stay there praising Him until after midnight in spite of having to get up the next morning at the crack of dawn.

The Houstons were getting stronger in the Lord, instead of hard and tough as some were. The lifeblood of faith was the difference between the tough ones that dried up as calluses and the strong ones that exercised their faith and built spiritual muscle. The strong ones kept their faith pumping by fellowshipping with other people of faith as often as possible.

Even during those depressed and very difficult times, the Bishop never saw God's people forsaken or begging bread. But some of those who hardened their hearts because of the devastating economic times, and stopped fellowshipping with the body of Christ, thereby no longer abiding in the Vine, lost their faith and the battle.

If ever people of faith need to "forsake not the assembling of themselves together" (Heb. 10:22), to encourage each other in the Lord, it is during the tough times when it is the hardest to keep the faith.

This can be especially hard to do when other people are responsible for our hardships, and often that is the case. Even the great billowing clouds of dust that rolled across farms bringing the gnawing pain of hunger to many, turned out to be a result of greed replacing stewardship.

Memories of those hard childhood days always flooded back when, as an adult, the Bishop read articles such as "Dust and the Nation's Bread Basket,"

"After World War I, the farmers of the Great Plains, enticed by high wheat prices, plowed up the grass and planted wheat. Year after year they worked the land, exhausting the soil. Just as the Depression of the 1930s rolled in, the rain stopped falling on the Great Plains. Stripped of the native grasses, which helped to anchor the soil, the land dried up and turned to dust, and then the wind began to blow. The worst dust storm occurred on April 14, 1935; the dust moved at speeds of 45 to 70 miles per hour over Colorado, Kansas, and Oklahoma, blackening the sky, suffocating cattle, and dumping thousands of tons of topsoil and red clay on homes and streets." [*]

Even on the hottest days, people had to keep the windows down in their un-airconditioned homes and still the dust found its way inside. Cloths were stuffed between cracks and around doors and windows, and still the dust found its way in. Many wore goggles to protect their eyes and kerchiefs over their noses and mouths to keep from inhaling the pervasively fine dust that filled the air. It settled on top of everything, including food and drinking water if they were left uncovered for even a short while.

---

[*] Copyright (c) Literary Digest 119 (20 April 1935): 10

And as if all that was not enough, the advent of the tractor begin to change things for the tenant farmer. Labor-saving machinery allowed land owners to farm more of their own land or to hire hands to drive tractors for them and keep more of the profits from crops.

John Steinbeck wrote about those day, in *The Grapes of Wrath*:

"The tenants cried, Grandpa killed Indians, Pa killed snakes for the land. Maybe we can kill banks - they're worse than Indians and snakes. Maybe we got to fight to keep our land, like Pa and Grampa did.

"And now the owner men grew angry. You'll have to go.

"But it's ours, the tenant men cried. We-

"No. The bank, the monster owns it. You'll have to go.

"We'll get our guns, like Grampa when the Indians came. What then?

"Well--first the sheriff, and then the troops. You'll be stealing if you try to stay, you'll be murderers if you kill to stay..."

"But if we go, where'll we go? How'll we go? We got no money.

"We're sorry, said the owner men. The bank, the fifty-thousand-acre owner can't be responsible. You're on land that isn't yours. Once over the line maybe you can pick cotton in the fall. Maybe you can go on relief. Why don't you go on west to California? There's work there, and it never gets cold. Why, you can reach out anywhere and pick an orange. Why, there's always some kind of crop to work in. Why don't you go there?"[*]

Those were the times and conditions that prompted the Houston family, who had lived in Oklahoma

---

[*] Copyright (c) 1992, *The Grapes of Wrath*, John Steinbeck, Author, The Viking Press, New York, Publisher

through the depression and the dust bowl, to migrate to California. It was also the impetus for Bishop Houston's prayers regarding a business of his own. One that would provide him with enough income to meet all his family's needs so his wife would not have to work outside the home. He also earnestly prayed and worked for a home that they could raise their children in without having to move due to some unforeseen development. God graciously granted all these requests.

Bishop Houston's childhood memories would never really be understood by anyone else as they had been by George, Lil, and the parents who gave birth to them. An era was passing, time was relentlessly marching on and there was no way to slow it down. There was so much Bishop Houston still wanted to do before his time on earth was up and yet he wanted to spend as much time as possible with Sister Minnie.

Fortunately, she understood the omnipotent call on his life, and since the two of them were one, she felt led to encourage him to answer, "yes," when invitations were extended to him. Over and over again, she assured him of her willingness to make sacrifices and forego the pleasure of having him by her side, as they both preferred. Observers had no doubt that duty was high on the list of priorities for both of them.

While they were working for Him, the Lord raised others up to share their burdens and to love them through their losses. They heard from many, including Robin and little Ralph, who surfaced from the depths of the witness protection program.

CHAPTER SEVEN

"And ye became followers of us and of the Lord, having received the word in much affliction....(I Thess. 1:6)

After several years of living in hiding, Robin and little Ralph were weary of the lifestyle. They had lived in a series of cities under several different names. The strain of the moves as well as having to watch every word they said to new acquaintances had taken a toll on them.

On one occasion, Robin had encountered an old acquaintance at a mall and, according to the rules of the witness protection program, immediately notified Federal Marshals who moved them that same night to a new city.

The next day they were in yet another strange city trying to remember another set of new names, while wondering what their old neighbors were thinking about their sudden disappearance.

Little Ralph had been receiving three forty-five minute counseling sessions a week with a psychologist he had just begun to trust. The sudden move meant they had to start all over again.

Then Robin got so sick she thought she might die and asked her contact at the witness protection program if her parents could come for a visit. She had been in the hospital for a lengthy stay and, not knowing if she would ever walk out, strongly felt the need to see them, but her request was denied.

Actually, they had been allowed to come see her only one time before, and the visit had involved a series of furtive maneuvers.

Her parents were given separate tickets under new names for each of the three legs of the flight. When they got to their hotel and called for room service, they were asked for their name and room number. Chagrined they said they would just call back (because they could not remember which name they had registered under, since they had already used five different ones that same day).

When Robin met with her parents over dinner, they had six U. S. Marshals at the adjoining table watching their every move. Suddenly several young hoodlums rose from a nearby table and started to move in Robin's direction. All six Marshals drew their guns on them, terrifying everyone around them. Fortunately no shots were fired at the young men, who turned out to be gang initiates trying to complete the requirements for full membership.

In spite of that bad experience and all the red tape that was involved, Robin felt that she must see her parents. After her request for an official visit was denied, she made a direct call to her parents. After making arrangements for them to come visit her, she was summarily expelled from the witness protection for breaching security. The Justice Program is proud of the fact that they have never lost a witness, and they obviously plan to keep it that way. However, Robin felt they were being unreasonably hard on her. And, recalling the latitude she had seen given to Jimmy "The Weasel" Fratianno, it was easy to understand why. It was also easy to understand the decision of the witness protection program.

Nevertheless, it had happened when Robin was sick, broke, and unable to make it on her own. The Houstons were sorry to learn that after living with friends for a while, she had finally ended up in a homeless shelter.

They were glad that she and Ralph were re-admitted after Robin wrote the President of the United States. It seemed right to them, as the diminutive and frail girl had taken as many risks as Fratianno to testify. Fratianno was a self-confessed murderer whose victims included his friends. Surely Robin deserved the same breaks Fratianno received.

Her riveting account of life inside the dark and ominous drug trade had informed the public of dangers they needed to address. And most important, her "no holds barred" testimony had sealed the fate of a terrifyingly vicious cast of characters. Bishop Houston smiled at the memory of his family and church members rejoicing when the trial dismembered one of the most insidious and dangerous drug rings in the country.

Because of their years of friendship with Robin and little Ralph, the Houstons understood their struggles as very few others could. The identity crisis and subterfuge were stressful to say the least. Regarding the similar plight of fallen angels, John Milton wrote the following in his book *Paradise Lost.* "Milton tells us their names had been removed as they were dismissed from heaven. Now they seek new names among men. They are never reconciled to their loss of identity; they continue to hunger for their old roles and names."[*]

All these considerations caused the Houstons to be in prayer once again for Robin and Ralph. How they hoped they would be able to cope with their plight in life and build a stable life for themselves.

The Houstons were always helping, but never asking for help for themselves. They seldom said a word to their friends about their own needs, so people counted

---

[*] Used by permission of publisher, Prentice Hall

it a privilege to discover something they could do for them.   Once while Bishop Houston was out of town, taking care of His Heavenly Father's business, Laverne asked Sister Minnie if she could pick up anything for her from the store.   She said she would appreciate some Ensure (a highly nutritious liquid meal), which Laverne gladly picked up.   Laverne had seen the product advertised but was surprised at how expensive the small item was, and of course that was only the tip of the iceberg compared to the other costs associated with a catastrophic illness.   She wondered, How does the average family bear the cost of being sick?

There had been several situations that made her realize just how difficult it must be to be assaulted financially when it is hard to just get up and make it through another day.   Not long after that, friends were very sad to learn that Bishop Houston had taken a part time job at the airport.

Laverne had been working very hard on an assignment for the Lord, and as a result, the Bartons' own income had dropped while Laverne's expenses had risen, so she was more aware of costs than she had previously been.   Tommy was doing an admirable job of producing enough business to cover all the household expenses she had previously helped with, but there was no money for extras, so it was quite an adjustment for them.

When Laverne mentioned that, and also the sadness they felt about Bishop Houston's part-time job, to one of their children, she was surprised at the reaction. Her dear child retorted, "Our Lord owns the cattle on a thousand hills, so why do some of His people have to struggle so?"

The question reminded Laverne of the responses of some Christians who experienced a severe recession that hit the oil-producing states. Since her family was one of them, she was familiar with the painful consequences.

Plummeting oil prices threw the economy into such a downward spiral that banks closed and people had to leave the state to find employment. That affected both Christians and non-Christians, just as a drought does. Some Christians became angry with God over their losses and hardships.

The angry ones were content with God raining on the just and unjust, but not with the reverse of that. Laverne did not want her children to develop the mindset of the angry ones. So, she firmly replied, "Honey, it is time for the church to grow up and for Christians to be more mature.

"Bishop Houston just back from burying his only brother and sister, but he has not whimpered. His testimony has never been greater than it is right now while he is quietly shouldering his family's burdens with great dignity. As he uncomplainingly goes to the airport to do his part-time job, he is teaching others how to bear their burdens."

Laverne's child accepted this strong message and responded by saying, "Yes, mom, I guess it is time to grow up spiritually."

Men who have taken jobs for which they are overqualified in order to provide for their families during hard times are shining examples of the humility of Christ. Not only did Bishop Houston do that, he also lovingly cared for his sick wife by going into the kitchen and, with hands as big as hams, cooking and washing dishes.

He even became quite good at baking cakes. Sister Minnie could always tell when he had not sifted the flour the proper number of times, but instead of complaining, she just lovingly reminded him of how it was best to do it. Bishop Houston smiled and thought that was the way it was with him and his parishioners. He could always tell when they hadn't been following God's recipe for a wholesome life, but like Sister Minnie, rather than berate or condemn them, he just continued to share what he had learned about how to get the best results from life.

Very few people knew Bishop Houston was carrying such a heavy load. Only close friends and family knew that he was keeping up with his work for the Lord while caring for a terminally wife and working part time to cover the additional expenses associated with her illness. He lived what he preached and his life was his greatest sermon.

In spite of sickness, death, and having to fight all manner of evil in order to rescue the perishing, his faith never wavered. Every day he lived, he was trying to be more like the Lord, and he could feel the Lord sustaining him and blessing him for his steadfastness.

He had lived long enough to know that there was no temptation or trial that comes to any of us that is not common to the condition of all mankind and that God is faithful not to put more on us than we can bear. (I Cor. 10:13)

To His own, God has always been faithful to lead them out of every difficult situation. Innumerable times, Bishop Houston had seen that reality come to pass in his own life and the lives of other Christians.

During the course of his life, there had been times of testing and there were times when God had shown Bishop Houston that he was one of those He had kept as the "apple of His eye." Those were precious moments when the presence of God communed with him and encouraged him to keep the faith while he was being led through deep, uncharted waters.

"For I know the thoughts that I think toward you, saith the Lord, thoughts of Peace, and not of evil, to give you an expected end." (Jer. 29:11) So, Bishop Houston clung to the promises of God and waited on the Lord for direction. He had no idea what the Lord had in store for him but felt that was something more.

Sister Minnie felt the same way. So when, in February 1995, her husband received an invitation to go to Nigeria to consecrate six African Bishops into the United Gospel Churches Association of Nigeria (UCCAN), she encouraged him to go. Some were shocked at this trip because of Sister Minnie's condition, but the Bishop and his ailing wife were in agreement and at peace with the decision. It is hard to explain how they understood so much about each other, but it was part and parcel of their relationship with each other and their Lord. In fact, it was even a part of their heritage.

Isak Dinesen, author of *Out of Africa,* observed the same sense of understanding and "knowing" among her close African friends. Among other things, they would often anticipate her unannounced arrivals at the train station, in spite of her having made impromptu travel plans.

When she found them waiting there to pick her up and asked how they had known she was coming, she reported that "they looked away, and seemed uneasy, as if frightened or bored, such as we should be if a deaf person insisted on getting an explanation of a symphony from us."[*]

So knowing as she did that some of Bishop Houston's greatest work lay before him, Sister Minnie was, even in the midst of her illness, infinitely patient in sharing the life of her husband with their Lord. In a comfortable and congenial way, both of them continued on, in one accord, with their lifelong commitment to submitting to God's plan for their lives. As Isak Dinesen

---

[*] From *OUT OF AFRICA* by Isak Dinesen, Copyright (c) 1937 by Random House, Inc. and renewed 1965 by Rungstedlundfonden. Reprinted by permission of Random House.

had recorded of their ancestors, they "had real courage...the true answer of creation to the announcement of their lot, the echo from the earth when heaven had spoken."[*]

Even in her frailness, Sister Minnie's erect and noble carriage bespoke a confidence of knowing who she was in Jesus and that she was never alone. Perhaps that was why she faced all life's trials, including innumerable medical procedures and cancer treatments, with a calm, brave, stoicism. Even with the death angel waiting in the wings and in the absence of her dearly beloved husband, she was at peace.

Nevertheless, since more than a few were questioning the wisdom of the trip, Bishop Houston prayed without ceasing that his dear wife would not pass away while he was gone.

---

[*] Ibid

CHAPTER EIGHT

" Before thou camest forth out of the womb I sanctified thee, and I ordained thee a prophet unto the nations."
(Jer. 1:5)

On this trip to Africa, Bishop Houston was not only carrying Sister Minnie with him in his heart, he was also carrying a burden for the people he was going to see. They had labored long and hard under dire circumstances in a country whose history was one of coups and countercoups. Even for himself, there were concerns, as the country was being governed by the Nigerian army, which had a notorious international reputation for gross violation of human rights. No one was immune, not even gentle souls who were working to improve the plight of the people. Later that same year, in November 1995, Nigeria would execute playwright Ken Saro Wiwa and eight other human rights activists. Anyone who came to help did so at considerable risk.

The observations of the UN Human Rights Committee were as follows: "The Committee is deeply concerned by the high number of extrajudicial and summary executions, disappearances, cases of torture, ill-treatment, and arbitrary arrest and detention by members of the army and security forces and by the failure of the government to investigate fully these cases to prosecute alleged offenses, to punish those found guilty and provide compensation to the victims or their families.   The resulting state of impunity encourages further violations of Covenant rights."[*]

Bishop Houston's ministry had been very different from that of most of his white colleagues.   He had pastored an inner-city church in Watts and his missionary endeavors had taken him into countries filled with strife. He could not help but marvel at the ways in which the Lord had ordered the steps of his life.

In this instance, it had come about as a result of being awakened with a call from a representative of Nigerian pastors working with seven different Pentecostal groups representing sixty different churches. It blessed his soul when men of God cooperated together to further the cause of Christ, so he did not hesitate to say that he would come and lend his support to their efforts.

He found it interesting to contemplate what his life might have been like if his parents had remained in Oklahoma.   There he would probably have pastored a country church and never even gone to the mission field at all, but God had other plans and for some reason, they had taken him to violent areas.

Perhaps he had more compassion for pastors in those environments because his own church was in an area where men of God, and the families to whom they ministered, were faced with more challenging struggles due to high crime rates and poverty. It was hard to say "why," but when he received a call from these Nigerian brothers, he felt he should go. He wanted to help in any way possible and as he prayed about what he might be able to share, he felt it would be a good idea to take a manual for the use of those who wished to establish an Episcopal form of government.

He had been to Africa many times, and this was his third trip to Nigeria. In 1980, he, Sister Minnie and

---

[*] www.amnesty.org/ailib/intcam/nigeria/index.html

their daughter, Pastor Carol, had brought a group from Bethel United Holy Church in Los Angeles to Liberia, Nigeria, and then on to the Holy Land. The short-term mission team, known as J.O.I. (Jesus Our Inspiration), gave the full time Liberian missionaries a much needed break from their daily tasks. After becoming personally acquainted with the people they had been supporting and gaining a firsthand knowledge of the work, the J.O.I. team had a much greater enthusiasm for the Salala Mission. As a result of that trip, the Houstons' church, Bethel United Holy Church, made a decision to more than triple the monthly amount sent to the Salala Mission and were faithful to maintain that level of giving for years to come.

In 1987, he replicated that trip and in conjunction with Bob Harrison, a good friend and former Billy Graham associate, took the team on to Keyna for the World Pentecost Convention. While in Kenya, which is on the east side of the vast African continent, they ministered to a tent city of refugees who had been banished to a locale some five miles out of the city. The speakers' platform was not completely covered, so the piano was about the only thing that stayed dry in the downpour that fell on the seven speakers. The crowd, numbering in the thousands, was so hungry for the message of hope that they were oblivious to the deluge.

That message of hope was just as needed in Nigeria, which is on Africa's west coast, and north of the equator, as is Liberia. For Bishop Houston, it wasn't possible to make a trip to Africa without thinking of Liberia, home of the Salala Mission that he had spent so much of his life assisting.

In spite of a civil war that turned Liberia into an inferno of gruesome hostilities, Bishop Houston still had hopes and dreams for the United Holy Church's Salala Mission. They had established the mission over half a century ago, but many of their plans had been put on hold due to the mayhem and terror that had engulfed the country. According to the Africa News Service, the war had "claimed the lives of 1 out of every 17 people in the country, uprooted most of the rest, and destroyed a once-viable economic infrastructure.

"The strife also spread to Liberia's neighbors, contributing to a slowing of the democratization that was progressing steadily through West Africa at the beginning of the decade and destabilizing a region that was already one of the world's most marginal. U. S. taxpayers footed a sizable bill -- over $400 million to date -- for emergency aid that arguably never would have been needed had their government used its considerable clout to help end the killing."[*]

The Association of Evangelicals in Liberia (AEL) had previously sponsored two reconciliation conferences, and even though some of the worst massacres were committed after them, neither they or World Relief had given up. However, while plans were being formulated for a third meeting, to which more than 1,000 leaders of the country's government, churches, and warring factions would eventually come, the Southern Baptists, Assemblies of God, United Methodist Church and other missionary and relief agencies had to evacuate their workers who, like everyone else, were coming under fire from armed rebels.

At this time, only God could have brought Bishop Houston back into this region of Africa where unprecedented attacks were taking place on peace keepers and civilians.

In Nigeria an estimated 500,000 to 2,000,000 people had died in the war that lasted from 1967 to 1970 when eastern Nigeria had attempted to secede. In 1979 civilian rule was restored but a second coup by northern

---

[*] http://www.africanews.org/usaf/liberia.html article by Reed Kramer

regimes brought this to an end in 1983. Since that time, Nigerians had been trying to escape the succession of oppressive northern-dominated military governments. Extensive rioting broke out in 1993 as a result of the army annulling long awaited democratic elections.

Now the international community was doing everything possible to help Nigeria make the transition from a military run country to one in which the civilian population had a democratic voice. Maybe then they could put their history of poverty, disease and starvation behind them.

In such an oil-rich country, it was a shame for so many to be living in destitute conditions. Greed, widespread corruption, mismanagement, and political turmoil separated the average Nigerian family from the benefits that should be accruing to a population whose country produced over 2,000,000 barrels of oil each day.

While contemplating that deplorable situation, Bishop Houston thought of something Dr. Martin Luther King, Jr. had said: "The curse of poverty has no justification in our age. It is socially as cruel and blind as the practice of cannibalism at the dawn of civilization, when men ate each other because they had not yet learned to take food from the soil or to consume the abundant animal life around them. The time has come for us to civilize ourselves by the total, direct and immediate abolition of poverty."[*]

As the fourth leading supplier of U. S. crude oil imports, it was possible for Nigerians to accomplish that goal but the first step was the establishment of a stable, democratic government. As with most African nations, it had been difficult for them to maintain a cohesive form of government. This was due, in part, to their own

---

[*] Copyright (c) 1963, *Why We Can't Wait*, by Martin Luther King, Jr.

population being comprised of more than 250 different ethnic groups.

Christian missionaries had made considerable headway with traditional faiths and that helped reduce tensions. However, the northern sector of the country, where the Hausa-Fulani people resided, was still predominately Islamic.

Bishop Houston chuckled at the memory of how surprised some Europeans were when they realized they, and their religions, were being quietly evaluated by the African natives among whom they lived and conducted business.

One had written, "It is an alarming experience to be, in your person, representing Christianity to the Natives.

"There was a young Kikuyu by the name of Kitau, who came in from the Kikuyu Reserve and took service with me. He was a meditative boy, an observant, attentive servant and I liked him well. After three months he one day asked me to give him a letter of recommendation to my old friend Sheik Ali bin Salim, the Lewali of the Coast, at Mombasa, for he had seen him in my house and now, he said, he wished to go and work for him. I did not want Kitau to leave just when he had learned the routine of the house, and I said to him that I would rather raise his pay. No, he said, he was not leaving to get any higher pay, but he could not stay. He told me that he had made up his mind, up in the Reserve to become either a Christian or a Mohammedan, only he did not yet know which. For this reason he had come and worked for me, since I was a Christian, and he had stayed three months in my house to see the *testurde* - the ways and habits, - of the Christians. From me he would go for three months to Sheik Ali in Mombasa and study the testurde of the Mohammedans; then he would decide. I believe that even an Archbishop, when he had had these facts laid before him, would have said, or at least have thought, as I said: 'Good God, Kitau, you might have told me that when you came here.'"*

While most people do not evaluate religions in such a deliberate fashion, still everyday lives speak volumes to those who are looking for spiritual answers. The way we live our lives has much more of an effect on others than what we say. More than we realize, others are usually, on a subconscious basis, either turned "on" or "off" to our beliefs by the way in which we live. Our life style says more about how we really esteem the tenets of our faith than anything else.

Our Lord said, "If you love me, keep my commandments." (John 14:15) In the sixteenth chapter of John, three times Jesus asked Peter if he loved Him. In response to each of Peter's affirmative proclamations of his love, Jesus admonished Peter to feed His lambs and sheep.

Feeding the bodies and souls of His sheep requires obedience and sacrifice, with some going to the mission field and some sending. Those going should be committed to a body of believers who are committed to them. Those sending should know the ones they are sending very well and work closely with them. Especially if they are not of the same denomination or church. It is important to know the beliefs of those being sent, so senders know what they are supporting. We have a responsibility to be wise stewards. Bishop Houston believes those being sent should be accountable to those doing the sending, as well as to God.

He encourages those doing the sending to see that those being sent don't have to worry about support. The

---

* From *OUT OF AFRICA* by Isak Dinesen, Copyright (c) 1937 by Random House, Inc. and renewed 1965 by Rungstedlundfonden. Reprinted by permission of Random House, Inc.

average church member may not know very much about missions, so Bishop Houston teaches that it is the responsibility of leadership to educate their congregations about the importance of integrating missionaries into the church. If we are brothers and sisters in Christ, we should act like brothers and sisters. We should be family. Then, even when our missionaries are half a world away, they are not as likely to feel so alone. Missionaries with close bonds are less likely to suffer from either loneliness or need.

Any relationship is a two way street requiring effort on both ends. When missionaries don't do their part in establishing and maintaining relationships, churches may view them as guest speakers. As such, they maybe appreciated while there but be perceived more as a visitor than as a part of the congregation. Bishop Houston views this as a growing problem with independent churches and missionaries. Usually, they don't have the kind of close relationships that he believes our Lord intended, or that both can benefit from.

Unless church leadership treats missionaries as they themselves want to be treated, missionaries may be given old clothes and treated as some treat the poorest members of their families. This is a real tragedy.

Missionaries have the same commitment to the Lord as pastors and deserve the same respect. We should do unto those missionaries who go as we would want others to do done unto us if we were going. If we don't, those going to the more hostile locales for long tours of duty may become disheartened. According to our ability, we should give unto them, as unto the Lord.

When we have live in a nice home, wear fine clothes and give God our old "hand-me-down" clothes, it is like tossing a dog a bone without any meat on it. Our Great and Mighty Creator is grieved when we offer inappropriate sacrifices. For many of us, tokens of our lives, such as used clothes or small checks are inappropriate gestures of our appreciation for all God has done for us. God may not accept second rate sacrifices insofar as the spiritual laws of seed time and harvest are concerned. Worse still, we may get to heaven and discover that we haven't laid up as much eternal treasure as we thought we had. God has always required a pure sacrifice...the first fruits...our best and foremost.

In the twelfth chapter of Romans, we read, "I beseech you therefore brethren, by the mercies of God, that ye present your bodies a living sacrifice, holy, acceptable unto God, which is your reasonable service. And be not conformed to this world: but be ye transformed by the renewing of your mind, that ye may prove what is that good, and acceptable, and perfect, will of God." If we love Him, we will seek to do that good and perfect will. Those who do make their lives a living sacrifice should be held up as role models to the church at large.

Missionaries who go to live full time in foreign, dangerous lands come the closest to living out those concepts. Better communication and understanding will enable all that love the Lord to do a better job of partnering together to feed His sheep and lambs.

Bishop Houston's trip to Nigeria was a result of those who had previously come and lived among the natives. They were most certainly a part of the great cloud of witnesses who would be watching as Bishop Houston consecrated the following men as Bishops:

- Rt. Rev. (Dr.) Samuel O. Fadeyi, the founder and general overseer of Gospel Light Mission International, Lagos
- Rt. Rev. (Dr.) Michael O. Adeoye, general overseer, The Living Gospel of Christ Church Inc., Lagos

- Rt. Rev. Daniel Ugochukwu, general overseer, Christ the King Church of God
- Rt. Rev. Joseph O. Adeagbo of Christ Gospel Assembly with headquarters in Lagos
- Rt. Rev. (Dr.) Michael A. Fadeyi of Gospel Faith Assembly and dean of the Christian Faith School of Theology
- Rt. Rev. (Dr.) Emmanuel Adekunle of AIM Ministry.

Nigeria's capital city of Lagos was a center not only of trade but also of the nation's religious community. Bishop Houston was looking forward to being there. It had blessed him to learn of the high level of cooperation among these men of God, especially since earlier visitors to Africa had recorded, "The prestige of the Christian religion in Africa was weakened by the intolerance that the one Christian church showed towards the other."[*]

The dedicated servants of God he was going to be with were known to be quite different. Foremost in fostering the spirit of brotherly love that brought them all together was His Grace, The Most Rev. Dr. Abraham Oye, Oyeniran, founder of the Evangelical Int'l Church, and the Pentecostal coalition known as the United Gospel Churches Association of Nigeria (UGCAN). Because of his exemplary commitment to the progress of the Kingdom of God in Nigeria, he was being enthroned and consecrated as Archbishop of this illustrious assembly.

The alliance was encouraged and supported by representatives from the presidency as well as representatives of other countries. Among those who would be in attendance was the new Israeli Ambassador to Nigeria, His Excellency, Mr. Gadi Golan and his wife, as well as the second secretary of the Embassy, Mr.

---

[*] From *Out of Africa* by Isak Dinesen, Copyright (c) 1937 by Random House, Inc. and renewed 1965 by Rungstedlundfonden. Reprinted by permission of Random House, Inc.

Hanan Goder, all of whom would be attending the ceremony.

Naturally, Bishop Houston was looking forward to all the related international festivities and receptions, the first of which would be for the Israeli dignitaries.

At the airport, the Bishop was greeted warmly and taken to the Federal Palace Hotel in Lagos where he would be staying and where the reception for the Israelis was to be held. Introductions were followed by jubilant, optimistic expressions of anticipation for the upcoming ceremony and for the future of the country itself. In the new Nigeria many believed there would be no economic adversity and all those living in exile would return from the U.S.A., Britain, Saudi-Arabia and other countries to help rebuild their beloved homeland.

The following day, the ceremony began with the procession of the Evangelical International Choir, which sang down the power and glory of God until the whole auditorium was filled with His presence. Then the Nigerian International Choir and Orchestra (NICO) performed, followed by the Barley Dancers, who brought 15,000 people to their feet in a standing ovation -- including the majestically attired ministers, bishops and even the new Archbishop himself, Dr. Oyeniran.

There were many fine speakers addressing the issues of the day. One of the strongest challenges made to those in attendance came from Prophet (Dr.) T. Obadare of WOSEM, who implored the heads of state, *"to make sure that members of the Federal Executive Council think of Nigeria first, before they think of their private homes."*[*]

That bold statement reminded Bishop Houston of Martin Luther King, Jr.'s own admonishments: *"The*

---

[*] April 12, 1995, Daily Times article written by Isaac Anumihe and Michael Ekwuribe

church must be reminded that it is not the master or the servant of the state, but rather the conscience of the state. It must be the guide and the critic of the state, and never its tool.   If the church does not recapture its prophetic zeal, it will become an irrelevant social club without moral or spiritual authority."

Bishop Houston breathed a silent prayer for the future of the prophets of God, especially Obadare who concluded his speech to the new bishops with a statement that made it clear he had counted the cost of speaking out. Chills went down the spine of many in the congregation when he said, "Evangelism is not an easy task. *As evangelists, you will be persecuted but you will conquer all temptations."*

Obadare believed it was time for the new bishops to be courageous and lead the country to reform as they were God's chosen people. The people were looking to them for direction and he believed church leadership should give it without being afraid of the consequences.

The newly enthroned Archbishop The Most Rev. Dr. Abraham Oye, Oyeniran emphasized that their positions as archbishop and bishops would be used to "uplift the name of our Lord and Savior Jesus Christ," adding that while "there are leaders in positions of authority in our nation, it is also pertinent for us to have people who take care of the spiritual aspects of the nation...."[*]

The following days newspaper coverage included the following remarks: "...Among the dignitaries were Archbishop Ralph Houston who performed the ceremony..."[*]

Bishop Houston chuckled at the newspaper's elevation of his title to Archbishop. It was also interesting

---

[*] Ibid
[*] An anointed Christian vocalist

to note that of all the dignitaries in attendance (including more than one Archbishop), that Bishop Houston was the one whose photograph appeared in the newspaper with Archbishop Dr. Oyeniran. It was quite an honor considering the incredibly high number of important people in attendance. To name a few of the categories, there were "royal fathers," chiefs, prophets, commissioners of education, professors, ambassadors, and several others.

This was an experience of a lifetime, and as his hosts graciously bestowed honor after honor upon him, Bishop Houston could sense the spirit of his mother and recalled her dying prophesy, "Your gift will make room for you and bring you before great men."

On this visit, it was great men *and women*, which included the Rev. Justus Awaji, Press Secretary to the newly-enthroned Archbishop, and more importantly, pastor of the Battle-Axe Women's Army, a newly formed international church.

There was a consensus among the distinguished guests who witnessed the enthronement of Archbishop Abraham Oyeniran and consecration of six Bishops that the ceremony was approved of God.

This was confirmed when the Israelis explained that according to Jewish tradition, God may indicate His blessings and approval of a king or spiritual leader by bringing rain during the consecration or coronation ceremony. Even though the ceremony was not held during the rainy season, at the exact time of the consecration, the heavens released a mighty downpour that flooded the vicinity of the Evangelical International Church, venue of the ceremony. One hour prior to the ceremony the scorching sun had been beating down on the multitudes. It was wonderfully uplifting and refreshing to have it give way to showers of blessings as Dr. Oyeniran was being enthroned as Archbishop and the six other ministers were being consecrated as Bishops. As soon as the ceremony was complete, the heavy down pour abruptly ceased and the sun began shining down on the freshly washed and cooled off earth.

The epochal occasion was concluded by a bountiful feast the likes of which Bishop Houston had never seen before. In attendance were the traditional rulers, spiritual leaders, members of the diplomatic corps, government representatives, and the happy and lively multitude of approximately 15,000. They just naturally broke up into people groups according to dialect or tribe. It was an incredible experience to see so many different customs and varieties of colorful native apparel.

For two days and nights cows, goats and chickens had been butchered and prepared for this occasion. Every aspect of this was fascinating to Bishop Houston. Much to the surprise of the workers, he was interested in mingling with them and observing their ways of doing things.

As Bishop Houston watched the natives use an air pump to inflate a recently slaughtered cow, then pour scalding water on it and scrape the hair off, he realized they were not wasting one ounce of edible substance...not even the hide. Some of the meat was cooked with greens and served over rice and some was cooked over a pit. All of it was delicious.

In a country that had seen much hunger and starvation, it was wonderful to see everyone get plenty to eat. Bishop Houston realized there was a great deal of appreciation over things most Americans take for granted.

As for him, he wasn't taking one moment of this experience for granted. It was unbelieveable, to be in the country of his heritage, as the guest of honor, at an event of such a multitudinous dimension.

The extensive guest list read like a "Who's Who" of Nigeria and there were also representatives from many other governments. Before Bishop Houston left this illustrious company, thirteen of the pastors paid him a special tribute by presenting him with a robe and headdress that were fit for an African Chief.

As he flew out over the coast, he looked down at beautiful Nigeria, which was so rich in natural resources, including gold, silver, coal, tin, iron, lead, forest and waterpower. He prayed Nigerians would eventually live the kind of lives these God-given assets could make possible. So many had nothing in a country that had everything. In the distance, there were swamps and mangrove jungles teeming with hippopotamus, rhinoceros, crocodile, monkeys, and parrots. Further north in the savannah grasslands resided buffalo, gazelle, elephant and gorillas. In the arid regions mimosa trees, patches of grass and acacia formed the habitat for giraffes, lions, hyenas, and antelopes.

In a land of such abundance, the people should be living comfortable, peaceful lives. Even poor Americans had more than most Africans and as Bishop Houston evaluated the reasons why, he concluded that it was most likely because it was still a predominately Christian nation. People have no idea how important that is until they have traveled to other nations where corruption and strife are rampant.

Even though most Christians fall far short of Christ's teachings, no other religion calls its followers to a higher standard of behavior toward their fellow man than Christianity. Visits to other countries always made Bishop Houston appreciate America, land of the free and home of the brave. He had visited many countries whose governments wouldn't even allow their men and women of vision to voice the need for change. That was an especially sad situation when those governments were failing to serve the needs of the people at the most basic levels.

Some of Nigeria's finest citizens, such as Nobel-prizewinning author Wole Soyinka, were forced to flee the country in order to live long enough to urge international action on behalf of his country.

Around the world, radical factions can, and do, assassinate men of vision, but in America it does not happen nearly as often as in other countries. Most importantly, our form of government gives voice to cries for change. Even those who have been assassinated still have a voice. After their deaths, their wisdom echoes through our minds, their dreams haunt us, and their challenges continue calling us to higher standards, long after they are gone.

As Dr. Martin Luther King, Jr. said, "Man is man because he is free to operate within the framework of his destiny. He is free to deliberate, to make decisions, and to choose between alternatives. He is distinguished from animals by his freedom to do evil or to do good and to walk the high road of beauty or tread the low road of ugly degeneracy."

Nations with a predominately Christian population have a better record of helping their citizens, and other people groups, than do countries where other religions predominate.

In Nigeria, Muslims heavily outnumbered Christians, and there were also many other religious beliefs and practices that varied from tribe to tribe, including ancestor worship that was common among the southern tribes. There were estimated to be as many who subscribed to various tribal religions as those who professed to be Christians. With so much opposition from the Muslims and tribal religions, Christians certainly could not afford conflict among themselves.

The church at large could accomplish a great deal through spiritual solidarity but without a spirit of cooperation, the more difficult problems would continue to grow. All over Africa, and around the world, persecuted Christians needed the support of America's Christian leaders. This was very much on Bishop Houston's mind after this trip to Africa.

Over the next twelve months, it would become even more evident, as Charles Colson's article in the April 1996 newsletter from *Intercessor for America* newsletter would so vividly point out.

"Waving branches and dancing rhythmically, the children chant, 'He is risen, He is risen!' They bang drums; their small bodies glisten in the African sun. These are Sudanese Christians, and from their Easter celebration you would never know that weeks earlier they were driven from their homes by soldiers, that they are celebrating in a refugee camp -- and that their memories are still raw with scenes of rape and murder.

"The Muslim government in Sudan has made it a crime to convert to Christianity - a policy enforced brutally. As the Khartoum government troops move south, where most Christians live, believers are given three options: convert, flee, or be killed. Thousands of children have been snatched from Christian families and many sold as slaves to buyers in Sudan, Libya and other Islamic countries. Thousands of women have been raped, others sold as servants or concubines. There are even reports of men being crucified.

"Sudan is not alone in acts of hostility toward Christians. Michael Horowitz of the Hudson Institute has collected evidence of widespread persecution throughout Africa and the Middle East. In Ethiopia last year, government troops raided the largest evangelical church, arresting most congregants. Many died in jail, their bodies thrown out to be scavenged by animals.

"In Pakistan, Christian evangelization is outlawed by a blasphemy law that prohibits speaking against Muhammad, punishable by death. A 12-year old child was recently sentenced to death and freed only by international pressure. In Saudi Arabia, the government offers rewards of up to $8,000 for information about secret worship services, which are then raided. In Iran, three prominent pastors were abducted and killed last year. Armenian and Assyrian Christian schools have been closed and taken over by Muslims. Christians have been arrested, tortured, lost their homes, jobs and businesses.

"Despite the gruesome evidence, the U. S. government inexplicably refuses to recognize what is happening. According to Horowitz, the Immigration and Naturalization Service often denies asylum to victims of anti-Christian terror. The INS even return them to the country they have fled - where they face imprisonment, torture, even death - in clear violation of U. S. laws granting asylum to religious refugees. Horowitz writes that current INS policy is 'a shameful blot on America's historic traditions.' Our nation was, after all, founded by religious believers fleeing persecution.

"Haven't we learned anything from history? For years, American leaders resisted acknowledging religious persecution by Communist governments. What will it take for our nation to wake up to Islam-inspired terror?

"Today Christians are more widely persecuted than believers of any other faith, says John Hanford, aide to Sen. Richard Lugar (R-IN). Does that startle you? 'On a worldwide basis,' Hanford explains, 'Christians are the most persecuted major religion in terms of direct punishment for practicing religious activities - public worship, evangelism, charity. Yet these tragedies are given scant notice even in the Christian press.

"It is time for us to use our pulpits and publications to cry out in defense of fellow believers. Each of us can write our political leaders, demanding that they reform

INS policy and make persecution of Christians a priority when negotiating with other countries."[*]

Bishop Houston believes many people would respond to those admonishments if the horrific conditions were more widely known. Like Chuck Colson, the Bishop believes we are able prevent history from repeating itself, if we just care enough to act. And we need to do so before Hitler like monsters kill millions more.

Bishop Houston challenges every individual Christian and every church to pay heed to the aforementioned problems and recommendations.

He also recommends reading *Unveiled at Last*[*] by Bob Sjogren. It has an excellent plan of action for every lay person and church leader. Bishop Houston has faith that improvements can be made in the African continent he loves, and throughout the entire world. With so many problems at home, we sometimes forget that "God so loved (all) the world that He gave His only begotten Son, that whosoever believeth in Him should not perish, but have everlasting life." (John 3:16)

The depressing, almost overwhelming problems of the world keep some people from even trying to do anything at all, but the world can be evangelized and helped. People can learn about how to get involved by reading books on missions and taking the "Perspectives" course. When churches began giving to missions and getting involved in the lives of missionaries, the quality of the church's walk with God is richer. The churches that are most actively involved in going into all the world and preaching the gospel, are the churches that are closest to the heart of God the Father.

---

[*] Intercessors for America, Box 4477, Leesburg, VA 22075
[*] Published by YWAM Publishing, a ministry of Youth With A Mission; P. O. Box 55787, Seattle, WA 98155

Bishop Houston has faith that improvements can and will happen in spite of how things now appears. That faith has grown to the level it is now at, in part, because he has seen so much improvement for his own people in America. His is the resilient and ever-increasing faith of a man who has risen from the cradle of slavery, immigrated from the dust bowl, survived World War II, ministered in Watts, and dedicated himself to world missions. With God all things are possible and the brave-hearted Bishop has lived long enough to see "impossibly" tragic situations change for the better. Believing it can happen is a big part of making it happen.

His unwavering commitment silences naysayers in much the same way that Caleb silenced his. Just as Bob Sjogren does, the Bishop encourages people to take up Caleb's battle cry of many centuries ago: "*We should go up and take possession of the land, for we can certainly do it.*" (Num. 13:30)

Bishop Houston is doing everything he can to help Liberian Christians retake their land. By operating within the framework of his own destiny, Bishop Houston now concentrates the majority of his efforts on building up the Salala Mission in Liberia, West Africa.

The faith to keep on helping Africans is a gift of God that enables the Bishop to gladly sacrifice for them. His sacrifices are quietly made on a daily basis. For instance, when the author of this book suggested it would be nice for the Bishop to have a new photo made for the book cover, he didn't say he wouldn't, he just very nicely refrained from doing so. Since he hadn't said anything, she wondered if he was too busy or had just forgotten it. So, once again she mentioned that it would be nice to have a photo of him in the resplendent attire featured in newspaper articles. Again he said nothing but later brought her a basic photo of him in a business suit.

She knew he was planning to make another trip to Liberia, where people were hungry. He didn't say he wouldn't spend the money for a nicer photo, he just quietly refrained from doing so.

Throughout his life the kind, compassionate Bishop has considered the needs of others, and limited his personal spending because of them. He has not begrudged the sacrifices, nor does he ever mention them. Most cannot keep up with his schedule of going and doing for others, which included thirty trips in 1998 alone. Crusading in his quiet, unobtrusive way, enables him to revolutionize the thinking of many, convincing them that the efforts of every individual do make a difference.

Much of his own inspiration came from his heritage, so, in a way, his work is an extension of his parents' work. They buoyed his faith (as he now does for others) through skilled and attentive parenting.

Bishop Houston's father, Oscar Houston, had planted moral values, more by example than by admonishments, and also gave him a strong work ethic.

Bishop Houston passes that training on to others. As he observes the number of modern parents who don't train their children in the ways of the Lord, his appreciation for his own parents grows. He feels privileged to have had such wonderful role models and attributes his blessings to them and the Heavenly Father of them all.

The Bishop feels no one could have had a better example of a great father than he did. His father was also an excellent role model of a kind and loving husband and trustworthy and faithful friend.

As instructed by God, in the sixth chapter of Deuteronomy, the Bishop's father taught his children the Holy statutes and commandments and as promised to those that do so, his days were prolonged. Even into his nineties, he was available to all his family for prayer and spiritual counsel.

Few people have a mother who is also their pastor and spiritual mentor, but Bishop Houston did. Early on, he learned that she was a fount of wisdom and spiritual discernment. Many times when he had a problem in his spiritual walk, all he had to do was spend some time with mom, and while in her presence the Holy Spirit would reveal and confirm what was going on. She convinced him that he could become whatever he dreamed of becoming, and she reveled in his success as both businessman and pastor. She often reminded her son that: "...no good thing will He withhold from them that walk uprightly." (Ps. 84:11)

Bishop Houston was certain he had been blessed to be a success because of his faith in God and the loving guidance of his parents. And there were others who had cultivated the good work begun by them. During his teenage years, the late Elder H. D. Green had been the Houston family's pastor and a sterling example of a great man of God. This man of prayer helped Bishop Houston to believe in himself and taught him how to be blessed by continually pointing out Ecclesiastes 11:1, "Cast thy bread upon the waters: for thou shalt find it after many days." So reliable had the dear saint found the message contained therein that he had taken to adding that the bread would be found with "butter on both sides." Bishop Houston laughed to himself as he recalled the number of times he had also found that to be true.

He had cast much bread upon the water in his work within the Original United Holy Church and the Salala Mission in Liberia. Some of the bread was found with butter added to both sides when a noted author (who preferred to remain anonymous) invited him to participate in an upcoming meeting with the Agency for Holistic Evangelism and Development (AHEAD).

Inspired by the vision of the Bishop Augustus "Gus" Marwieh, known as the "Billy Graham of Liberia," AHEAD was established to promote the self-sufficiency of the Church in economically-disadvantaged areas, so it could develop and manage resources to support national and world-wide evangelism. For Bishop Houston, the most exciting aspect of this courageous vision was that AHEAD's pioneer project would be in Liberia.

Liberian saints had been subjected to atrocities of the worst kind. During the time Bishop Houston was in Nigeria performing the consecration service for UGCAN, the Associated Press was reporting the following about Liberia:

"Buchanan, Liberia -- Thousands of civilians are trapped by fighting between rival factions outside Buchanan, and the countryside is covered with the bones of those who did not reach safety, survivors say.

"People interviewed Thursday in the port city of Buchanan said rebels were destroying homes and killing people suspected of collaborating with rival groups. UN officials say two groups...are fighting for control of the region.

"About 500 people are arriving each day in Buchanan, where 65,000 displaced civilians are already staying. Buchanan, 60 miles south of the capitol, Monrovia, is controlled by African peacekeeping troops has long drawn people displaced by Liberia's 5-year-old war.

"Recent refugees said about 10,000 civilians remain trapped by fighting and face starvation. Robert Jaykpah, who escaped the fighting, said bones of people who died along the way were 'scattered all about the bushes everywhere.'

"Most of the new arrivals are women and children -- men either being killed or forced to join rebel forces, they said.

"Liberia's war was supposed to have ended with a peace accord faction leaders signed in December. Disarmament of the estimated 60,000 fighters was to have begun April 1, followed by the election of a new government in November.

"The accord, however, collapsed like countless others before it because of the warlord's inability to negotiate a power-sharing agreement."[*]

AHEAD's visionaries, who were preparing to invest themselves in a decimated country with virtually no remaining infrastructure, were certainly proving Proverbs 28:1 to be true, "...the righteous are bold as a lion." Without supernatural resiliency, strength, and faith, these men of God, especially the Liberians, would not be making plans to help the approximately 1.5 million uprooted Liberians who would be returning once a peace accord was cemented. In many ways, they were echoing Paul's message in I Thess. 2:2, "But even after we had suffered before and were shamefully entreated...we were bold in our God to speak unto you the gospel of God...."

Many men at the age of 69, as Bishop Houston was at that time, had already been in a rocking chair or on the golf course for four or five years, but not Bishop Houston. He had no plans for "retiring" but was pressing forward with a fire and determination that equaled the Biblical Caleb.

Many times, Bishop Houston had laughed knowingly while reading Caleb's declaration, "Forty years old was I when Moses the servant of the Lord sent me from Kadesh-barnea to espy out the land; and I brought him word again as it was in mine heart. Nevertheless my brethren that went up with me made the heart of the people melt: but I wholly followed the Lord my God. And

---

[*] *War-Time Liberia*, Friday, 24, March, 1995, "Thousands Trapped in Liberia (AP)

Moses sware on that day, saying surely the land whereon thy feet have trodden shall be thine inheritance, and thy children's forever, because thou has *wholly followed* the Lord my God. And now, behold, the Lord hath kept me alive, as He said, these forty and five years, even since the Lord spake this word unto Moses while the children of Israel wandered in the wilderness: and now, Lo, I am this day fourscore and five years old. ...yet I am as strong this day as I was in the day that Moses sent me: as my strength was then, even so is my strength now, for war, both to go out, and to come in. Now therefore give me this mountain, whereof the Lord spake in that day; for thou heardest in that day how the Anakims were there, and that the cities were great and fenced: If so be the Lord *will be* with me, then I shall be able to drive them out, as the Lord said." (Josh. 14:7-12)

Just as Joshua blessed Caleb and gave him Hebron for an inheritance, so Bishop Houston believed that some day, the Lord would bless him and give him the opportunity to do the things in Liberia that had burned in his heart for so many years. Like Caleb, he was as ready in his latter years as he had been in his younger years to take the land for the Lord.

It was possible that some of his vision would be accomplished in conjunction with the visionaries of AHEAD and he was looking forward to the upcoming meeting. Having been both a businessman and pastor, he liked their proposed concept of training students to become self-supporting evangelists or business owners whose profits would be used for Christian ministry. He agreed wholeheartedly with Bishop Marwieh's vision to deploy Owner/Trainers who would model both effective business practices and Christian discipleship while tithing a portion of their corporate profits to the church.

As Bishop Marwieh had written, "And never before in human history have those projects been so needed.

Three billion people have never heard of Jesus Christ, an impossible challenge for western missionaries alone. Furthermore, these people have unprecedented economic needs. One out of every three Africans, for example, lives in "absolute poverty" (*New York Times*, June 19, 1994), meaning they are unable to meet their most basic needs.

"World evangelism is too vast to be done by Western missionaries alone and to be financed by Western money alone. Economic self-sufficiency can enable the Third World church to send out its own evangelists and missionaries. I've seen it work."

Of these plans, Edward R. Dayton, retired Vice President of World Vision, had made the following endorsement: "'AHEAD' is a much needed solution to the problem of how to carry out the mission of the church in a way which both proclaims the Gospel and demonstrates the Gospel."

Tony Campolo, Professor of Sociology at Eastern College had said, "I was duly impressed with AHEAD's vision and commitments. It is the next step in the development of the world mission enterprise...."

Bishop Houston prayed this would prove to be a living reality and planned to do everything possible to make it so. From the window of the plane he kept the African Continent in view for as long as he could. God knew that as long as he drew a breath, it would be in his heart and his prayers.

CHAPTER NINE

"For to me to live is Christ, and to die is gain." (Phil. 1:21)

Yellow roses covered Sister Minnie's casket and cascaded down the sides, blending beautifully with a cornucopia of floral arrangements. The profusion of color was arranged on a gracious semicircle of steps ascending to the platform of Nashville's Christ Church Pentecostal, where rich tapestries adorned the chairs in which her speakers were seated. Rising up behind them were terraced rows of green-robed and golden-throated choir members who would soon be, as Minnie had humbly requested, singing her favorite songs. Above the choir, a white dove dominated the majestic stained-glass artwork that provided the backdrop for the baptistery. On either side of the baptistery stood green-marbled columns that were flanked on either side by walls of windows through which one could see the rain falling on the trees and the mist that rose up on the hills of Tennessee.

Minnie had asked the Lord for seventy years of life and that He not take her home to be with Him until she had an opportunity to grow back the hair she had lost to chemotherapy. The Lord surely considered these small favors, and delighted in answering them for one who had served Him so faithfully. In death, as in life, she was fashionably composed, with every detail attended to, right down to her beautifully coifed hairdo and lovely manicure.

Long before the need arose, she had selected her casket and consulted with her family about the funeral. Plans had been made for daughter Carol, Pastor of Bethel Unspeakable Joy Christian Fellowship, Inc. (founded by her paternal grandmother, Daisy L. Houston, and formerly known as Bethel United Holy Church) to eulogize her mother, as Bishop Houston had done for his mother. Many who gathered for Sister Minnie's funeral, had also been in attendance for Daisy's, affectionately known to them as "Big Mama."

After Big Mama's passing, her husband, Papa Houston, was doted on and recognized as the patriarch of their extended family -- which included members of their church. It was most convenient for them to be attentive, as Papa Houston now resided just across the street from the church in the Daisy Houston Senior Manor, which Bishop Houston had built to provide for the church's elderly members and in honor of his mother's memory. Papa Houston, now 92 years old, had never expected to live long enough to bury two of his three children and the wife of his only surviving child.

For many decades, the closeknit church family had fellowshipped together and been there for each other in both the good and bad times. In even the saddest of circumstances, they had offered up sacrifices of praise, and He had not failed to honor their faithfulness. As promised in Isaiah 53:3, "He had borne our griefs, and carried our sorrows..."

As "Great Is Thy Faithfulness" softly played, Minnie's husband and children gathered around the casket for their last earthly look at one they had loved for so long. Some kissed her tender face while others touched the still graceful hands that had cooled their fevered brows, wiped their noses, changed their diapers, cooked, cleaned, and served them in a thousand different ways.

Behind them, many unrelated members of the congregation brushed away tears at the memories of "Mother Minnie," as she was known to many, loving and caring for them as her own. Bloodlines had been transcended by the love and spiritual ties that bound them all together, regardless of race, age or station in life, as children of the Most High God. Many of them had blessed and broken bread together with the Houstons as often as they had with their own relatives. Most had had the Houstons join them at the bedside of a loved one or pray with them for friends or family members who were lost or in trouble.

The synergistic sum total of their shared lives was now diminished with Minnie's passing. There was now one less person who would understand and enjoy the memories of the time they shared together. A cast member had disappeared, and the play would never be the same again.

Some wondered if there would ever be wives and mothers like her in the future, since today there weren't many women who were content and fulfilled by devoting themselves to creating an atmosphere of love and generosity within their home, church, and community. Toward that end, both Minnie and her husband had agreed that he would make the living, while she made life worth living.

Both had dedicated themselves to cultivating a bountiful, cooperative garden of friendships and relationships. Through acts of kindness, they had planted a variety of seeds, watering them with love and fertilizing them with a generosity of spirit. Continual forgiveness had kept the weeds of life from choking the nutrients out of the soil so that much fruit of the spirit was produced for the cooperative benefit of all associated with them.

As Carol and Ron gently closed the lid on their mother's casket, many hoped and prayed that others had been taking notes while she lived and walked among them as a prime example of a loving, giving, woman of God.   Before the service was over, two outstanding women, Montelle Hardwick, wife of Christ Church's senior pastor, and Arthur Hicks, one of the Houston's Nashville neighbors, declared they wanted to model their own lives after Minnie's. In response to this, many others breathed a heartfelt, "Amen."

Innumerable dimensions of Minnie's personality were reflected upon by relatives, friends, and church leaders. As Nashville Pastors Rodney Beard, Bill Smith, and Hilly Hicks shared what Sister Minnie had meant to them, it was clear that these were not surface relationships. These young pastors and their wives had sat at the Houstons' kitchen table many times seeking prayer and guidance.   With the Hicks also being neighbors, Sister Minnie had been like a grandmother to their little girls, Brett and Lindsey, renting videos for them and delighting in caring for them when their mother, Arthur, had an appointment.

Daughter-in-law Vicky recalled how Minnie would lovingly and attentively care for her and Ron's five children when she was a working mom in Los Angeles. She was glad it had not been necessary for her to work outside the home since coming to the Nashville area and that she had been able to participate in her mother-in-law's care during Minnie's extended illness.

Many considered it a privilege to care for Minnie, and perhaps no one had done more than Dr. Pam Williams, one of the Houstons' "adopted" daughters. Living within a block of them, she was a constant caregiver who continually brought medications and liquid nutritional supplements to Sister Minnie.   As the Houstons' wide circle of family and friends ministered to them, they drew closer to them and each other. This resulted in, among other things, Vicky and Ron asking Pam to be their newborn daughter's Godmother.

Brianna's birth brightened everyone's lives, but most of all those of her grandmother and Godmother. In addition to showering her with love and attention, Pam also delighted in buying her gifts....and her generosity did not stop there. Pam's Christmas list included all of Vicky's family and of course, Mom, Dad, and Carol. These were not transitory relationships -- they were lifelong bonds established through mutual love, respect, and commitment. Ralph and Minnie Houston were the reason for them, or perhaps it was Big Mama and Papa -- no, it was the God they served.

They, like the saints of old, did not consider themselves to have attained perfection in this life but they surely had "press(ed) toward the mark for the prize of the high calling of God in Christ Jesus...." (Phil. 3:14)

Tommy and Laverne Barton were among those who considered themselves blessed to be a part of the Houstons' circle of friends. While Bishop Houston was in Africa the previous March, they, along with many others, had checked with Sister Minnie on a daily basis. After Bishop's return, Tommy continued to faithfully check on them on an almost daily basis until Minnie passed away on September 5, 1990.

Since that happened to be Bishop Houston's 70th birthday, Laverne wondered if Sister Minnie's spirit had chosen to depart rather than live another day in the body that was no longer able to make him a birthday cake, as she had done for the past forty-seven years, but perhaps it was just a coincidence.

In any event, before the sun rose Carol called to let the Bartons know Sister Minnie had passed away and Tommy immediately went to be with Bishop Houston. When he arrived, he found Dr. Jerry Crooke, a dear friend and fellow member of Christ Church, at the Bishop's side. Together they remained with the Bishop for as long as they were needed.

Laverne stopped in later with a cake as she thought that was what Sister Minnie would have wanted her to take. Many were reflecting on what Sister Minnie would have wanted in the days ahead. Because there were so many wanting to come, the funeral was delayed, allowing time for everything to be planned to perfection.

As Carol began eulogizing her mother, explaining how she had struggled with her mother's suffering until the Holy Spirit revealed the beauty of the saint who endured it with such patience, one could not help but notice the stained-glass dove in the background. Of course, it was representative of the Holy Spirit.

During her mother's long illness, Carol had grown and matured spiritually. As Sister Minnie's strength decreased, the power of God increased in Carol. Ever so slowly, her mother's vast spiritual strength, which had been the wind beneath Carol's own wings, was replaced with the power of the Holy Spirit. Like the white dove behind her, she was now strongly soaring through heavenly places on spiritual air currents undiscovered by many.

A similar transference of power also seemed to be taking place in the Bishop's life. Considering his age, it seemed strange to him, but he was sure it was happening. Shortly before Minnie's death, she had said to him, "Ralph, I'll be leaving you soon. My work is over but you have a task to finish. Be faithful to finish your task."

What was that task? he wondered. Retracing his sixty year journey with Christ, he remembered that it had started with a special call that resounded in his ears many times since. "Ralph, I've chosen you. I've ordained you. You are mine. Let me use you." His answer had always been, "Yes, Lord."

It had been hardest to answer, "Yes, Lord," when the Lord asked him to give up his role as pastor of Bethel Church. Under his leadership it had grown from fifty-six members to over 300, and the church had increased its budget enough to furnish its pastor with a comfortable salary and a full-time secretary. He was just beginning to enjoy those benefits when God said, to him, "I want Bethel." When he was sure it was God, he answered, "Yes." It wasn't easy but he had always desired, above all things, to be led by the Holy Spirit.

Following that relinquishment, God spoke to him again: "I want your business. I gave it to you and I want it back."

The business had always provided security for him and his family. It made him feel independent, but he had always been aware that it was God's gift to him. God was responsible for him showing a profit with it for more than thirty years now. As he was contemplating this, God once again spoke to his heart, "I want it back." It was clear now that God wanted his all, and he answered, "Yes."

As he contemplated the comfortable income he would realize from the sale of the business, the Lord made it very clear to him that the money and income was His and He wanted that also. All these years he had said, "Lord, this is yours" but now he was being put to the test. Remembering how God had blessed both the business and the church, he had the faith to once again answer "Yes," and to begin a new phase of his walk with God.

With his soulmate now gone, and having left him with confirmation that there was still more for him to do, he was wondering what in the world it might be.

The meeting with AHEAD had gone very well. In fact they had offered him an all-expense-paid trip to

Liberia but he had declined because of a firm decision to devote himself to Minnie in her remaining days. He was glad he had made that decision. They had both enjoyed the many visitors they received during those months and most of all, the time together.

In the midst of the funeral, those past expressions of love still comforted him as did those he now received from family and friends who came to the funeral. With the late Bishop Samuel M. Crouch having been Minnie's pastor in the 1930s and the pastor who married them in 1948, it was a joy to have his great-niece, Sandra Crouch there representing the family.

During the late '70s, Carol formed Sonrise International, a talent agency designed to secure ministry dates for Christian artists. She had been blessed to represent the Crouch twins, Sandra and Andrea, as well as Walter Tramaine, Edwin Hawkins, Daryl Coley, Shirley Miller, The New Jersey and Los Angeles Mass Choirs, Donn Thomas, and Debbie McClendon-Smith. So the Houstons had more friends available to them to provide exceptional music than most. Ron Houston, Daryl Coley, Shirley Miller, and Myrna Rochelle were among those who contributed to making Sister Minnie's funeral memorable.

Pastor L. H. Hardwick, Jr. did a beautiful job of officiating with the help of Dr. Paul Martin, pastor of Denver's 1,800 member Macedonia Baptist Church. Other speakers included Evangelist Bob Harrison; Songwriter Terri McFadden; Associate Pastor of Bethel Unspeakable Joy Christian Fellowship Church, Inc., Olive Buie; longtime friend Sharron Scott and family members Helen Tillery and Glenn Houston.

More than one person had fond memories of Minnie's Kitchen becoming an income-producing operation each time there was a fifth Sunday in the month. Via an announcement at church and through word of mouth, she soon had as many as 200 to 300 coming to her house for a $5.00 "all-you-can-eat" Sunday dinner. For five years, she carried on the venture that had been started to replace the church carpet. By doing so, she funded many a worthwhile project for the Lord with her delicious barbecue, ham hocks, greens and yams.

Sister Minnie was remembered well for giving of herself. Even on her and Bishop Houston's thirty-ninth wedding anniversary, instead of gifts, they requested donations for the mission in Liberia. The $2,000 that came in went to fix up the missionary's house at the Salala mission.

As President of the Interdenominational Ministers Wives Alliance, she issued a challenge that resulted in the organization of a banquet featuring *Happy Days* television sitcom star Henry Winkler as the guest speaker. The proceeds were used to refurbish a cabin at the McLaren Hall Children's Home.

When the funeral home employees remarked that Sister Minnie's funeral was one of the most impressive memorial services they had ever attended, no one doubted it. While Bishop Houston did not speak at the service, perhaps his graveside comments will be remembered as long as anything else that was said that day.

After thanking God for the gift of such a beautiful woman, he lightened everyone's spirits by saying, "I can't wait to get to heaven and tell Adam that I had a better wife than he did!"

In the weeks and months following Sister Minnie's funeral, Bishop Houston sought the Lord about what he should do with the remainder of his life. Then came the assignment. "I want you to minister to my Church leadership, for they have stolen my Church from Me, and I want it back. The Bishops, Pastors, and Leadership have claimed my Church to be theirs. They have attempted to run my Church, to lead my people without consulting Me. They have forgotten that my Church has an appointed administrator, The Holy Spirit. The Holy Spirit is not given space in their planning. Therefore they have forgotten that it is, not by might, nor power, nor intellect, but by my Spirit that the Church is led. They have forgotten that I've come to seek and save the lost, not to build fancy Churches nor to form great choirs nor build great institutions, but to seek and save the lost."

That message from God was confirmed when Bishop Houston attended an installation service at the Trinity Baptist Church in Los Angeles, California. Dr. Elliott J. Mason, Sr., the retiring minister delivered an awesome sermon in which he revealed that God had given him the same message.

Bishop Houston held Dr. Mason in the highest regard, knowing he had enjoyed a distinguished career in ministry since he was a teenager. He was well-known as a man who possessed an exciting blend of spirituality and intellectuality, but most of all, he was loved as a humble man of prayer.

In conjunction with the message Dr. Mason and Bishop Houston had received from the Lord, Dr. Mason had formed a special prayer ministry for pastors and leaders. Upon conferring with him, Bishop Houston felt that their spirits were knitted together and that they were of one mind and one accord. God was moving in His Church, and these two men had been chosen for a special ministry. Like Bishop Houston, Dr. Mason was also called upon to give up a great church and depend upon God.

While God was very clear in His assignment, Bishop Houston was given a warning that the task would not be easy. He was told that many would question his motives and some would not receive the message but he was not to fear, for God's grace was sufficient. Bishop Houston thanked God for His faithfulness, knowing He could be relied upon.

He had previously found it challenging to fulfill the vision God had given him but he had also found that when God cannot move through one group, that He simply raises up another to fulfill His purposes. Those who are completely faithful will cross the finish line with Him.

His mind went back to an earlier trip to Liberia, where during his sixteen days of ministry at the Salala Mission Academy, he had met with twelve pastors and leaders who were very discouraged with the denominational church. Bishop Houston's visit had been delayed for one month because the National Church requested that he attend a Board Meeting to see if he could get approval for an official church trip. After much debate, he was finally denied their approval for an official trip.

(Hoping that his resignation would strengthen the effectiveness of the General Mission Board, he had previously resigned as Bishop of Missions, in favor of another Bishop, and remained an unofficial member of the Board.)

In spite of not being able to get this visit approved as an official one, it seemed the will of God for him to go to Liberia, and God had confirmed it. The Liberian brothers made a pledge of unity and began praying for the Original Holy Church, of which they had become a part.

Over breakfast, Bishop Houston unloaded his burden for this mission and the lack of denominational cooperation concerning it to a Gohona missionary. The missionary assured him God had planted him there in the Robert Field Airport Hotel on Dec. 17, 1986, to encourage his soul, and he asked that they go to his room for prayer.

God's anointing came upon him as he prayed, and heaven came down and ministered to Bishop Houston as they wept and praised God together. He knew he must go on and obey God regarding the mission and his denomination. God had chosen him for these assignments and he must be faithful regardless of the obstacles.

Considering the challenges that lay before the Bishop, God must have looked down on him, as He did Adam in the garden of Eden, and said, "It is not good that the man should be alone." (Gen. 2:18) Because of Minnie's lengthy illness, the mourning process had actually begun before her demise and even though family and friends had been most attentive, both before and after her death, Bishop Houston sensed, within months of her funeral, that the Lord was ready for him to take a wife.

CHAPTER TEN

"There is no man that hath left house or parents, or brethren, or wife, or children, for the kingdom of God's sake, who shall not receive manifold more in this present time and in the world to come life everlasting."
(Luke 18:29-32)

One evening, on his way home from dinner at the Bartons, Bishop Houston told his good friend Bob Dorsey, also a recent widower, that he had proposed to Betty Jones, the sister of one of his lifelong friends, Bishop Raphel "Ray" Fortier, Jr. Betty Fortier was her maiden name, and she certainly wasn't a stranger to the Houston family.

The Houston and Fortier families had ties that reached back to their school days. During that time, the Houstons lived on 122nd and the Fortiers on 123rd. In 1942, Ray Fortier, Jr. and Ralph Houston had graduated together from Jordan High School in Watts. Shortly thereafter, they were inducted into the army.

War catapulted these young eighteen-year-olds from the warm nest of their family and friends into a world of soldiers from every conceivable background. Many were unchurched and escaped their apprehensions and loneliness by drinking and chasing after prostitutes. Even though Bishop Houston had heard firsthand accounts of what to expect, it was a daily challenge.

He made a decision to focus his energies on excelling, and shortly after his seven weeks of basic training at Fort Leonard Wood, MO, he was elevated to the rank of Corporal. In 1943 there were very few black commissioned officers in the Army but he fought to make his way up the ranks. He was motivated in part because of the disrespect young white officers were showing toward the older black soldiers. With many of them being as old as his father, Ralph Houston, who had been taught from his mother's knee to respect his elders, found that a bitter pill to swallow. So he worked hard to become a Sergeant. From that position of leadership, he had some authority and the ear of other leaders.

Unknown to those other officers, was the fact that Ralph Houston, a dedicated soldier who excelled at everything, was carrying the papers of a conscientious objector in his pocket the entire time. It was a private matter that he often wrestled with, wanting to serve but abhorring the thought of killing. He was as discreet about that internal struggle as he was about his opinions of soldiers who were fighting venereal diseases and having drunken brawls among themselves when they should have been concentrating on preparing themselves to fight the enemy.

It wasn't easy living in the barracks with them and he longed for his Christian family and friends. Without wholesome companionship, he was more tempted than he would have been otherwise to indulge in some of that activity himself, resulting in another quiet but serious internal struggle. It wasn't easy contending with that or the reactions of other soldiers to his own personal decisions to abstain.

Being very sociable by nature and having enjoyed a great deal of popularity back home, it was rather disconcerting to be treated as an outsider. Yet he could not become one of the young men who were busy sowing their wild oats, and bragging about it, without being untrue to himself and his beliefs.

Lonely, single, and far away from home, he longed for his Christian family and friends. Not finding one, he developed a friendship with Ed, a likable man with whom he worked. Ed was a "brother" who wore his uniform well. Together the two of them were in charge of a battalion mess hall in which over six thousand men were fed three times a day, so he and Ed were considered very important persons on base.

They were frequently given certain privileges such as visiting the battalion PX during off-duty hours where they had a chance to meet and talk with the ladies who worked at the Post Exchange, unmolested by the other fellows. In other words, they had the inside track to establishing relationships with those attractive young women. Before he knew it, he was beginning to impress a young lady who became very fond of him.

As the friendship grew, her friends began asking her why Ralph hadn't invited her to spend the weekend with him, as Ed was doing with his newfound friend at the PX. Then the soldiers in the barracks began to ask the same question and it wasn't long until it was rumored that he was "funny," and he became the laughingstock of all the girls in the PX.

As the rumor spread through the barracks, the tight leash he kept on his emotions snapped under the constant ridicule, and he grabbed one of the smart alecks closest to him by the neck. He had almost choked him to unconsciousness before the other soldiers were able to pull him off the offender. Realizing what he had done, he was crushed. He didn't even want to kill the enemy, much less an ally.

He'd had enough and decided to put the rumors to rest by proving his manhood. When he asked his lady friend to spend the weekend with him, she must have wondered at the mixed reaction she got from him as she accepted.

As the weekend approached, a battle raged within him. Like any virile young man, he longed to go, but he had a higher calling on his life, one that gently bid him stay away. What was he going to do? In addition to wanting to go, he felt he had to go. How would he ever make it through his tour of duty with the constant ridicule he would face by canceling?

Just a day or two before the date, God intervened. Perhaps if it had not been for the demonic taunts and false accusations, God would not have given him the miracle of a Christian friend, but the word of God is true: "When the enemy shall come in like a flood, the spirit of the Lord shall lift up a standard against him." (Isa. 59:19)

In this case the Lord lifted up a standard in the form of an ally, his high school friend, Rafael "Ray" Fortier! Only God the Father knew how shocked and overjoyed Bishop Houston was to look up from his work of overseeing the chow line to see Ray's face in a group of newly arriving soldiers. They saw each other at the same time and with an outburst of surprise, they ran to greet each other. Then Bishop Houston led him into the kitchen to give him a special meal.

Upon hearing of the tormenting ordeal Ralph had been through, Ray assured him God had brought them together to strengthen each other, as he had been having some trials of his own. The fellowship and encouragement enabled Bishop Houston to cancel the date that he had made for all the wrong reasons.

In his heart, he knew that rendezvous would have been even more of a mistake than his last serious temptation. In that situation, he was at least "in love," with a high school sweetheart. At the young age of fifteen and a half, they were very close and serious about the relationship. Still, he believed that he could not indulge in an out-of-wedlock sexual relationship without paying a spiritual price for doing so, and refrained.

He was honest about his own natural desires being as strong as any other teenager's, but he knew he had been chosen by God for leadership, and the strength of his character was developed by each decision. Yet it seemed there was always another challenge on the horizon.

After he got out of the service, it continued. At the age of twenty-two, it was spiritual pride that almost got him into trouble. He had boldly testified of God's ability to keep young Christians from sexual immorality, if they dared to commit themselves to Him, when a beautiful, young temptress walked up to him after the meeting and flirtatiously cooed that she didn't believe a word of it.

If any woman ever possessed the taunting and seductive spirit of Jezebel, this attractive and mischievous homecoming queen certainly did. And when she threw down the gauntlet of an invitation, he accepted it. It took a lot of willpower to nip that in the bud, but he did, and he did not play with fire anymore.

However nothing had been as hard for him as the trial in New Guinea. If he and Ray hadn't had each other to lean on, the two men, who are both Bishops today, may have had destinies thwarted, as Esau did when he traded his for bread and a pottage of lintels.

God went to great lengths to protect the destinies of these two young soldiers. When Ray and Ralph had a month together at Camp Stoneman, California, their port of embarkation, they did not expect to see each other again until after the war was over, if they survived it. Surely it was a part of God's preordained plan for these two men who would eventually become brother-in-laws to end up serving and praying together during the war.

The most important matter about which Bishop Houston was praying all during the war was that he would never have to take the life of another man. Now, after nine months in New Guinea, he boarded a ship that would take him into the heat of the battle and began wondering if he could participate in the invasion of the Philippines without killing.

During the week-long voyage, a ship close to them took a bomb in the aft section, near the fourth hole, blasting bodies off the nearby ship and into the sea. Transfixed by the horror of burned and bloody, mangled, and dismembered soldiers, Bishop Houston was frozen in place. Even though he remembered orders to clear the deck and go below, he was so paralyzed with fear that he was barely able to take shelter under a nearby gun turret. Instinctively he began praying, "Dear God, please don't ever let me ever be *frightened* like this again...."

And God answered that prayer.

Under fire they approached the Philippine island of Mindora on a landing craft that quickly spilled out two hundred soldiers into waist deep water. With a heavy pack on his back and rifles over his shoulders, Bishop Houston and another soldier carried a cooking range while running through the waves, hoping to reach the shore and cover of its thick foliage before they were hit.

As a part of the seventh wave of troops to hit the island, they could hear those who landed before them engaged in battle further inland. Advancing toward the action, their unit repeatedly alternated between charging forward, then diving for cover. When they dove into a rice paddy, they immediately were assaulted by the report of gunfire and a terrified scream.

In horror, they saw one of their own platoon leap up from the cover of the rice field, run forward, and then dive for cover. Adrenaline pumping, every man in the unit waited breathlessly, listening to the thunderings of the distant battle in front of them and the booming sounds of the destroyers shelling the beach behind them.

On command, they raced forward with hearts pounding through their chests and aching legs screaming out in pain. Crossing the same stretch of territory from which the screaming soldier had just barely escaped, everyone one of them was looking for the sniper.

Then they dove for cover and landed on thousands of protesting field mice!   As the mice scattered, a nervous, suppressed laughter rippled through the rice paddy as the soldiers realized their comrade had not been fired upon, he had discharged his own weapon fleeing the bed of field mice!

Fortunately the fighting tapered off and then ceased before their unit was involved. Setting up camp, the cooks, of which Bishop Houston was one, quickly began preparing a meal. To keep the morale of the troops up, they were under strict orders to always serve the meals on a timely basis.

As he cooked, he thought of meal times back home and his mother's prayers. While she certainly realized that the sons of many fine Christian families would be lost at war, she was certain that hers would be coming home. Perhaps it was that sense of "knowing" that prompted her to write, "A thousand shall fall at thy side, and ten thousand at thy right hand; but it shall not come nigh thee." (Ps. 91:7)

The night it came closest to him, Bishop Houston, then Sergeant of the Guards, had just gotten up to relieve the guards when he heard enemy planes approaching. Then the engines were cut, making it impossible to know which camp they were headed toward. The enemies' modus operandi was to glide in over their target and surreptitiously drop their bombs on sleeping camps before cranking up their engines for a quick exit. Since the Bishop's own camp hadn't been hit thus far, he had never before heard the rattling sounds he had been told to expect when a bomb was coming straight for you.

But this time he heard it! Diving under a truck for cover, he yelled out a warning just before the earth shook with the deafening impact. The concussion rocked the truck he was under, causing him to look up just as a second bomb hit the hammocks, exploding sleeping soldiers and debris sky high.

The night air filled with desperate, painful cries of, "Mama, mama, help me, mama." It was the young soldier who had discharged his rifle upon hitting the field mice. Now he was dying, after being blown in two. He did not suffer long and for that everyone was grateful, but Bishop Houston saw too many wonderful young men lose their lives during his tour of duty.

It could have been two or three times as bad if America's best military minds hadn't devised a plan to capture every third island in a chain of fifteen, thereby neutralizing the others by cutting off supplies to them. Under General Douglas MacArthur's brilliant leadership the strategic islands were bombed from the air and sea before ground troops routed the enemy from hills, jungles and caves.

To those doing the routing, it seemed that the world was being run by a bloodthirsty puppeteer on whose orders a legion of demons had been loosed upon the earth. Every day, those involved in capturing the five islands wondered when and how this madness would end, and when the rain would stop.

During the monsoon season their dirty, wet clothes clung to their weary limbs and the troops went for weeks without being able to get out of their boots even one time. Dead tired, they would sometimes awaken to find the Japanese had mistaken a nearby beach for a landing field and bombed it during the night.

The ever-present danger kept the young Bishop earnestly praying that God would protect him and that he would not have to kill another man. Day after day he prayed and continued to serve with valor until he was sent home in 1946 -- having the completely filled out but unfiled papers of a conscientious objector in his pocket the entire time.

Because of his natural, God-given ability to get along with people, he was not treated badly in the service, but many of his black brothers were. At times it seemed that even though the black soldiers served faithfully that the then segregated army had become a blatantly racist institution intent on belittling them. Loyal black soldiers were often given the worst duty just because of their race. Without their faith in God, many would have become angry young men, and understandably so. But like so many of our black unsung heroes, they, by the grace of God, courageously endured the insults and still embraced the country they had been sent to defend.

Of those times, Benjamin O. Davis Sr., the only black American General in World War II, wrote:

"The colored man in uniform is expected by the War Department to develop a high morale in a community that offers him nothing but humiliation and mistreatment. The Department has failed to secure the colored solder protection against violence on the part of civilian police or to secure justice in the courts." The Army, he continued, was spreading those attitudes beyond the South.

Davis, even as a General, was denied admittance to the white officers' clubs. In spite of this shameful and disgraceful treatment, more than a million black men and women served gallantly in World War II.

One of them, Vernon Baker, now age 77, was finally, on January 13, 1997, invited to the White House to receive the Medal of Honor. He was one of only seven black soldiers given that award for their World War II valor. According to the Associated Press, the other six were awarded "posthumously to Staff Sgt. Edward A. Carter Jr. of Los Angeles; 1st Lt. John R. Fox of Cincinnati; Pfc. Willy F. James Jr. of Kansas City, Mo.;

1st Lt. Charles L. Thomas of Detroit; Pvt. George Watson of Birmingham, Ala.; and Staff Sgt. Ruben Rivers of Hotulka, Okla.

"Fox, James, Rivers and Watson were killed in action. Carter died in 1963 and Thomas died in 1980.

"'We've all been vindicated,' Baker said. 'To those that are not here with me, thank you fellas, well done and I'll always remember you.'"[*]

While men and women were away serving their country, it was changing. For instance, in the South, tenant farmers, already victims of grinding poverty, found themselves replaced by the mechanical cotton picker that could pick 1,000 pounds an hour, while a good field hand could only pick twenty. This and other inventions were the catalyst for the nation's transition from an agricultural to industrial economy -- resulting in massive numbers of Americans moving from the simple country life to the more complex and stressful life of city dwellers.

In a time when there were few social programs to serve as safety nets, most left the security of their rural roots and extended families, with very little money on which to begin their new lives. Of the 4.5 million non-white migrants who primarily relocated to twelve of the nation's largest cities, most were African-Americans who found refuge in their churches. The dramatic population shift, and attendant cultural revisions started before World War II was over and did not end until the 1960s.

Contributing to those changes were the World War II experiences of African-American men and women who were treated much better by foreigners than they were by their own countrymen. It was an eye-opening experience, and when they came home, they had new ideas about the kind of lives they wanted to build for themselves and their families.

---

[*] Copyright 1997, Associated Press 1/13/97

As they worked to change unfair employment practices and social inequities, the white population resisted change, and pressure grew. While Christian men and women struggled to address these issues, in some instances the internal conflict was as almost as great as the one they faced externally. But by the 1960s, African-Americans had endured all they could of being limited by their skin color to mostly low-wage service or health care jobs, such as maid, custodian, nurse's aide, restaurant worker, clerk or security guard.

The movement culminated with the challenging messages of Dr. Martin Luther King and others like him. If necessary they would make the ultimate sacrifice so their people could be free from oppression, and of course Dr. King did. His assassination shocked and shamed the world into implementing the changes for which so many had been hoping and praying for so long.

Considering the burdens under which they labored, perhaps nothing was more amazing than the black women, who, in disproportionate numbers, had been left to make a living and raise their children all by themselves.

Betty Jones, the woman to whom Bishop Houston had proposed, was one of these incredibly strong women. Very few had managed their lives better than she did, which, in part, could be contributed to having come from a stable, Christian family.

Bishop Houston knew Betty's background very well. She was the fourth of eight children born to Gladys and Rafael Fortier, Sr. Two of her sisters and one brother were born in a northeastern sector of Los Angeles known as Boyle Heights. Before she was born, the family had bought a place in Watts because Betty's father had always wanted to live in the country. At that time, Watts was rural enough for a family to have chickens, turkeys, hogs and a cow.

Betty's maternal grandparents and one of her mother's older sisters purchased an acre in Watts -- on which her grandparents' house was moved - - somewhere around 9th Street in downtown Los Angeles. It was only a short distance from their house on Mona Blvd., at the southeast edge of Watts, to the John St. (later renamed E. 114th St.) home in which Betty was born.

Then another of her mother's sisters, Ruth, moved with her family from Hollywood to E. 113th St. This was great as the two houses actually backed up to each other so the families could go back and forth by simply opening a gate and stepping across an alley. Naturally, Betty and her siblings, grew up with close ties to the maternal side of her family.

Watts was a racially diverse community, where it was not uncommon to find some non-blacks who believed that all the neighborhood's African-American families were related. Of course, this was due to them not being familiar with the close friendships that African-Americans typically develop and often maintain for a lifetime.

While Betty was related to only five of the families in the Watts community, many believed they were related to the Houstons also, considering how much time the children spent together in each other's homes, as well as at church and school. It was easy to understand why that was a prevalent misconception. These close ties made it easier for Betty to seriously consider Bishop Houston's "out-of-the-blue" proposal.

Interestingly enough, Betty's maternal grandfather actually came from Nashville, where Bishop Houston now resided. After her grandfather left Nashville, he moved to Arkansas where he met and married Betty's grandmother. They had five boys and three girls, which was exactly what Betty's parents later had themselves.

With such a large family, their budget had been tight, as had that of the Houston family. The tradition in her family, as in his, was for the more prosperous members to help those who needed some help. It was nice that they thought alike in this important area.

As Betty reflected over that, she remembered dear Aunt Cora, the oldest of her mother's sisters. She was a college graduate who taught school for a while before deciding to devote herself entirely to her own four children. Her husband was a very hard-working man with his own business, causing many in the family to perceive Aunt Cora's family to be absolutely rich, and perhaps they were. If not by banking standards, at least they were in spirit, as they always helped Betty's parents when the need arose.

Especially during the Great Depression, when times were extremely hard for Betty's family. They owned their own home and rental property, but they, like almost everyone else, didn't have very much money. So it was a real hardship on Betty's parents when their tenants were unable to pay the rent. To make matters worse, Betty's parents often had to feed them. This additional burden eventually resulted in her parents losing the rental property. However, Betty's family was able to hold on to their own home. Losing the rental house was rather sad; it had great sentimental value because two of Betty's younger brothers were born there. Fortunately, the family still owned the home where Betty and her two younger siblings were born.

Betty was well suited to be the Bishop's wife as she, like him, possessed both a generous heart and a good head for business. In Betty's case, this was due to the confluence of her heritages from both sides of her family. Her parental grandfather was from the beautiful and exotic French Island of Martinique, a land of lush mountains, rain forests and black sand beaches. Even today, Martinique citizens have such a strong aversion to appearing subservient that some people think them rude.

Perhaps it was that influence that bid her grandfather to open a cigar factory in his backyard rather than work for anyone else. This very interesting and independent man, who spoke four languages, met and married her grandmother in Louisiana, after which they moved to California in search of a better life.

Betty's dad, born in L.A. as the youngest of fourteen children, did not like school because the other children teased and tormented him about his stuttering. Prior to becoming a Christian, he, like his father, was not prone to take insults lightly and frequently got into fights with his antagonists. Before graduating from high school, he took a job as a bricklayer, and finding much appreciation for the speed with which he worked and the quality he produced, he decided this was the way he would make his living.

Betty's brother and Bishop Houston's lifelong friend, Ray, grew up with the same speech impediment that had plagued his father. Even though he had a personality that enabled him to cope with it more easily, the Lord still saw fit to heal him of this affliction when he was 26 years old. Of course, that certainly made him a more effective minister of the Gospel. However, even before he was healed, or trained in the ministry, Bishop Houston's mother had recognized the call on the young man's life and opened her pulpit to him.

Ray and Betty had loved the Bishop's mother, "Big Mama" dearly and found her to be a source of constant encouragement in their walks with the Lord. Thank God for the United Holy Church's position on women in ministry, which was based on "For ye are all the children of God by faith in Christ Jesus. For as many of you as have been baptized into Christ have put on Christ. There is neither Jew nor Greek, there is neither bond nor free, there is neither male nor female: for ye are all one in Christ Jesus. And if ye be Christ's, then are ye

Abraham's seed, and heirs according to the promise."
(Gal. 3:28)

Just as "he," a generic term, refers to both men
and women in much of today's literature, so there are
some places in scripture when it is applicable. Of course,
there are also places where it does refer just to men but
still, women do, according to the tenants of the United
Holy Church, have a place in ministry. Therefore, both
Ray and Betty were encouraged in their work for the Lord
by their natural and spiritual mothers, among whom were
"Big Mama" and Mother Mattie Cummings.

If not for the influence of her church family, Betty
might have sought after social status, as she was
encouraged to do by her dad's sister, the much loved and
admired Aunt Vi. This influential and generous aunt had
done very well for herself in Chicago, in part because of
her social skills and connections. Even though Betty
could see the merit in following that path, she was not the
partying type. While Betty very much appreciated the
lovely Christmas presents she, and other family
members, received from Aunt Vi, she remained true to
herself and God's will for her life, which included caring
for her family and serving the Lord.

The Fortier family began their journey with the Lord
as a result of her dad being converted when Betty was
just a few months old. It happened, strangely enough, as
a result of a fiery accident that took place when her dad
was filling his truck tank with gasoline. He was in the
alley behind the house when the gas exploded, engulfing
him in flames, and there was no one there to help. By
instinct people tend to run away, when ablaze with a fire
that overwhelms them. By the grace of God, Betty's
father had clear, divine revelation that he should cover
himself with his coat to extinguish the flames and was
able to do so.

That experience saved him both physically and spiritually. It resulted in him promising to serve God for the rest of his days, which he did.

Therefore, Betty was blessed to grow up with a Christian father who never smoked, cursed, fought, or drank alcohol. Except for the fervent prayers of her father, Betty might not have even lived to adulthood as she was such a thin and sickly child that her family feared losing her.

However, thanks be to God, Betty overcame her weak start and grew up to be, in every sense of the word, a very strong individual with leadership abilities. She was also a beautiful, fun-loving girl with an enchanting laugh.

During her high school years, she, like all her friends, wanted to walk down the halls in one of the "Lettermen's" sweaters. She and her best friend knew some of the athletes, but they didn't have boyfriends, so Betty asked Ray's best friend, Ralph Houston, if she could wear his. He was a football star and big man on campus. Sporting his sweater made her the envy of all her friends. They became even more envious when Ray went into the service and left his car with her. She and her friends had lots of fun with that!

Betty graduated from high school before her 18th birthday, and because she couldn't begin work immediately, she began training in a government sponsored program known as the National Youth Association (NYA). After coming of age, she considered going to college but instead opted for a job opportunity with the U.S. Postal Service. After six months there, she took a job with Douglas Aircraft in Long Beach. Shortly thereafter, for the first time in her life, she faced open and blatant racial prejudice.

It was a real shock, as she had grown up in a rather interracial family with relatives who actually looked white, and naturally so, as they were as much white as black. In her neighborhood, school, and church, she had friends of other races. But when she applied for work at the aircraft plant, she encountered people who hadn't lived among people of different races, as she had. In some ways, it was sad, as they were so limited in their view of the world.

Early visitors to Africa discovered that Africans were often more familiar and comfortable with other races, making them more a man of the world than the white man who had heretofore known only the ways of their own people.

Betty and Bishop Houston had both learned to cope with this unfortunate situation and this was yet another area in which they had much in common.

Still the situation at the aircraft plant was particularly difficult, as some of her co-workers went out of their way to treat her unfairly. Their resentment grew when she and a lovely white girl became close friends. Betty could not understand this unfair treatment since all her life she had always enjoyed cross-cultural friendships.

She had found that while skin color, hair texture, languages, and customs may vary, most human beings have the same basic needs and desires. With all mankind having so many common denominators, she wondered why some people had so much trouble interfacing with other ethnic groups.

Betty reveled in the diversity that is evident in all of God's creation. To her, it was wonderful that the Lord gave us mountains and prairies; salt water and fresh water; seashore and desert; apples and oranges; dogs and cats, etc., etc.

When our hearts are in one accord with our all inclusive Creator, we will enjoy all He has created for His and our pleasure. "Shall any teach God knowledge? Seeing He judgeth those that are high. One dieth in his full strength, being wholly at ease and quiet. His breasts are full of milk, and his bones are moistened with marrow. And another dieth in the bitterness of soul, and never eateth with pleasure." (Job 21:22-26)

This was Betty and the Bishop's outlook on life, and at every opportunity, she enjoyed getting acquainted with all the wonderful people and places Her Heavenly Father had created.

Like Bishop Houston, Betty possessed a generosity of spirit that enabled her to overcome the prejudice. In fact, she had only been at the aircraft plant about nine months when a girlfriend invited her to share a berth and accompany her on a trip to Brooklyn. Not only was this Betty's first trip to the East Coast but her friend worked for black superstar Ethel Waters, so it was most exciting.

To understand the pride African-Americans take in the success of one of their own, it is necessary to consider how much many have overcome to achieve their goals. For instance, Ethel Waters was born into extreme poverty in Chester, Pennsylvania, shortly before the turn of the century. While still attending convent school, she married for the first time at the age of 12 and by 13 she was working as a hotel chambermaid. By age 17 she had transitioned into a nightclub singer who was billing herself as "Sweet Mama Stringbean," and she quickly rose to new heights of professional excellence as a recording artist and actress.

In 1951, her autobiography, *His Eye Is on the Sparrow,* was published and became a best seller. Thereafter, she worked on television and toured with Billy Graham evangelistic crusades until she died in Chatsworth, California in 1977.

The sweetness of her success can be fully appreciated only by those who have overcome as much. To those still trying to succeed, Ethel Waters was a source of inspiration and hope. Betty was one of millions who viewed Ethel Waters as a role model, so it was a double blessing to make a cross-country trip with one of her associates.

Even at this young age, Betty had found favor with the Lord. For the future work she been chosen to do, she would need a world-view. This trip was a part of the Lord's education for her. Among other things, Betty learned that some of America's cities began as settlements that predated many of Europe's modern cities and countries. In fact, history first recorded that Brooklyn and Long Island were discovered and claimed by the French more than half a century before Pope Gregory XIII introduced the Modern Calendar and during the era in which Michelangelo was just completing the ceiling of Sistine Chapel.

The trip was one of those memorable adventures that broadened her horizons at an early age. Not everything about the trip was wonderful though as Brooklyn experienced some frightening blackouts during Betty's visit.

When she returned home, she became interested in the benefits of obtaining a federal job and landed one with the Navy, where she worked for three years. There she met Itella Walker, who liked Betty so much that she wanted to bring this girl into her family. Due to Itella's matchmaking, Betty met her son when he came home from the service. They were married and had a son, Theodore "Teddy" W. Jones, Jr., but the marriage did not last. The immature and spoiled young man left and returned numerous times. He finally moved to Oklahoma permanently, abandoning his wife and five-month-old son. From that day forward, Betty was a single, working mom.

In such cases, the church can provide much needed support -- especially in an inner-city environment where there is enormous peer pressure on fatherless youngsters. Betty provided more stability than most single moms by remaining close to both her family and church. These support systems enabled her to become a homeowner and active member of the community while she worked on her next Federal job for more than thirty-four years.

During those years, she lived in the same neighborhood with the Houstons, where they fellowshipped and worked together on many projects for the Lord.

At the young age of 13, Betty had began working with Ray and Ralph, bringing neighborhood children to church. When they were old enough to drive, they wore their cars out carrying them back and forth, hoping and praying the efforts would keep the youngsters away from the many dangers they faced during their most vulnerable years. Wholesome activities, solid teaching, and an abundance of long-suffering love made a difference in the lives of many.

When Betty became a single, working mom, she thought back on those days and the good they had accomplished. Realizing the growing number of children who needed that kind of underpinning, she started a Sunday School in her small five-room home, as there were some children who would come there who weren't comfortable going to church.

She regularly ministered to approximately thirty children in the dining room of her little house. Then she bought a larger home and converted part of the garage into a permanent place for them to meet. They had many wonderful times. When she was able to plan outings, Bishop Houston always made the church van available to them.

This community outreach grew to the point that she decided to establish the "Rafael Fortier Youth Foundation," in memory of her dearly departed father.

She donated the little five-room home to it for the permanent use of the neighborhood's children.

Betty's father had taught his children to care for others by his own acts of kindness, just as the Bishop's had. Many times she had seen her father take clothes and food to the poor people in Mexico and in the housing projects. It did not matter what race they were or what their beliefs were, if they were hurting, he would help. Her father and mother often pitched a tent and held meetings near the produce areas of Tipton and Prixler California. Migrant workers who had toiled in the fields from sunup until sundown welcomed both the practical and spiritual gifts brought to them by the Fortiers.

In the tradition of her parents, Betty did a lovely job of fixing up the Foundation House and continued ministering to the children in the neighborhood, particularly those in the Imperial Court Projects. Their needs pulled at her heartstrings and she welcomed them with open arms.

In addition to regularly scheduled meetings, there were special ones for all the holidays. Parents were appreciative of their children being invited to have a good time while learning songs and scriptures. Their favorite was the 100th Psalm, "Make a joyful noise unto the Lord, all ye lands. Serve the Lord with gladness: come before His presence with singing. Know ye that the Lord is God: it is He that hath made us, and not we ourselves; we are His people, and the sheep of His pasture. Enter His gates with thanksgiving, and into His courts with praise: be thankful unto Him, and bless His name. For the Lord is good; His mercy is everlasting; and His truth endureth to all generations."

This neighborhood outreach was so successful that Betty received an award from the Federal Government and was honored to have it presented to her by Bob Hope.

In addition, Betty did volunteer work at the La Padrino Downey Juvenile facility where Pauline Montgomery, one of her good friends, was Chaplain (and later became Senior Chaplain). For eight years Betty donated her time to do weekly counseling and also led the song services. At the same time, Betty was caring for her son, helping her own aging mother and assisting one of her church mothers, Mattie Cummings. As the needs of her family increased, it eventually became necessary for Betty to give up all outside activity to care for them.

During this time Betty was moving up the career ladder. By the time she retired, she had advanced from a file clerk to Chief of Outpatient Clinics at the Veterans Administration Medical Center in Long Beach, California.

Never one to sit back and take it easy, after retiring, this financially comfortable woman began working for her nephew, Pastor Plummer, at a church-run day-care center where she rediscovered the joy of working with little ones.

Her life was a satisfying one, and she was pleased with the contributions she had been able to make to her family, church, and community. Among other things, she was enjoying her term as President of the Los Angeles County Chapter of the Women's Christian Temperance League, in which she had become very active. She had traveled all over the country to national conventions and had even attended international conventions in Canada and Australia. Still, she felt the Lord had more work for her to do.

It was at this time in her life that the phone rang and she heard Bishop Houston say, "Betty, how would you like to spend the rest of your life with me?" If she accepted Bishop Houston's proposal, she would be able to do more of the things she longed to do, and those were exactly the things Bishop Houston was doing.

Betty had been single for forty-seven years, and Bishop Houston had been married forty-seven years. What a paradox -- and now he was asking her to marry him. Betty thought about her father's objections to her first marriage and believed that he would not object to this one. He had passed away at the rather young age of 62 or she would have consulted with him, but really there was no need. In many ways he and the Bishop were alike, as both were big-hearted men who loved and served the Lord.

When she thought of the building Bishop Houston had done at Bethel, it reminded her of the church her father had constructed in the Fresno area. She laughed when she thought of her father packing up his family, including Betty's son, Teddy, and taking them on the road. Traveling throughout the country he never missed an opportunity to put either the Word of God or his tools to good use and did so many times in Nebraska, New Mexico, and Colorado. Yes, in many ways her father was much like the man who was asking her to marry him. God had blessed her father in all his ways, just as He had blessed the Bishop.

Then Betty's thoughts turned to her son, Teddy, and it was comforting to know he already thought of Bishop Houston as a father figure, as did many of the other children who had grown up in his church. There was no doubt that Teddy would approve, as he had been included in so many church and family functions that he already felt as if he were a part of the Houston family.

One of the most memorable occasions occurred when Teddy, at the age of four, had been the ring-bearer in the wedding of Bishop Houston's sister, Lillie Mae.

The event would conclude at the Houston's home and keep the little tyke up way past his usual bedtime, so it was decided that he would just spend the night there. However, with so many out-of-town guests, there would be a lot of new faces at the house and that caused Betty to wonder if she would get a call saying he wanted to come home. She needn't have been concerned though. The little lad just slipped his small hand inside the Bishop's enormous one and felt right at home.

There certainly wouldn't be as much of an adjustment period as some blended families have to go through because all the children knew each other well. Bishop Houston had always treated Teddy and the other children at church as his own, so the Houston children were accustomed to sharing their dad and would have no reservations themselves. It had always been their parents' practice to bring young people into their home.

Recently, upon hearing that Teddy was having some problems, the Bishop had invited him to come to Nashville and live with him. This kind invitation came at a time when just about all help and avenues of escape were exhausted for Teddy. When he arrived, he got a great deal of help from the Bishop, which resulted in Teddy reestablishing himself with Christ Jesus. Because of that, Teddy survived one of the worst times in his life.

With all things considered, is it any wonder Betty consented to marry the wonderful man who asked her to spend the rest of her life with him?

In the process of making plans to merge the two households, Betty said she would not feel comfortable moving into the home Bishop Houston had shared with his late wife. Minnie was Betty's own lifelong friend. Along with other family members, Betty had twice come to Nashville to see Minnie during her extended illness. They all loved each other in the Lord and each of them had a high sense of propriety, which accounted for Betty feeling as she did.

Bishop Houston understood completely and agreed that they should have a home of their own. Loving Bishop Houston as he did, Tommy Barton delighted in helping them find the perfect home. All the while, he was wondering what in the world the Lord had in store for this dynamic duo. After a beautiful wedding ceremony attended by more than 500 people and a subsequent settling down period, it begin to become clear to everyone.

CHAPTER ELEVEN

*"Because thou hast been my help, therefore in the
shadow of thy wings will I rejoice." (Ps 63:7)
"For I delivered unto you...
that which I also received." (I Cor. 15:3)*

While God has promised that with the same
measure we give, it shall be given unto us, that should
never be our motive for giving, as God simply will not
accept the sacrifices of those who "give to get" -- and no
one can deceive God.

Bishop Houston believes God always richly
blesses those who give for the right reasons, but that it is
not always in dollars, as exemplified by this passage of
scripture: "My dear friends, you surely haven't forgotten
our hard work and hardships. You remember how night
and day we struggled to make a living so that we could
tell you God's message without being a burden to
anyone. Both you and God are witnesses that we were
pure and honest and innocent in our dealings with you
followers of the Lord. You also know we did everything
for you that parents would do for their own children. We
begged, encouraged, and urged each of you to live in a
way that would honor God. He is the one who chose you
to share in his own kingdom and glory." (I Thess. 2:9-12
CEV)

If financial blessings had been guaranteed to the
apostles and their spiritual children, Paul would not have
had to do any tent making, as the congregation would

have been able to support him easily, without it being a burden on them. However, that was not the case, so he gladly worked, as did Bishop Houston, because of his love for God and His children. All who give of themselves and their resources simply because they love Him and want to obey will reap rich blessings.

An added benefit of giving only for the right reasons is that it makes one immune to the manipulative practices of those false prophets "which come to you in sheep's clothing, but inwardly they are ravening wolves." (Matt. 7:15) Immeasurable damage has been done by those who pervert the word of God and use His Holy promises for their own selfish purposes. It is one of the most despicable sins, and just as Jesus drove the money changers out of the temple, so He will deliver swift judgment to those who "destroy souls; to get dishonest gain." (Ezek. 22:27)

But to the wise steward and cheerful giver, He has promised, "Give, and it shall be given unto you; good measure, pressed down, and shaken together, and running over, shall men give into your bosom. For with the same measure that ye mete withal it shall be measured to you again." (Luke 6:38)

With Bishop Houston having given much of his time and resources to help others, just as promised, much was given to him. Rather than simply relax and enjoy it, he kept right on giving those things he received of God, to both lay persons and ministers.

His championship attitude toward life proclaims, "But thanks be to God which giveth us the victory through our Lord Jesus Christ. Therefore, my beloved Brethren, be ye steadfast, unmoveable, always abounding in the work of the Lord, forasmuch as ye know that your labour is not in vain in the Lord." (I Cor. 15:57-58)

Even those who have observed Bishop Houston's life from afar know that he is a brave man with a big heart, but those who have been close to him through life's fiery trials have been amazed at the way in which he has remained "steadfast, unmoveable, always abounding in the work of the Lord." Yet he has not been rigid, inflexible, or dogmatic. Reasonableness, combined with love and respect for others, has enabled him to grow in favor with God and man -- as Christ did.

Those traits contributed to the accomplishments he had already seen and the ones that he would see in the future. However, the primary reason he was able to fulfill his God-given destiny was that he lived out the admonishment, "Be thou faithful unto death." (Rev. 2:10)

Even before his feet hit the floor each morning, he is seeking the guidance of the Holy Spirit regarding what the Lord would have him do that day. That sacrificial offer proceeds from a thankful, loving heart, which is rewarded daily with a new and fresh anointing of the Holy Spirit. It coats his heart with a spiritual oil that keeps offenses rolling off him like water off a duck's back. Without the daily cleansing, refreshing, and anointing, he would surely have been caught up in disputes that would have distracted him from realizing his God-given destiny because as Christ said, "...it is impossible but that offenses will come...." (Luke 17:1)

In addition to being steadfast, faithful, and forgiving, he is also continually serving those in need, be it with spiritual encouragement or food for the body.

God honors those who serve Him with a humble heart by being with them. In fact, it is His very own presence that draws many people to men and women who serve God, even though they may not know why.

Their spirits long to be in communion with His spirit which is in and around those who abide in Him. It was for that sweet communion with God's presence that they were created and even before they have learned about the ways and teachings of God, the yearning is there. It is only in God's presence that they find peace, wholeness, and contentment.   Until that connection is made, the soul is searching, searching, searching -- until the heart becomes sick.

As life progresses, storm clouds gather for those who don't have a God-given purpose in life. Therefore, a growing number of older Americans are becoming more and more heartsick, even to the point of medicating themselves against the ever-increasing pain of depression, loneliness and isolation.   Bishop Houston believes that more than ever, they need to connect with their Maker and fellowship with those who are involved in God-ordained activities that would give their lives significance. Without it, the entire being deteriorates until physical illness overtakes them and they die.

Most doctors can't help those individuals very much because what they really need is communion with God, who can heal all manner of illnesses, be they physical or spiritual. Many times the presence of God abiding in His children has a healing effect on others, as it did when Paul's shadow fell upon the sick and they were healed.   The more time we spend in communion with Christ, the stronger the presence of God is in us, which results in those around us seeing supernatural things happen. It's not always because of what we say or do, sometimes it is just a matter of His presence with us.

Also, when the children of God pass the baton, and recipients are faithful to finish the course, that same Spirit travels with them. As Dr. Mark Hanby wrote in *You Have Not Many Fathers*, "The flow of spiritual progression and digression flows from generation to generation.

"...The first generation of the Church was awesome and mighty. The shadows of the apostles healed the sick, and offering-thieves dropped dead in the middle of meetings. Buildings literally shook with the power of God as believers prayed and God answered. Lame men leaped and dead women were raised to life. Deacons held city-wide crusades, healed the sick, and cast out unclean spirits. The unchurched Gentiles spoke in tongues before a sermon was ever finished. Cities rioted, demons fled, and prison gates flew open. Prophetic voices predicted famines, future arrests, and storms at sea. Apostles spoke and sorcerers fumbled in blindness. Apostles preached and thousands upon thousands repented and were baptized in a single day. The world was turned upside-down in a single generation.

"This first generation of the Church, who passed on the inheritance of the saints to the next generation of believers, gave us the blessings we enjoy today...."[*]

Many are enjoying blessings because Bishop Houston has passed on the spiritual inheritance he received. If asked, some of them might not be able to remember many of his words of wisdom or identify exactly how he helped them. At times, Bishop Houston is himself oblivious as to how he has helped people, but if he had not been steadfast, faithful, serving, and willingly available to those needing a touch from God, those individuals would not have been helped. There have been times when it has been as mysterious as the instances of people being healed by Paul's shadow passing over them.

Perhaps insights can be gained through this verse, "But unto you that fear My Name shall the Sun of Righteousness arise with healing in His wings." (Mal. 4:2) That may explain how people were healed by the apostles' shadow passing over them. When the Sun of Righteousness (with healing in His wings) rises over those who fear His name, *He gives them a healing shadow.*

---

[*] Copyright (c) 1996 - Dr. Mark Hanby, author *You Have Not Many Fathers* Destiny Image Publishers, Inc./P. O. Box 310/Shippenburg, PA 17257

There are two reasons why the author of this book, believes that to be true. One, God has given her that divine revelation and two, she and her husband, Tommy, have experienced it in their own lives as they have been in Bishop Houston's spiritual shadow.

Many times, those who have been healed or helped fail to give thanks to God or to show appreciation to the person through whom God has worked, and that is wrong. Therefore, Tommy and Laverne gladly give public thanks to God for what He has done in their lives through Bishop Houston. They also express their love and appreciation to Bishop Houston for the many times he has been available for them.

As author Joyce Landorf explains in *Balcony People*, we should be happy to be in the balcony applauding what God is doing through the lives of our brothers and sisters in Christ. She writes, "'Don't just pretend that you love others: really love them." (Rom. 12:9), 'Love each other with brotherly affection and take delight in *honoring each other*" (Rom. 12:10, italics added).

"When balcony people love, they do take extraordinary delight in "honoring each other." They are *not* in competition with each other, and they particularly do *not* keep score.

"It seems to me that too few of us honor one another. We are too interested in our own welfare, our own successes, our own achievements. We are intimidated by someone else's gifts or talents. We become so busy climbing the ladder of our own triumphs that we resent taking the time to pay homage to some someone else. True balcony people love with honor and respect.

"In the sixteenth chapter of Romans, Phoebe was described as a dear Christian woman. Paul tells the church in Rome to 'receive her as your sister in the Lord, giving her a warm Christian welcome.' Then he goes on to advise, 'Help her in every way you can for she has helped many in their needs, including me.'

"Paul continues to teach the balcony people concept by example when he writes next, 'Tell Priscilla and Aquila "hello." They have been my fellow workers in the affairs of Christ Jesus. In fact, they risked their lives for me; and I am not the only one who is thankful for them: so are all the Gentile churches.'

"Later in that same chapter, Paul says, 'Remember me to Mary, too, who has worked so hard to help us.' Paul has no trouble being a loving balcony person to women, nor does he struggle in the least with respecting Priscilla, Mary, and other women for their work in the church. In fact, he comes right out and calls them co-workers. I suspect several women were partners with Paul in the Lord's work, and I do not mean they cooked and served the Wednesday night potluck supper.

"The entire sixteenth chapter of Romans is, in my mind, the biblical 'balcony person' passage. It is where Paul practices what he preaches. He cheers all those dear people in Rome from the balcony of their minds. He gives no false compliments, no build-up of one person and belittling of another but straight from the balcony, he gives his love.

"My favorite balcony motto from Paul is that marvelous sentence, 'Whatever you do, do it with kindness and love' (2 Cor. 16:14)."[*]

Tommy and Laverne Barton are delighted to be two of many who are in Bishop Houston's balcony, expressing their love and appreciation for him.

One of the attributes they find most pleasing is the way in which he is a balcony person for others, frequently encouraging both men and women their ministries. The

---

[*] Copyright (c) 1984 by Joyce V. Heatherley, Balcony Publishing

many examples given in this book are only a representative sampling.

Bishop Houston encourages people because he really cares about them realizing their full potential and he helps them to do so. The characteristics of a sincere and genuine balcony person are characteristics of God Himself. Balcony people typically rise to the top because they grow in favor with both God and man, as Jesus did. They love and sacrifice for others as Jesus did. They also praise others publicly and privately.

In this area too, a balanced approach serves the body of Christ well. In fact, a balanced spiritual diet is equally as important as a balanced nutritional diet, or perhaps even more important. While too many pleasant things to eat will adversely affect one's health, very few enjoy their lives without some foods that fall into that category. And since our Lord was often breaking bread with the disciples and celebrating days of spiritual significance with feasts, it seems that He did indeed mean it when He said He came that we might have life and have it more abundantly.

Perhaps Jesus was cautioning his followers against another type of overindulgence when He tempered their exuberance. In response to the seventy followers who came joyfully exclaiming, "Lord, even the devils are subject unto us through Thy Name." Jesus, wanting them to know how insidious and dangerous pride is, answered them, "...*I beheld Satan as lightning fall from heaven.* Behold, I give unto you power to tread on serpents and scorpions, and over all the power of the enemy: and nothing shall by any means hurt you. Notwithstanding in this rejoice not, that the spirits are subject unto you; but rather rejoice, because your names are written in heaven." (Luke 10:17-20)

We should keep our priorities well-balanced and in order. Never should we forget to give *God* the glory, lest we also fall, but just as God allows us to enjoy the warmth of the sun on our back, so He also allows our hearts to be warmed when the Sun of Righteousness shines down on us and makes our shadow and our work effective for eternal purposes.

Prayer, appreciation, and acknowledgments stir up the gifts of God that are within us. Even when God was sternly addressing the sins of various churches in the book of Revelations, He also acknowledged the things they were doing right in order to encourage them to continue doing those things. Some pastors follow God's example and find that they get more of the behavior they desire when they affirm and praise it.

Bishop Houston does that and he also comforts, as the Holy Spirit has comforted him. Only God knows how many have taken refuge in Bishop Houston's shadow, but more than a few have found a respite there from the scorching wilderness of life. There, innumerable discouraged souls have been refreshed in the shady comfort of a giant spiritual oak.

All too often, recipients fail to Praise God for His blessings or to thank His servants who have sacrificed of themselves so that others can enjoy the blessings God has given them to pass on.

By giving thanks and honoring those who are mature and wise enough to handle it properly, the church could give the younger generation the role models they need to learn how to become great spiritual oaks themselves.

The importance of good role models was made clear by an article written by Beverly Heirich, a national award-winning writer and lecturer. Concern for the country sent Ms. Heirich searching for answers. She asked a classroom of bright students who their heroes were, allowing them to chose from those living and dead.

"Three said, 'Michael Jackson.' One said, 'My parents.' Two said, 'Michael Jordan.' Another said, 'Magic Johnson.' One said, 'Jesus.' Another said, 'My mother.'

"But more than half the class shrugged their shoulders, looked bemused, or answered laughingly, 'No one! No way!'"

Ms. Heirich wrote, "The words 'No way!' reminded me of a warm November day in Hawaii many years ago...when I had asked George Foster, a young baseball star, to tell me about his heroes....

"'I had three heroes when I was a little boy growing up in Alabama and later in California: Willie Mays, my big sister and my momma.

"'Willie inspired me to play baseball. My big sister taught me about Jesus and planted deep seeds of faith.'

"George paused a moment and grinned broadly. 'But it was my momma who filled me with determination not to give up when things got hard.'

Then George told Ms. Heirich about a serious injury he had sustained some years age. It was so serious that doctors told him he would be lucky to simply walk normally again and advised him to forget about playing big league baseball. Several downcast coaches and medical personnel had told him how sorry they were, but George's momma had a different message. Brimming with confidence, she emphatically said, "George, God can make a way out of no way!"

George recalled, "'...It took a lot of hard work, a lot of faith, and a lot of prayer, but before long I was running better and faster than I ever had before. The doctors were amazed, but momma and I weren't. We just grinned at each other because we knew it was God who did it. He made a way out of no way. Just like momma said He would.'"

"When George finished telling his story, we were silent for a moment. Then I heard him say softly, almost as if speaking only to himself. 'Kids need heroes. Heroes leave footsteps for kids to walk in until they grow big enough to find their own direction.'"[*]

Bishop Ralph Houston has been an excellent role model as husband, father, businessman, civic leader and a man of God. For that reason, the author of this book is making presentations to film and television producers about his life story. With no script or book available, the story still garnered a considerable level of interest at the most recent American Film Festival in Los Angeles. This past week a New York filmmaker was in Nashville and talked with Laverne about it. Because he was pleased with the results of a highly acclaimed film he produced about another African-American man of God, it is likely that he will be our producer.

This generation can be reached more effectively through the media than any other way. *L.A. Times* Film Critic Kenneth Turan, in his movie review of *The Prince of Egypt* mentioned that the miracles portrayed therein could make a believer out of an atheist. He also acknowledged that it is likely to encourage viewers to read the story in Exodus. It is also expected to be a highly profitable venture.

Speaking of profit, it was reported that Catholics produced *Spitfire Grill* as a fund-raiser. Not only did they do quite well with it financially, they also took first prize at the Sundance Film Festival.

If we will use the tools the good Lord has put at our disposal and teach with stories as Jesus did, we can teach compassion, courage, tenacity, and truth, instead of sexual behavior that leads to grief, gratuitous violence, profanity, and greed. Films are a cost-effective way of

---

[*] Excerpts from "Nashville Eye" a *Tennessean* article by Beverly Heirich

going into the highways and byways. Doing so with this story would be highly effective as people would find the extraordinary risks Bishop Houston has taken to help others most entertaining and challenging.

They would also be intrigued with flashbacks to the younger days of a man who is the grandson of a slave growing up in the dustbowl and maturing in World War II. The country has never needed faithful, steadfast role models more than now, and Bishop Houston is an excellent one.

Even pastors need to see this story. While most have received more education than those of previous generations, some haven't been taught as much about having faith that can move mountains and make them stand tall in the face of severe problems. If we ever needed more courage and cooperation, we need it now. Our country's problems can't be dealt with unless pastors and church members pull together to help others as Bishop Houston and the members of Bethel did to help Robin and her son.

In this fast-paced culture neither pastors or members have as much time to be quiet and seek the mind of Christ about issues. Patience and public relations skills are in short supply, resulting in the church being in a weakened condition.

According to Brooks Faulkner, pointman for a new program at the Baptist Sunday School Board here called LeaderCare, "An estimated 225 pastors are fired from their churches every month. At this rate they say all 35,000 pastors will be gone in thirteen years. 'The hurt and pain are more common than I ever dreamed'."[*] This is a problem affecting the church at large.

---

[*] Excerpt from "Pastors Take Next Step When 'Lord, help" isn't Enough" A *Tennessean* article by Religion Editor Ray Waddle

The bar of expectations is being raised to increasingly higher levels in the fields of education, income, physical fitness, etc. but not in the area of morality and goodwill. Even the church has become accepting of sins that are weakening and destroying us. Churches and the population at large need role models of long-suffering, overcoming faith in the face of the problems facing everyone in the country today.

Many people believe education is the answer, but education as it now exists isn't meeting all of society's needs.

Plano, Texas, is surely one of the better educated, more affluent communities in the country, yet it is plagued with woes. According to the January 1999 edition of *Texas Monthly*, Plano, Texas has become a "Teenage Wasteland," where kids are frequently strung out on heroin. Or they're on trial for distributing it! Plano's students are also suffering from a variety of stress-related ailments. Eating disorders, ulcers, and insomnia are only a few of the side effects of trying to measure up to their parents' sky-high expectations. Prior to this latest round of bad publicity, Plano's teenagers made the country sit up and take notice with their high rate of suicides.

The enemy is attacking from the inner-city to the suburbs while the church fights this modern war with dated weapons. Emmy-winning producer and best-selling author Bob Briner challenges the church to consider the culture-shaping arenas of television and filmmaking as mission fields. In *Roaring Lambs* he makes an excellent case as to why we should be as willing to send people into these areas just as we are sending people to China.

To understand the impact these venues have on the culture, read *Hollywood vs. America* by film critic Michael Medved. It is an "explosive bestseller that shows how - and why - the entertainment industry has broken faith with its audience." (And how expensive that has been for the entertainment industry. The more profitable and enduring productions are the films and television programs of substance and quality.)

Steve Allen endorsed Medved's book by saying, "Everyone - left, right and middle - is perfectly aware that we are in a period of cultural and moral collapse. But some people don't want to concede that the popular media bears part of the responsibility. Michael Medved's book should convince them that it does."[*]

Bishop Houston encouraged the author of this book in her endeavors to establish contacts to promote worthwhile films long before he was a subject of one of them. He, like many others, believes it is important to make films about people who are good role models.

When testifying before a Senate Subcommittee Hearing on violence in television, Marvin Kitman, TV critic, *Newsday*, stated, "...TV programming should be filled with stories that glorify society's real heroes, the ones who save lives, the ones who take care of old people or the handicapped, the ones who sit and work in universities and laboratories, courthouses, hospitals, or kindergartens. How boring? There is no such thing as a boring situation, only boring writers who can't make it come alive without killing or bombing...."

To encourage the behavior we want more of, we should affirm it with recognition. Christians give more of themselves than anyone, typically juggling many more demands than those who do not attend church. Our lights should not be under a bushel.

Especially the lights of those who have served faithfully for fifty or sixty years. Those giant spiritual oaks can be a source of encouragement that keeps young

---

[*] *Hollywood vs. America* Copyright (c) 1992 by Michael Medved, Harper Collins Publishers, Inc.

pastors from burning out and giving up. We should also affirm the positive relationships that keep our churches together to serve this generation of hurting and shattered families.

Role models like Bishop Houston and Bethel would challenge young and old alike to make more contributions to society. In this culture where men and women are living longer and have a great need for significance, there is a marvelous opportunity for the church to do more to improve our neighborhoods and our country. He is a wonderful example of how a "retired" businessman and pastor can serve. And it is very rewarding.

For instance, after Bishop Houston performed the wedding ceremony of Rodney Beard and his bride, Charlene, he, along with a Board of Elders, ordained Rodney to pastoral ministry and helped him organize the Living Word Church. Beginning with only three members, it has grown to a membership of over 600 within a short four years and is still growing. Not only has Bishop Houston been a counselor and mentor to the pastor, he has also been a servant to the church by, among other things, counseling with its members several hours each week. At 73, and with enough accolades to last a lifetime, Bishop Houston is still serving God by feeding His sheep.

At Bishop Houston's request, the following personal example is also given. Bishop Houston first began his work with Tommy and Laverne when their friendship took on new dimensions as they visited terminally ill friends together. While praying about those and other areas of deep concern, a unity of spirit began to develop between the Houstons and the Bartons. So, when Laverne had a need of her own, it seemed perfectly natural to call Bishop Houston to see if he could help.

When Laverne placed that call to Bishop Houston, she had been in communication for three years with a missionary whose husband had been brutally murdered in a children's home founded by him, his wife and their four children.	Their situation was so dire that Laverne believed that the same God who carried them through it surely could and would carry any of us through anything. If people knew all the story, they would know God could carry them through *any challenges* they might face in their own life. She believed people needed to know that.

For that reason, Laverne worked with other church members to get a play produced and scheduled for an upcoming missions conference.	It had been on the agenda for the previous missions conference but was "bumped" and rescheduled.	Now, there was some discussion of postponing it again. Laverne asked Bishop Houston if he would intercede for the project.	Then she went to her flower garden to work and pray for peace in her own heart and for peace in the hearts of all concerned.	She was especially praying for Glena Jacobs and Alice Kiester, who had written the play, selected cast members, and conducted rehearsal after rehearsal.

Bishop Houston soon called to say he had gone to the church and worked everything out.	That was no small feat, when considering the number of options available to a church of approximately 6,000 members.	Especially one located in Nashville, Tennessee, "Music City USA," with many highly talented members. And since those are frequently complimented by visiting speakers and artists known on a national or even international basis.	In fact, a Russian celebrity was being flown in for that missions conference and a nationally known preacher was also speaking.	Nevertheless, because of Bishop Houston's intervention, *A Call to Courage* remained on the agenda.

The insert in the church bulletin read as follows: "Barbara and Bill Robinson answered God's call ten years ago when they went to Lebanon to serve as missionaries. It has been an unbelievable ten years. We are very pleased to present a play entitled, *A Call to Courage,* about their extraordinary commitment, at 7:00 p. m. on Wednesday, September 1, 1993, which is the last evening of the missions conference.

"Don't miss this unforgettable story of faith. It will sustain us all as we face our own personal challenges.

"It is incredible to have Barbara here with us for the missions conference. Last month nearly 500,000 refugees fled from Southern Lebanon in what the Associated Press called 'a human catastrophe of tragic magnitude.'

"In response to our request for her to come be with us, she wrote:

"'Due to recent fighting in the area we have been without electricity for some time now, and our generator has been down as well. During these uncertain times, it seems impossible for me to join you. Yet we walk by faith and not by the things we see, so I don't lose hope of being with you. I don't know the price of a ticket, nor do I have easy access to finding that information, yet I know God is able to do all things well in His time. I am enclosing a photo taken recently by my son (perhaps to recognize me at the airport with!).'

"That wonderful letter, combined with a comment Barbara had made in an earlier letter about wanting to see her mother who is well into her seventies and that she has not seen in ten years, really touched our hearts and arrangements were made to bring her here. We know you will be blessed by the drama and by her."

Due to the aforementioned fighting having totally destroyed the infrastructure in Barbara's area, it took an incredible amount of work on Laverne and Tommy's part, as well as a giant leap of faith, to get Barbara to America. They authorized a $1,600 charge for the ticket to their American Express card, but not before calling Bishop Houston to see if he thought they should do it. He said he felt it was ordained of God and that he would help them raise the money to cover the cost of the ticket if the offering from the church didn't.

Because of Pastor Hardwick and Sister Montelle's extraordinary kindness in taking an offering and the generous giving of their congregation, the expenses were more than covered. Barbara also had enough extra money to travel around the country to see family and friends she had not seen in years.

Barbara made many new friends during that 1993 trip. One of those new friends later gave Barbara a $100,000 gift that allowed her to purchase a home when the children's home closed. To Laverne it seemed God had given Barbara the same kind of homecoming that a few war heroes received when they returned from their tour duty to find their community had built a home for them while they were away defending their country. That was a wonderful ending to an old black and white movie Laverne once saw, and she thought it would be the perfect happy ending for *A Call to Courage,* a film based on the Robinsons' true story, but that was a future development.

During the 1993 trip, so many people were inspired and helped by the play that Laverne began working to get the story told on a larger basis, never dreaming how hard it would be or how long it would take.

The following year, Emmy-winning producer and best-selling author Bob Briner included Laverne's work on a film project based on the Robinsons' story in his book, *Lambs Among Wolves.* The film project was in the early stages of development, yet he included it with the highly successful endeavors of twenty-two other "Roaring

Lambs," who were having a positive impact on the culture. Laverne hoped and prayed it would come to pass, and believed it would.

Former Tennessee State Senator Norma Crow, had brought the work to Bob Briner's attention. She had also traveled with Laverne to the Middle East on one of two trips Laverne made in conjunction with her work with the Robinsons. Unbelievable events happened on both trips. As the work progressed, Laverne gained a greater appreciation for Bob Briner's comments about viewing the venues of television and filmmaking in much the same way the church views China or other challenging mission fields.

Bob Briner had also written about the faith and sacrifice that would be required of Laverne and her husband Tommy before the film, television program or video was produced. He may have had those unique insights due to being personally acquainted with the seventeen-year journey of faith and sacrifice CBS producer Ken Wales made to get *Christy* produced.

In March 1996, six years after Bill Robinson was viciously murdered, Ken Wales invited Laverne and Barbara to his home. During that visit he gave them permission to tell a publisher he had a working relationship with that he was interested in the project.

For Laverne, that was wonderful, but that did not seem to be the case for Barbara. Barbara mentioned that the publisher was affiliated with the same denomination as another Christian ministry that had a foreign operation near the children's home. It was the same Christian ministry that had employed three men Barbara alleged to be responsible for instigating Bill's murder. Barbara declined going to that publisher.

The relationship between Barbara and Laverne grew increasingly tense following that decision. They finally ended up having "no small dissension and disputation," as Paul and Barnabas did in Acts 15:2. It was a heartbreaking situation that took a long time to get over, but Laverne has.

In the end, all who continue abiding in the Vine find that God redeems many unfortunate situations and uses the end results for His Glory, as He is in this situation. "And we know that all things work together for good to them who love God, to them who are called according to His purpose." (Rom. 8:27)

The disagreement was the catalyst for Laverne looking into those difficult aspects of the story, that hadn't been dealt with properly in the script because she did not know enough about them. Now she does. After much prayer and reading, she has come to terms with those lamentable issues. So some good has come from it, and there is more to follow.

However, during the midst of the storm, Laverne's faith was so seriously damaged that without Bishop Houston's help, she probably would not have been able to go on with her work.

In fact, she was still in a downward spiritual spiral when Bishop Houston called and asked her to come to his home to meet a woman named Robin Byrd who wanted to discuss the possibility of having a book written and/or a film project developed.

CHAPTER TWELVE

"The angel which redeemed me from evil..."
(Gen. 48:16)

Robin and her son were now out of the witness protection program. While young Ralph was completing his last year of high school, she was looking for a writer and/or producer.

As Laverne listened to all that had transpired, she thought, Not one in a thousand pastors would have led their family and church to help this woman and her son, especially after learning Robin had a contract out on her life! Not one in ten thousand would have continued helping her after discovering she was also wanted by the FBI. And God knows that not one in a million would still be trying to help her now that she was living out in the open.

However, being a man of legendary loyalty, Bishop Houston was still doing all he could to help Robin, and he had the full cooperation of his new bride in these endeavors. Just a few months earlier, Sister Betty, suggested that they advance several thousand dollars to Robin to keep her out of trouble, and they had. Even with that generous assistance, life was so hard that Robin became suicidal.

Before making her final exit, Robin called Bishop Houston to say good-bye and to thank him for all he had done for her and her son. Surprisingly, the Lord had

Bishop Houston respond rather bluntly. He told her plainly that she would "hurt like hell," if she attempted to take her life, but she would not die. Nevertheless, after Robin hung up, she did swallow enough pills to kill herself.

She was near death when Bishop Houston and Sister Betty visited her in an out-of-state hospital. Just as Bishop Houston had prophesied, she hurt like hell but did not die.

After God raised Robin up, Bishop Houston arranged a speaking engagement at a church where many young people were strongly influenced by hearing about the hard life she'd had as a result of getting involved with the drug business. Everyone present believed it would make a lasting impression and serve as a deterrent to others. Laverne hoped there would be many more speaking engagements like that for Robin. She even worked in conjunction with Bishop Houston to schedule one in his home.

Believing that would be a continuing trend, Laverne was surprised to be led in a different direction with the development of the work she planned to do. It happened as a result of being awakened in the middle of the night with the strong impression that she should get up and read II Kings 2:2. Padding through the darkness, she found her Bible and turned on a lamp. While reading the verse about the Lord sending Elijah to Bethel, the Lord revealed to her that she should write the story she was researching not from Robin's point of view but from Bishop Houston's. Then she came to understand that God planned to use what Bishop Houston and his church, Bethel, had done for Robin as an example to others.

Having no idea how Bishop Houston would feel about that, Laverne still immediately told Robin what the Lord had revealed to her and what she must do. Not long after that, Laverne met with a producer she had previously pitched the story to. When she ran the new vantage point by him, he liked it even more than he had the first time.

In fact his level of enthusiasm was so high that he took Laverne to see his entertainment attorney who had been with a major network for more than a decade and who had formerly served on the Board of Governors of the Academy of Television Arts and Sciences. He also liked the project from the Bishop's point of view.

Finally the producer took Laverne to see one of his friends who happened to be a William Morris agent. When he said that vantage point seemed right to him as well, and also commented on how interesting it was that these remarkable stories were coming to Laverne, she felt God was certainly confirming His direction to her. Even though her experience was limited, it was enough to know it isn't always that easy to get people involved in creative endeavors to see things the same way.

Bishop Houston also confirmed it by giving her permission to proceed. Then he gave the project a jump start by providing her with forty or so pages of an autobiography he had started long ago. As she read through it, she was amazed to read something God had spoken to Bishop Houston many years earlier, "Ralph, I want to use this place "<u>Bethel</u>" as an example!"

Those confirmations were a healing balm on Laverne's wounded spirit, but she was still so heartsick over the other project that she had spent so many years working to develop, that she just could not move ahead. She needed help from someone who had been through the same kind of experience.

As Billy Graham wrote in *Hope for the Troubled Heart*, "hurting people need someone to help them up. To encourage them, to support them, to let them know they're not alone. Who are the helpers, the comforters for the times when we're bleeding and need a transfusion of love?

"We can talk about God being our Comforter, but that doesn't absolve us of our responsibility. He has given us a special assignment. The Apostle Paul said: 'Praise be to the God and Father of our Lord Jesus Christ, the Father of compassion and the God of all comfort, who comforts us in all our troubles, so that we can comfort those in any trouble with the comfort we ourselves have received from God' (II Cor. 1:3-4)

"...Being available is difficult, because it takes time, but being sensitive to the small amounts of time we can give could really reap large rewards in someone's life. It doesn't really matter what we say to comfort people during a time of suffering, it's our concern and availability that count."[*]

Bishop Houston was available for Laverne and Tommy, both of whom were devastated by the strange turn of events. Bishop Houston did not know it, but as he shared the story that Laverne would write, he helped her. By learning that he had gone to Liberia with the money in hand to build a clinic for the Salala Mission, only to find that there was no gas and no cement, she realized that God's visions don't always take shape in the time frames that we expect. In Liberia the work was postponed because of a coming civil war. Laverne believed her own work may have been delayed because of civil war in the body of Christ.

Because Barbara believed employees of another Christian ministry had instigated Bill's murder, there were a lot of unresolved issues. Since Laverne had the assignment of telling the story, these troubling aspects affected her deeply. By the time she came to terms with it, she had come to understand very well something

---

[*] Copyright (c) 1991 by Billy Graham, Publisher, Word Book

practicing psychiatrist Dr. M. Scott Peck had written in the *Road Less Traveled*.

"Confronting and solving problems is a painful process, which most of us attempt to avoid. ...The very avoidance results in greater pain and an inability to grow both mentally and spiritually.... Suffering through the changes can enable us to reach a higher level of understanding."[*]

Laverne did suffer through the process of confronting and solving the problems in which she had become involved. She ended up with a higher level of understanding of herself and the story she had now been working for years to develop. And she grew spiritually.

It was strange that Laverne and Tommy's faith had been raised to its highest level ever by the Robinsons' story of faith and it was finally taken to the lowest level it had ever been because of it.

During the time when it was at its lowest, Tommy lost his precious mother and Laverne lost a dear sister. Laverne also agonized over her mother who had suffered a severe stroke in the midst of those losses. It was painful to see her Mother struggling to remember her own name.

Laverne's kind, loving mother, Rosa Lee Lansford, was a fount of spiritual wisdom and a prayer warrior who frequently touched God on her children's behalf. To understand her level of faith, it is worthwhile to mention that she once took a shovel and personally dug the foundation for a church she built. Later, as she was praising God and laying the hardwood floor, she got carried away and almost completed that task by herself as well.

---

[*] Copyright (c) 1978 by M. Scott Peck, M. D., author, A Touchstone Book published by Simon & Schuster, Inc.

She was Laverne's inspiration, as Bishop Houston's mother was to him. Laverne was grieving over her mother's condition and the deaths of their loved ones. She was also becoming increasingly aware of the loss they would face if her mother did not pull through, as there wasn't anyone else capable of interceding for the family as her mother had.

The culmination of all these things resulted in Laverne's faith and confidence being so badly shaken that she could not go on with a new project until she heard from God about the previous one.

In order to get away from everything and seek Him, she attended a Christ Church spiritual retreat at which Pastor Carol Houston was the speaker. It was there, in the healing shadow of the Houston family, her own church, and that great cloud of witnesses who wants to see all of us overcome, that God encouraged Laverne by once again confirming her calling to make His beautiful stories known.

As Ruth Whittinhall, another retreat attendee, told Laverne, a complete stranger, about what had happened to her dear son, Laverne felt this was not a coincidence.

Back in October 1989, Ruth's parents had come to her home to deliver the tragic news. Her father put his strong arms around Ruth and hugged her tightly while gently saying, "Baby, Ronnie was killed tonight while riding his bicycle."

Going limp, Ruth cried out, "No, please no, Oh, God, no." Her father held her up, as over and over Ruth said, "No...no...no" Thinking of their sleeping children, Ruth did everything she could to suppress the scream rising up in her throat and was enabled to do so by the desire to protect them from the pain she was feeling.

When Ruth's two sleepy-eyed stepsons, came in to see what was wrong, their dad hugged them to himself and told them what had happened. As the teenage boys fought back tears, Ruth prayed her twelve-year-old-daughter, Natasha would not wake up. Ronnie, four years her senior, had always been the perfect big brother. Ruth could not bear the thought of telling her about Ronnie's death right now.

The next morning with swollen eyes and heavy heart, Ruth waited for Natasha to wake up. Fresh, hot tears flowed down her cheeks as she remembered how happy Ronnie had been when Natasha was born and how he was always so loving and protective of her. It seemed like only yesterday when Ruth had found almost all his stuffed animals in Natasha's crib and asked, "Ronnie, why did you do this?"

With hands on his hips, little Ronnie had replied, "Because I love her."

Smiling, Ruth had said, "Well, Ronnie, she has her own stuffed animals. You don't have to give her all of yours."

He said, "I didn't give her *all* of mine. I still have my Pooh bear." Ruth hugged and kissed her generous little darling. Later she found his constant sleeping companion, Pooh bear, had also been given to Natasha.

The hardest thing Ruth ever did in her life was to tell Natasha that Ronnie had been killed. Natasha cried as if her heart would break. Ruth so much wanted to take away the pain, but there was nothing she could do, except hold her while the tears flowed down both of their faces.

After the funeral, Ruth's pastor called to say how angry he was about Ronnie's death, and that puzzled Ruth. However, many months later, after the shock and denial stages wore off, she came to appreciate his remarks, as they kept her from feeling guilty for her own struggle with anger. The whole grief process was an emotional roller coaster ride. Ruth drove to Ronnie's grave one day and, like a hysterical child faced with an overwhelming situation, just sobbed, "No, no, no..." Then looking into the heavens, she cried out to God, "*Why*???"

Her pastor had assured her God was bigger than her anger and grief and that it was okay to feel and express these very natural emotions. By the time she left, she was hoarse and exhausted.

In March, the drunk driver who had killed her precious son was sentenced. Even though he had a history of DUI arrests, and was therefore given the maximum penalty the judge could impose, he only received a five-year sentence. Furthermore, because of the early-release program, the perpetrator could be out of prison in a year.

"This man should go to jail for life," Ronnie's father, Ronald Cole Jr., said angrily. ...Instead of buying a class ring, I bought a headstone," Cole told Circuit Judge Robert Boylston. "Instead of buying a prom tux, I bought a casket....I have to live with the fact that he was murdered by a drunk."[*]

Like Ronnie's father, Ruth's ex-husband, Ruth too was still struggling. It was hard to hang onto her faith, when the first thing she encountered every morning was the devil cackling, "Remember, your son is dead...remember, your son is dead." Over and over he emotionally and spiritually slapped her in the face with that taunting phrase, "Remember, your son is dead...remember, your son is dead."

Nightmares invaded her sleep and there was no peace to be found when she was awake. It was very hard, and with Mother's Day looming ahead, it was getting worse. At times, the anger, a very natural part of the grieving process, threatened to engulf her and she was afraid she would become a bitter person if she did not overcome it.

---

[*] Copyright (c) *Sarasota Herald/Tribune*, March 15, 1990

The emotional roller coaster ride continued. At times, she was strong for Ronnie and at other times, she was even angry with him for not having been more careful and for leaving her. Very, very few people knew she had these dark, angry feelings or that sometimes she just could not bring herself to go to church. Of course, her husband Bill knew and he never judged her. He just loved her and waited.

Some days Ruth thought of taking a big bat, walking through the house and just demolishing everything in it...everything. Realizing this thing was bigger than she was, and that she wasn't getting out of it alone, she responded to an altar call given at a meeting by the Full Gospel Businessmen's Association. Shortly after a sermon on anger and forgiveness, she found herself standing in front of a man, about her father's age, who had his son by his side. She briefly explained that her 16-year-old son had been killed by a drunk driver about six months ago and that she really did not want to hate the man who killed him. To do so would make her hard and bitter, resulting in the loss of personality traits that were the essence of who she was as a person.

The man asked Ruth, "Do you forgive the man who killed your son?" Ruth replied, "Well, the Bible calls for me to forgive him. He is my enemy, needless to say...he wiped out my son...but still I pray for him. Every single night before I go to bed, I pray for him."

"Do you pray out loud?" the man asked. Ruth said, "No, I don't pray out loud about that part." He told her to pray out loud and then had her, phrase by phrase, repeat aloud after him. "By the grace of God...I forgive..."

He stopped and asked Ruth, "What's his name, Honey?" Withdrawing her hands from his, Ruth tearfully exclaimed, "I can't do this!"

He reached out, took her hands back, looked her right in the eye and intently said, "That's right, you can't, but God in you can." When they finished their prayer, Ruth realized it did make a difference to pray out loud. Every day since then, she has prayed out loud for her son's murderer. It is a matter of dying out to sin daily so anger will not build up in her heart and the root of bitterness take hold. A single prayer of forgiveness was not enough for the pain with which she lived on a daily basis. To remain victorious, she had to pray for him daily as a way of keeping her own sinful nature under control, and read her Bible.

One day while doing so, she came across a caption of "Forgiveness for the Sinner," in her NIV Bible. Followed by, "If anyone has caused grief...the punishment inflicted on him by the majority is sufficient for him..."

Ruth thought, *What*?!? Well, I guess being in jail is punishment enough, but he probably won't serve much more than a year...

Nonetheless, Ruth realized the Lord was showing her that his punishment was sufficient for him. Reading on it seemed that God was speaking right to her from His word, "...Now instead you (Ruth) ought to forgive and comfort him..."

She could not help asking God, "*Comfort him? Comfort him? Me*, comfort *him? Come on God*, you've got to be kidding me. *Me*, comfort *him? I'm the one who needs comfort here.*"

The Lord spoke to Ruth's heart, "No, you are to comfort him."

Ruth read on..."so he will not be overwhelmed by excessive sorrow..."

Then she read, "The reason I wrote you (Ruth) was to see if you would stand the test and be obedient in everything." Ruth thought, Ouch!

"If you forgive anyone, I will also forgive him." Ruth realized the Lord wanted her to be His instrument in this and through her obedience, she could give this man the peace she had come to know when her own sins were forgiven. Feeling it was not right for her to rob someone else of that peace, she read on, "And what I have forgiven...I have forgiven...in order that Satan might not outwit us. For we are not unaware of his schemes."

Ruth realized that the Lord was inviting her into a partnership with Him, so that, together, they could do battle and defeat the enemy. Then the Lord clearly spoke to her heart, "Ruth you are going to buy a Bible and send it, with a letter, telling him how much I (Christ) love him."

Ruth bought the Bible and even had the name of man who took her son's life imprinted on it. She sent it in care of the Prison Chaplain, who soon called her and said, "You know a lot of people talk the talk but you are really walking the walk. I can't tell you how much this has affected my life today."

For the remainder of his prison term, Ruth corresponded with the man who took her son's life. The responses she received were highly respectful and most appreciative of her kindness. When he was released, the prison chaplain told Ruth he was attending the church he pastored, and Ruth felt her work was finished.

Satan was not allowed to rob Ruth of the beautiful, kind personality God had given her. By entering into partnership with Him, she was able to bind the enemy and keep him from doing any further damage in her life.

Many times Laverne had heard Bishop Houston speak of entering into partnership with God. Now, she was gaining a better understand of what that meant and how to do it. Laverne realized that regardless of the losses, we must do as Ruth did and as Bishop Houston recommended. If we don't go on with God, Satan will be able to compound our losses by stealing certain aspects of our personalities from us, and our future.

Laverne felt these incredible stories had tremendous value as they were testimonies of God

Himself as revealed through the lives of His people who surrendered to His desire to redeem even the tragedies. It didn't seem possible that Laverne was meeting people with such amazing testimonies by chance. She thought, God must be leading me.

After the retreat, Laverne began working on the second assignment she'd received from the Lord. She had written four chapters of this book when Bishop Houston said, "Laverne why don't you make this our book and write about our involvement with Barbara in it."

Sadly, Laverne sighed and said, "Bishop Houston, I won't lie about it." To which he responded, "Of course not."

Dejectedly, Laverne suggested, "With all that has happened, I'm not sure the story should be told."

Without hesitation, he firmly answered, "The Holy Spirit will lead you."

Upon returning home, Laverne knelt at the chair in front of her computer and lifted up her hands to God, praying, "Dear Lord, you know that more than anything in the world, I want to stand before you with clean hands and a pure heart. Since we cannot know our own hearts, I am asking You in some clear unmistakable way to show me if You want me to write this story."

Then she opened up her Bible, completely at random, and read, "...What thou seest write in a book...." (Rev. 1:11)

As Laverne sat down to write what she had seen, she realized this was the second time Bishop Houston had kept the project on track when Satan tried to derail it.

As she worked with Bishop Houston's story, it meant a lot to her to see that in spite of many delays the Lord was finally bringing to fruition the vision He had given him so many years ago regarding the Salala mission in Liberia. Regarding her own vision and work, she looked forward to the day she would receive the kind of wholehearted support Bishop Houston was now receiving from people like Bishop Gus Marwieh who had written:

"I can scarcely find words to describe adequately my profound gratitude to you for your kindness in accepting our invitation to participate in the forthcoming Executive Planning Conference by the Board of Directors of AHEAD (Agency for Holistic Evangelism and Development). This conference will be historic and I am so glad that you will be there with your tremendous expertise and experience.

"The purpose of the conference is for the Board of Director of AHEAD to get the best of counsel from the various Christian business and professional men and women being invited as the Board seeks to develop a plan of action for its two-phase program for the evangelization of third world nations. Phase one concerns the economic enablement of indigenous Christians so they will be able to support adequately the evangelization of their individual nations. Phase two concerns the establishment of an institute of missions and technology for the training of self-supporting missionaries who will be deployed to every sector of the nation in which AHEAD will be active.

"Planning to use Liberia as a beachhead for the launching of this vision, AHEAD has won the interest of Jim Halcomb, who sees Liberia as an opportunity to develop a Christ-centered post war national development program that could make Liberia the South Korea of West Africa. Jim Halcomb is a champion among counselors to corporate America. He has been a corporate counselor for the past 35 years to business executives from over 5,000 corporations and agencies such as Xerox, AT&T, RCA, IBM, J.C. Penney, Exxon, American Express, Kentucky Fried Chicken Corporation, Avon Products, B. F. Goodrich, Honey, CBS and U. S. Government

Agencies such as the U. S. Navy, U. S. Air Force, U. S. Postal Service, U. S. Public Health Service, and NASA as well as many Christian organizations such as World Vision International, Campus Crusade for Christ, and Lausanne II.

"The conference will consist of a series of brainstorming sessions that will be conducted under the general supervision of Jim Halcomb who will serve as facilitator. The sessions will be done along the lines of Halcomb's Five Steps to Executive Planning. You will find the explanation of the five steps in the enclosed document entitled, *Halcomb Associates Demonstrates Boardroom 2000...."*

Laverne could see that God, in His timing, which included the conclusion of Liberia's civil war, was bringing about the God-given vision that had burned in Bishop Houston for so long. It gave her hope for her own endeavors and helped her to see that God often works things out in unimaginable ways.

Once again she was thankful for the way in which God had blessed her family through Bishop Houston, but God still had more surprises in store for her. As she wrote, it soon became apparent that there were two books in the making and when she and Bishop Houston discussed separating the material, Laverne asked if she could finish the more difficult one first as it carried with it a burden she had borne for many years now. Due to his understanding of what she had been through and with a mature patience developed during his many years of serving the Lord, he said, "Of course."

That freed Laverne up to complete a forthcoming book about the journey the Lord led her and her husband Tommy on as a result of their response to the tragic news of Bill Robinson's murder. That book and this book improve the chances of the stories being developed into film projects.

In *The Art of Adaptation,* Dr. Linda Seger wrote, "Adaptations are the lifeblood of the film and television business. Think about how many of our great films come from books, plays, and true-life stories: *The Birth of a Nation, The Wizard of Oz, Gone With the Wind, The African Queen, Casablanca, Shane, High Noon,* and *Rear Window* to name a few. Even the classic *Citizen Kane* was loosely based on the true-life story of William Randolph Hearst.

"Most Academy Award and Emmy Award-winning films are adaptations. Consider these amazing statistics:

- 85 percent of all Academy Award-winning Best Pictures are adaptations.
- 45 percent of all television movies-of-the-week are adaptations, yet 70 percent of all Emmy Award winners come from these films.
- 83 percent of all miniseries are adaptations, but 95 percent of Emmy Award winners are drawn from these films."

The aforementioned statistics bear out the personal advice Laverne received from CBS producer Ken Wales, who convinced her that a book would help immensely in the development of the film project.

Knowing Laverne had spent years of her life and thousands of dollars developing that film project, Bishop Houston certainly wanted to see her complete the task.

However, Bishop Houston's unique understanding went far deeper as he was in a similar place himself. While he yearned to help the people of Liberia, he also had another burden that he needed to get off his shoulders before he could fully devote himself to doing so.

That burden involved the split that had occurred in his beloved denomination more than twenty years ago. It was an issue he had not been in a position to address until May 1996, when after fifty-three years of ministerial experience, the oldest Pentecostal body in the United States elected him to its highest office, that of General President.

After returning home from the convention at which the election had taken place, Bishop Houston began seeking God as to his assignment. That resulted in God leading him to Isa. 58:12, from which he came to understand that he was to be a "repairer of the breach...."

That revelation brought back memories of a national leadership meeting of Pentecostal/Charismatic Churches of North America (PCCNA), at which efforts were being made to further the cause of interracial reconciliation. In response to being asked for his input, Bishop Houston advised PCCNA leaders that he could not respond, as his own denomination was divided. That heartfelt statement prompted the distinguished body of leaders to gather around him to pray for healing within the United Holy Church.

The PCCNA's movement stirred Bishop Houston's soul. Like many others he believed Sunday morning should not be the most segregated morning of the week. In the days of the Azusa Street Revival, the racial walls had melted under the power of the Holy Spirit. White ministers were ordained by black officials and everyone worshipped together regardless of color or station in life.

The interracial services irritated society's prideful groups, motivating them to bring political and social pressure against both black and white worshippers. It grew more intense as a result of African-American Pentecostal leaders encouraging pacifism during World War I. Pastors with interracial followings were jailed and whites were strongly discouraged from attending integrated services. FBI surveillance of men like C. H. Mason, founder of the Church of God in Christ, contributed to the atmosphere that drove blacks and whites apart and eventually resulted in the lynchings that followed World War I.

Even divided, the number of American Pentecostals had continued to grow to an estimated 15 million. Having worshipped together in the past, many were desirous of doing so again, but there were differences. Politically, most whites were conservative while African-Americans were more often liberal. Traditionally, most African-American leaders leaned toward a stronger form of church government than their white counterparts.

Having grown so far apart, could the two groups come back together? Could seventy years of racial division be healed?

"Delivering the keynote address to assembled delegates, PCCNA National Chairman, Bishop Ithiel Clemmons, focused on the theme, 'First Century Pentecost for 21st Century Witness and Ministry.' Citing the outpouring of the Holy Spirit as recorded in the Book of Acts, Clemmons noted the early believers received a new surge of spiritual strength not only for personal transformation, but also to give them the ability to deal with the social tasks they faced.

"'We'll never understand what happened in the Upper Room until we look at the disciples' attitude toward the outside world,' Clemmons stated. 'Early believers faced a world of need around them. God gave them power sufficient to take on the big task of making a difference on several fronts -- thought and theology, morality, economics, racism, and world evangelism.'

"Focusing on the present, Clemmons cited three frontiers the Church is confronting: racism, prosperity, and the 'encumbrance of adaptation' to societal norms. On racism, Clemmons shared, 'The Church must move from behind the stockade of platitudes and generalities. The Pentecostal Church faces the task of making brotherhood and sisterhood a reality." He warned against a Church caught up in a prosperity ethic where profit motive reigns and gaining wealth is the chief goal. Thirdly, Clemmons cautioned the Church not to try to accommodate every nuance of the times. 'Our purpose is not adaptation to the world, but the transformation of the world.'

"'The task of changing the world is a big one--a task which requires Pentecostal power to accomplish. 'But God doesn't waste His power,' Clemmons stated. 'He gives His power only to people who need it, who tackle something bigger than they can handle.' On the issue of reconciliation, Clemmons adds, 'The issue is too big for us. Unless God helps us, all our planning and talking will be only platitudes. But when we come to the end of ourselves and rely on God's power, that gives Him opportunity to open the door for a fresh touch of His Spirit.'

"Dovetailing with frontiers and challenges the church is facing were addresses, "The History of Women in Ministry" and "Releasing Women in Ministry" by Dr. Cheryl Sanders and Reverend Sheri Benvenuti respectively.

"Prolific author, educator, and Associate Pastor for Spiritual Life and Leadership Development at Third Street Church of God in Washington, D. C., Sanders noted that women were very instrumental in leadership ministry during the early years of holiness/Pentecostal movements. Yet, in ensuing years, the trend declined sharply. 'Women in Gospel preaching have been an indicator of church vitality,' Sanders stated. 'But it is the nature of paganism to despise women. Revival will be marked by the partnership of men and women, with women involved in every aspect of leadership. Gifts, not gender, qualify women for positions of spiritual leadership.'

"Assistant professor of social ethics at Southern California College, Costa Mesa, Sheri Benvenuti noted that as denominations formalized the role of women in ministry declined. 'The idea of authority became the center of discussion.' she observed. 'This was a reversal from the early days when servanthood was the focal point. But it is incomprehensible that the Holy Spirit would fill women with His power and presence only to demand they remain silent. It is imperative that the Church realize that as women become more assured of their calling and are affirmed by their leaders, they will rise to the occasion.'"

Bishop Houston's heart was stirred by the messages delivered. He wholeheartedly agreed and had been preaching similar messages himself. He remembered that his mother had preached holiness and Pentecostalism in houses, churches, or anywhere else she had the opportunity. Then there was his daughter Carol pouring herself into ministry. Surely she was as full of fire and promise as any man. He hoped the church would listen and take heed.

He believed they would. As he contemplated the effects of that, he breathed a silent prayer for the women who were called to the traditional roles of wife and mother. They must be appreciated and valued within the church, as they are its bedrock. They were the prayer warriors that moved heaven and earth, as well as the glue that held families and churches together. Whoever coined the phrase, "The hand that rocks the cradle, rules the world," certainly knew what she was talking about.

The Bishop's late wife was one of those called to the traditional role. Her prophetic words often rose up in his spirit, "Ralph, I'll be leaving you in a few days, but you be faithful to finish the task God has set before you."

At the time the statement was overshadowed by the grief of losing his wife of almost half a century. Over and over again she had proven her love for him, and it wouldn't be long before the saint would be departing from his side. It was too early for the words to take on the meaning they did now as he remembered them. He wasn't ready to receive and act on them until the Holy Spirit completed the work of comforting him.

While Bishop Houston was relaxing in his recliner late one evening, the presence of the Lord filled the room and a voice spoke the name, "Betty." With that one word, Bishop Houston understood what he was to do and welcomed an end to his loneliness. How blessed he was to have the void filled and to know that God cared about every aspect of his life. With a helpmate by his side, he was ready to complete his destiny.

Shortly thereafter God moved him into the position of his denomination's General President. As its chief executive officer, he began working for reconciliation within the United Holy Church, with the full support of General Vice President, Bishop G. W. Thornton, General Second Vice President, Bishop Leamon Dudley, Sr., General President, and Emeritus, Bishop J. A. Forbes, Sr.

That spirit of cooperation confirmed the message he received from God during an early morning devotion. He was looking over the wooded area behind his home in Middle Tennessee when the Spirit of the Lord spoke to him, "I've chosen you for a task. Read Isa. 58:1, "Cry aloud, spare not, lift up thy voice like a trumpet, and show my people their transgression, and the house of Jacob their sins."

Then he was led to Isa. 58:12, "And they that shall be of thee shall build the old waste places: thou shalt raise up the foundations of many generations; and thou shalt be called, the repairer of the breach, the restorer of paths to dwell in."

Bishop Houston's denomination had split in 1977 and while there was nothing he wanted to more than seeing it restored, it hardly seemed possible. Founded in 1886 as the United Holy Church of America, it was the oldest Pentecostal denomination in the country. When the split occurred, Bishop Houston went with the larger division comprised of approximately 300 churches, known as the Original United Holy Church International.

At the time of Bishop Houston's election as the denomination's General President, no serious efforts had been made to repair the twenty-year breach. Even though Bishop Houston knew there were strong elements within the two groups that were comfortable with the division, Bishop Houston felt Christ was saying, "I want my church to be one. I've asked my Father to make them one."

It was a theme that resonated throughout the Old and New Testaments. From Ezek. 37:19, where it is written, "Thus saith the Lord God; Behold, I will...make them one...and they shall be one in mine hand," to John 17:22-23 where the words of Christ are recorded, "And the glory which You gave Me, I have given them, that they may be one just as We are One...that the world may know that You have sent Me, and have loved them as You have loved Me."

While knowing that it was ordained of God, there were also feelings of doubt and fear, as Bishop Houston dared to obey. Upon doing so, he began to see the same move of the Holy Spirit that he seen at the PCCNA reconciliation meetings.

In late 1997, Bishop Houston contacted Bishop Odell McCollum, President of the United Holy Church of America and discovered that God had spoken to him as well! It also helped tremendously that the two men had enormous respect for each other and knew each other's backgrounds well.

As a young man, Odell McCollum had pastored the House of Prayer for seven years prior to accepting a position as Bishop H. H. Hairston's Assistant. Following Bishop Hairston's death in 1964, the eloquent minister was invited to assume the pastorate of the Gospel Tabernacle in Columbus, Ohio. For more than thirty years, Bishop McCollum had served both his congregation and his denomination with distinction.

Before the New Year dawned, Bishop McCollum and Bishop Houston had made arrangements for 25 of their Bishops to meet in Nashville on January 20-21,1998. They were pulled together by the beliefs they all shared.

Both bodies believed their denomination had been built upon the foundation laid by the prophets and apostles with Jesus Christ Himself being the Chief Cornerstone. It was readily acknowledged that they could be more effective for Him together than they were apart. With the power of the Holy Spirit wooing them together, as He had the 120 disciples on the day of Pentecost, they realized that they needed to be in "one accord" in order to render their highest and best service unto their Lord. For this body that had sprung from the tenants of the Great Revival and the Second Great Awakening, there was now anticipation of yet another Great Outpouring.

After much fasting and prayer, more than forty Bishops and seventy members of the General Leadership of both branches met again on March 9-10, 1998, in Greensboro, North Carolina, the place where the denominational division had taken place. Then in May 1998, they went to their separate conventions with "Make them one..." ringing in their ears. At both conventions, the people responded to the proposed reunification with, "Thank God the division is over!" With joy and peace reigning in the hearts of all, they began planning a great celebration for the year 2,000.

It reminded Bishop Houston of the PCCNA meeting where Jack Hayford had proclaimed, "Look if you will from the heavenward side of things and see where you have been -- two separate streams," said Hayford. "But now look! Not only is there a new purity but multitudes more who will gather at one mighty river."

The excitement and euphoria rivaled that of the PCCNA attendees when a white pastor unexpectedly stepped forward to wash the feet of a black bishop. Not only did the bishop accept the gesture of forgiveness, he then washed the feet of the white pastor. That same loving, forgiving spirit reigned over all the participants of the United Holy Church.

These testimonies are so precious to our Heavenly Father and to the body of Christ. As it is written in Rev. 12:11, "And they (the saints) overcame him (Satan) by the blood of the Lamb and by the word of their testimony...." Through these testimonies, others find the faith to move forward and overcome.

For that reason God commanded the children of Israel to make a memorial of stones so that "this may be a sign among you, that when your children ask their fathers in time to come, saying, what mean ye by these stones? Then ye shall answer them, that the waters of Jordan were cut off before the Ark of the Covenant of the Lord; when it passed over Jordan, the waters of Jordan were cut off: and these stones shall be for a memorial unto the children of Israel forever." (Josh. 4:6-7)

We should remember what God has brought us through and the kindness He has bestowed upon us. Our testimonies should be offered up as a praise offering to Him and stand as an encouraging memorial for those who will come after us.

This book is Bishop Houston's stack of stones, his testimony and a record of the wonderful things God has done for him and others who have been in his shadow. Surely he is one on whom the Sun of Righteousness has shone, bestowing on those in his shadow both healing and blessings.

EPILOGUE

"The Glory of this latter house shall be greater than of the former, saith the Lord of Hosts: and in this place will I give peace, saith the Lord of Hosts."
(Hag. 2:0)

Bishop Houston's heart overflows with thanksgiving, to which anyone who knows him will attest. His mouth is full of praise to God and blessings for His people. Very few have bid farewell to the Bishop without hearing a heartfelt, "Bless you," on the way out the door. God delights in him, all his children and grandchildren. From them a new generation is rising up to bless God and the world in which they live, and one of the most prominent is the Bishop's beloved daughter, Pastor Carol Houston.

Bishop Houston is overjoyed at the spiritual fruit being borne in Carol's life. Because she had many talents and options in life, it was only by the Grace of God that she followed in his and his mother's footsteps.

When Carol graduated from the University of Denver, Colorado, with a Bachelor of Arts Degree, her postgraduate studies indicated a variety of interests. As she took classes in health education, recreation, gerontology, educational administration, and speech communication, Bishop Houston patiently watched and waited to see what the Lord would do in her life. Of course, he was most pleased when she decided to attend

Fuller Theological Seminary in Pasadena, California, where she studied Missiology.

He was so proud when, due to her pattern of excelling in every endeavor, she was listed as one of the academically acclaimed students throughout America in "Who's Who Among College Students" and "Who's Who Among Outstanding Women Entrepreneurs."

Initially it seemed Carol might opt for a business career, as she certainly had a natural God-given talent for it. In addition to doing an excellent job of managing A & A Barrel & Drum Co. Inc., she had also managed the business affairs of several Christian physicians and singing artists. However, she really came into her own when she began devoting herself to full-time pastoral ministry in January 1991.

In addition to being the pastor of Bethel Unspeakable Joy Christian Fellowship Church, Inc., she founded God Said It Ministries, Inc., designed to teach communities about how to use the power of God to break satanic strongholds. As a result of having taught secondary education for five years in the public school system, she was acutely aware of how much parents need to be equipped with that knowledge.

Just as Bishop Houston's own work had extended beyond the church and into the community, so Carol's leadership roles were far reaching. In addition to her other endeavors, she was recently appointed to serve on the Board of Trustees of Westmont College in Santa Barbara, California.

As Dr. Mark Hanby wrote, "Those in ministry today must develop the heart of a father and raise up a generation of sons and daughters in a 'double portion' anointing...."[*]

---

[*] Copyright 1996 - Dr. Mark Hanby, author with Craig Lindsay Ervin, Destiny Image Publishers, Inc. Shippensburg, PA 17257-0310

Bishop Houston had devoted his life to that end. When he considers Carol's age and what she has accomplished thus far, he has every reason to believe she's received a double portion of the anointing that is on him, and that is saying a lot!

Bishop Houston had a generous spiritual inheritance that he had not squandered. With every character driven decision, he built on it. He was a faithful administrator of it in smaller things and God continually increased the level of opportunities that came his way. In all endeavors, Bishop Houston was ever mindful that he must not fail the Lord. Whether working with the church or with those outside the church, Bishop Houston always made every effort to walk uprightly before God.

As a result, he found God continually granted him favor with those in Christian circles as well as with those he worked with in business, civic, and governmental affairs.

From Mayor Tom Bradley's office to the City Council, from the County Board of Supervisors to the Police and Fire Departments, his calls were always welcomed and returned.

Bishop Houston developed an excellent reputation as a facilitator with a talent for getting things done while being respectful and considerate of the opinions of others who were also in positions of authority.

That was one of the most significant reasons he began to be called on as a leader of leaders. It started with him being asked to serve as treasurer and later as president of the Interdenominational Ministerial Alliance of Greater Los Angeles, to which approximately sixty members of the community's clergy belonged.

The membership expressed their appreciation of his service and approval of his effective leadership by electing him to serve three years in succession, a first for the organization. Members of the Ministerial Alliance had to vote to suspend the rules of the by-laws in order for him to serve the third year. However, the Bishop's work in progress was deemed important enough to warrant doing so. When he completed it, he presented his position paper putting forth the black community's attitudes toward the mandatory (and highly volatile) school busing controversy. The report was well-received and strongly supported by the Ministerial Alliance. As their President, Bishop Houston then delivered the highly acclaimed report to the Los Angeles School Board.

The report became a vital part of the L. A. School Board's decision-making process. It also garnered city wide recognition for Bishop Houston, making him well-known both as a spokesperson for the community's clergy and African-American voters.

Shortly thereafter, he was asked to join black leadership in Sacramento to lobby before the Senate and Assembly in support of a bill dealing with school desegregation and busing. Consequently, Bishop Houston was invited to sit in counsel with State leadership that included the Governor of California. Then, the Rev. Jesse Jackson called upon Bishop Houston to serve for two years as treasurer of his Push for Excellence Program.

Subsequently, Bishop Houston was invited to be the Pentecostal representative to an organization known as "The Gathering," which comprised some 300 interdenominational ministers representing over 175 churches in the greater Los Angeles area. During the formation stage a nationally known member, Dr. Thomas Kilgore of Los Angeles' Second Baptist Church, was acclaimed its first president and Bishop Houston as treasurer.

Afterwards, Bishop Houston was elected to succeed Kilgore as the organization's first elected president. This was an interesting development as

Pentecostal ministers aren't usually considered the most viable candidates to lead organizations desirous of dealing with social and political issues. But Bishop Houston was different from most of his Pentecostal colleagues who preached mostly spiritual solutions. Being a business man the Bishop was more in touch with the angst of people who worked outside the church world. He knew they needed faith to sustain them *while* circumstances were improved, *not in lieu of* them being improved.

So he was well-known as a spiritual man devoted to changing things. As its membership had expected The Gathering's fame spread across the United States under Bishop Houston's leadership.

Soon other cities were establishing similar organizations, resulting in higher levels of cooperation among their spiritual leaders. Together they were more effective in praying about and acting on issues of common interest.

While serving as President of The Gathering, Bishop Houston was called upon to aid the United States Legislature in writing an Immigration bill and this brought him exposure on a national level. A few months later, at the request of an aide to the President, he was back in Washington, along with four other Bishops, to discuss the feasibility of government funds being channeled through nonprofit Credit Unions for the purpose of aiding in urban development.

When the Reagan Administration cut back welfare benefits, the Los Angeles Times called Bishop Houston for an interview. He suggested it was a positive development for the black community as the changes would force people to become self-sufficient. The reporter was interested in many of the Bishop's opinions and wrote a lengthy article about them.

The Lord often gave Bishop Houston quite a platform from which to proclaim his beneficial messages, even though he wasn't one of Los Angeles' half-dozen 'name' pastors and he didn't have one of the larger churches in the city.

All these opportunities to contribute once again brought to mind his mother's dying prophecy, "Your gift will make room for you and bring you before great men -- and you don't have to push it, just be a Christian."

What a treasure that prophecy had been to him and what a joy to see it brought to pass innumerable times. He was thankful for all of it. His life had been so full and rich that there wasn't much more anyone could want.

God had enabled him to build and remodel a $700,000 church and a $1,500,000 Senior Citizen Apartment Home, where elderly members of Bethel were lovingly cared for by those whose lives they had nurtured.

Everything accomplished through Bethel was a result of their concerted efforts, working together as God intended. Some had planted, some watered, and God gave them a bountiful harvest.

Members of Bethel rejoiced as much as his family and friends over the crowning achievement of Bishop Houston's life, the reunification of his denomination. Without the underpinning of their prayers, it wouldn't have been possible.

In the midst of higher profile activities, Bishop Houston did not neglect ministering to the day-to-day needs of his church congregation or his family. Sam Barnett's comments are representative of the love and care Bishop Houston gave his congregation:

"Thanks for asking us to contribute to Bishop Houston's book. We are delighted to do so, as he is one of the most compassionate and caring men we have ever known.

"We joined his church in December, 1980, when it was known as Little Bethel United Holy Church. The years we belonged to his church were happy and joyous times.

"However there was a time in our lives when we went through a tragic and very emotional period, but we didn't go through it alone. Bishop Houston was always there for us. If we called him about any situation, he was never too busy to pray for us or come to our home and be with us. He was, and still is, loved by many.

"He is the reason I am a Deacon today. Because he believed in me and trusted me with responsibilities, I've done everything in my power to live up to his expectations in fulfilling my duties related to my position in the church. It has been my privilege to serve in a greater capacity since being elected Chairman of the Deacon Board, all of which I owe to Bishop's confidence in me. Bishop Houston's messages and words of encouragement will stay with me all the days of my life.

"There is one other situation I would like to mention. When my son was murdered in 1983, I went to work that morning as usual. In shock, I was just going through the motions without talking about what had happened.

"My wife called Bishop Houston and he immediately came to our home. When he discovered I wasn't there, he came to my place of employment to see if I was all right. That touched me deeply. I will never forget Bishop Houston. The many kind words and deeds of this compassionate man were truly a blessing to my family."

Bishop Houston's youngest son, Kim, spoke for all the Houston children when he said, "My dad is not only a special man but he has been a great inspiration to me throughout my life. He is a superb example and role model for anyone to follow.

"During my pre-adult years he was always there for me to talk with about any problem that I had to face. He is very caring and wants to see not only me but all his children succeed.

"When I think back to some of my most disturbing times, I remember that he was always there to share some encouraging words and thoughts on how I could overcome my problems. He always told me to believe in myself and to hold onto my faith and trust in God. With that, I could achieve anything that I ever dreamed of doing.

"He also instilled in me the value of hard work and dedication. With those two values there isn't any obstacle that I can't overcome. If there was ever anyone I want to pattern my life after, it is my father.

"He is indeed a great man and most importantly has been a great father. All through his life he has worked very hard to help other people. He always gives of himself and makes himself available for his family or anyone else who needs him

"I thank God for the father He gave me because without him I would not be the person I am today. My father means the world to me and I am eternally grateful for him."

From California to Tennessee and on to Liberia, West Africa, the voices of appreciation ring.

As Dr. Jerry Crooke's wife Scottye wrote, "To stand in the Bishop's shadow must be closely akin to standing in the shadow of the Almighty. Though the Bishop's frame is enormous, it does not even compare to the size of his heart!

"I don't recall the first time Jerry and I were introduced to the Bishop, I only know that God brought us together. Over the period of the subsequent years, we developed a very strong, lasting bond between us. I remember once being summoned to the platform at Christ

Church and, not wanting to be noticed, I slipped over beside the Bishop where I felt safe, secure and *hidden*. It reminded me of Psalm 91:1, 'He that dwelleth in the secret place of the most high shall abide under the shadow of the Almighty.'

"Because of the Bishop, Jerry and I now have a heart for mission. This hunger grew gradually out of time spent listening to his stories and those of his missionary friends. Those conversations developed in us a real desire to fulfill the Great Commission in our lives.

"However, we were to soon to learn that there are missions and then there are missions! As Jerry and I were wasting away in the poorest villages of the Ukraine, coping with bedbugs, broken-down buses (or no buses at all), outhouses (if we were lucky), and no running water, we remembered how Bishop Houston was treated like royalty on his trips to Liberia. Compared to our accommodations, his Liberian house sounded like a palace. Furthermore, since he has been supporting them for over twenty-five years and returning there regularly to help, he has friends who cook and chauffeur him around.

"One night as Jerry and I lay in our foreign bed, wishing we could take a nice, hot bath, we started wondering where we went wrong! Even though our own outreach did not exactly line up with our expectations, it was a precious time. We came to realize that no matter what the circumstances, God's heart for His people is always blessed as we step out in obedience and we in turn are blessed by His people.

"Nevertheless, I can assure you that my next mission trip will be spent in the Bishop's shadow!"

When Bishop Houston read Scottye's comments he laughed and said he hoped their mission trip with him was all they expected it to be. Some of his own have not been!

On one occasion, while he was dining with a group of missionaries in Liberia, he excused himself to go to the men's room. Unbelievably, he discovered his prostrate had swollen so much that he could not pass a single drop of urine. Even though he had not had any previous problems of this nature, he knew he was in serious trouble. About two hours later he was in a doctor's office in Monrovia having a catheter inserted. Then he traveled about fifty miles back into the African bush to the Salala mission.

Two days later a village nurse removed the catheter. However, within twenty-four hours, he needed it again, but it had been thrown away. Since catheters were not readily available in Liberia, he did not know what to do. When he found out he could not get an earlier flight out of the country, Satan told him he was going to die. Sensing the spirit of defeat, he strongly rebuked it and declared, "In the name of Jesus, I am going to stick with my schedule."

The Holy Spirit impressed upon him that he should not eat or drink anything, even though the doctors had advised him to drink plenty of fluids. While on this total fast, he traveled with several missionaries to a town about forty-five miles away. The journey seemed agonizingly long as pain shot through his body with every jarring bump they hit while traversing the rough, pothole filled road.

Several hundred Liberians were eagerly awaiting their arrival, but the great excitement turned to sadness and grief when they heard of Bishop Houston's condition. He was their guest of honor, the featured speaker for the services they had planned. Their concern touched Bishop Houston deeply. He prayed for strength and God gave it to him. For two days, he ministered to the people in spite of the pain. And he was ministered to, as many prayers went up for his healing.

On the return to the Salala Mission, the Bishop asked the driver to stop so he could attempt to relieve himself in the bush. He stepped out of the car and into a horde of flesh-eating army ants that immediately attacked him. These were ants that most people have only seen in the movies, stripping trees and carcasses clean in a matter of minutes. Fearful of seeing this happen in real life right before their very eyes the Bishop's friends hurriedly rushed to pull him away while simultaneously knocking the ants off. But the ants were moving up his legs at such a pace that he could only escape by jumping out of his pants, right there in broad daylight!

Following his encounter with the army ants, they drove into the night searching for a village clinic that was open, and Praise God they found one! The nurse on duty looked everywhere and finally found a catheter. What a relief!

Two days later it had to be removed and another could not be found. For the next four days, there was no further relief. Thank God the Bishop was able to board a flight to America. When he arrived in New York, he considered entering a hospital there, but decided to hold out until he was home with his family. About an hour and a half before landing in Los Angeles, he thought he would die from the excruciating pain.

Having called ahead, he found his family waiting at the gate ready to take him directly to the hospital where a doctor was waiting. As he was hurriedly prepped for surgery, he thought about all the missionaries who live among foreign people on a full-time basis and breathed a prayer for them. Even though his own mission trips were short term, he had faced enough dangers to know how much faith they must have and what sacrifices they make to minister to others.

Because of the additional strains faced by career missionaries, usually only able to come home every few years on furlough, Bishop Houston holds these saints in the highest regard. He considers them to be the "Special Forces" in God's army. Unfortunately many American Christians, not realizing their needs, fail to care for their missionaries properly. Bishop Houston has made every effort to do that and to show them the respect they deserve. In November 1997, he designated the West African Region of Cote D'Ivoire and Liberia as the Eighth District of the Original United Holy Church, International.

He plans to be in the trenches with the missionaries there in Liberia as often as possible. Much work remains to be done there and at home as well, but he would rather be there. In fact, he and Sister Betty are praying about relocating to Africa.

Family and friends would miss them sorely if they were to go. To the logical mind, this is incomprehensible, as the most serious health crisis Bishop Houston has faced in his life happened there. In addition to limited medical facilities for the normal range of health problems, there is also the added threat of tropical diseases, some of which the Bishop has experienced personally.

On one occasion when the death of an African associate bid him leave the states quickly, before he could get the usual regiment of shots, he ended up with the dreaded malaria disease. This resulted in him suffering with chills and fever, violent shivering, excruciating headaches, as well as nausea, vomiting, and urine which turned so dark red it almost looked black. He believes he only survived by the miraculous Grace of the Almighty.

It is that same Grace that makes Sister Betty willing to serve by the Bishop's side on either a short- or long-term basis. This is truly incredible, as both Sister Betty and Bishop Houston have been prudent planners who've made provisions for their latter years to be comfortable. On every trip to Liberia they pack an abundance of tuna, Spam, and other nonperishable foods to make sure they have enough to eat while there. They also pack food to take to others.

The needs of Liberians override the inconvenience and risks. They cannot forget the people who are driven by gnawing hunger to eat the very leaves of the banana trees, or any other edible thing they can find.

Still, it is amazing to think the Houstons are actually considering a move there. It is especially awesome to those who haven't climbed high enough up the mountain of faith to become acclimated to its thin, pure air. While it may be a breathtaking consideration to many, the Houstons see it differently. Because they have had God as their guide for longer than most of us have lived, they have learned to trust Him more.

They have no plans for retirement and are kept young by the God-given visions toward which they will work for as long as they live.

Bishop Houston plans to live every day to the fullest and to meet the Lord in the same condition Moses was in when he met God..."with eye not dim, nor his natural force abated." (Deut. 34:7)

It is that persevering spiritual strength that makes people all over the world feel fortunate indeed when they find themselves in the Bishop's shadow.

Order Form

Send orders for

IN THE BISHOP'S SHADOW

to
Bishop Ralph Houston
P. O. Box 2171
Antioch, TN 37013

Please send $15.00 for each book requested plus
Shipping charges of $4.00 for the first book
and $2.00 for each additional book.
Please add 8.25% Sales Tax
for books shipped to Tennessee addresses.

If paying by credit card, please complete the following:

Visa ___, Mastercard ___, Optima ___, AMEX ___, Discover ___.

Credit card number: _____

Name on card: _____

Expiration date: _____

Order Form

Send orders for

A Call to Courage

to
Laverne Barton
P. O. Box 2171
Antioch, TN 37013

Please send $15.00 for each book requested plus
Shipping charges of $4.00 for the first book
and $2.00 for each additional book.
Please add 8.25% Sales Tax
for books shipped to Tennessee addresses.

If paying by credit card, please complete the following:

Visa ___, Mastercard ___, Optima ___, AMEX ___, Discover ___.

Credit card number:_____

Name on card:_____

Expiration date:_____

Special Quantity Discounts

Available
for
Organizations
and Corporations
making bulk purchases.

Order to:
Re-Sale
Raise Funds
Give as Gifts

For more information
Please write to:
P. O. Box 2171
Antioch, TN 37013